TEACHING WORD ATTACK SKILLS

FOURTH EDITION

TEACHING WORD ATTACK SKILLS

FOURTH EDITION

Lee Ann Rinsky
DeAnza College
Cupertino, California

Gorsuch Scarisbrick, Publishers
Scottsdale, Arizona

ISBN 0-89787-524-9

10 9 8 7 6 5 4 3 2 1

Copyright © 1978, 1980, 1984, 1988 by Gorsuch Scarisbrick, Publishers

All rights reserved. No part of this publication may be reproduced, stored in a retrieval system, or transmitted, in any form or by any means, electronic, mechanical, photocopy, recording, or otherwise without the prior written permission of the publisher.

Printed in the United States of America.

Preface

This fourth edition of *Teaching Word Attack Skills* has again been revised according to suggestions offered by users and elementary teachers-in-service, and according to recent research in the reading area. A comprehensive report, *On Becoming a Nation of Readers* by the National Institute of Education, emphasized in its philosophy the underlying philosophy of this text—namely, that phonics instruction is effective when it is carried out in meaningful context, that attention must be given to other word attack skills, and that comprehension must be the goal in reading.

Method books in reading for teacher education are very concerned with the process of reading but generally devote only a small section to the details of word attack skills. These books may provide only limited charts of our sound–symbol system and minimal instructions in phonics. Additional important word attack skills such as context clues and structural analysis are likewise neglected. It is frequently assumed that teachers already have this knowledge or need only a little instruction to master it. I make no such assumption, based on the needs of many students in my classes, both graduate and undergraduate, who have little or no background in word attack skills and who will be responsible for teaching in the classroom.

I believe teachers need an in-depth background in word attack skills for several reasons: (1) to understand the rationale and the scope and sequence of the reading program or approach they will use; (2) to be able to diagnose the reading skill needs of students they will be teaching; (3) to perceive the interrelatedness of word attack skills and understand how the emphasis changes as students progress through the grades; and (4) to be able to evaluate materials on the market, many of which purport to teach students to read but in actuality are little more than glorified phonics approaches.

I have written *Teaching Word Attack Skills* as a result of teaching many courses in reading and in recognition of the need for a pre-service and in-service teacher self-instructional manual in word attack skills. The organization, presentation of information, and suggested learning methods of this text will facilitate acquisition of the needed background in word attack skills. In addition, the linguistic and historical insights provided here will clarify some of the more complicated sound–symbol relationships.

This new edition includes revisions and updates in all the resource categories and in the games and activities sections. Since the major change in materials has been in the area of computers, this section has been considerably expanded. Because of the influx into American schools of a large Asian population, clarification of the differences between the American and Vietnamese sound systems has been added. Where applicable, current research in reading readiness is included and interpreted. Teaching suggestions have been expanded with some new techniques offered for working with students who have difficulties with decoding.

The section on phonics analysis, as before, systematizes the needed background, with students learning about variant consonants, blends, consonant digraphs, single vowel sounds, vowel digraphs, diphthongs; the variety of ways the letter *y* is used to encode; the conditioning effect of the letter *r;* and the special combinations *ci, ti,* and *si.* Following a discussion about reading readiness, procedures for introducing a beginning sound–symbol relationship are detailed, and the controversy about blending techniques is outlined. The difference between analytic, synthetic, and "linguistic" phonics is explained, and sample lessons of each type are included. The importance of sight words is detailed and several basic sight word lists are included, with suggestions for teaching them. Structural analysis focuses on compound words, affixed words, and syllabication. Difficulties encountered by students with these words are explained with suggested procedures for teaching. The importance of context as an aid in decoding is discussed. Various ways of using cloze to teach the use of context clues is explained with sample passages provided. Included are suggested lessons in teaching dictionary skills. There is a final section on the use of the computer in the classroom.

As a further aid to learning these word attack skills and their interrelatedness, this manual includes periodic generalizations set off with boldface type as well as periodic checkups for the readers. Most sections, whether relating to a particular phonics relationship or a feature of structural analysis, have a built-in short review and self-check. In addition, there is an overall review of each major part. Guidelines for teaching the skills and answers to questions that teachers frequently ask are also included. Because of special considerations with speakers of nonmainstream English, a separate section deals with dialect differences including Black English, the language of the Spanish-speaking child for whom English is a second language, and the Vietnamese child.

The research done during the revision of this manual reemphasizes that success in reading seems to be based primarily not on the methods and materials used, but on teacher competency and on the amount of time students actually spend in reading. This basic theory is supported by the report mentioned earlier, *On Becoming a Nation of Readers*. In this report, the National Institute of Education also claims that the time students spend in reading in school is actually very small—approximately seven minutes a day in primary grades and fifteen minutes a day in intermediate grades. This certainly needs to be changed. Reading is far more than a collection of discrete word attack skills; moreover, teachers of reading must be concerned with developing not only the skills of reading but also the love of reading.

I would like to thank the teachers and the students who reviewed this book and who offered many suggestions for its improvement. I also wish to acknowledge the many worthwhile suggestions made by members of the editorial and production departments of the publisher.

Contents

PART 1
Understanding Phonics 1
Support for the Use of Phonics 2
The New Debate 3

Section I. Consonants 4
Single Consonant Letters 5
Consonants With More than One Sound 5
    The letter *c* – The letter *g* – The letter *s*
    Quick Self-Check I 7
Consonant Blends 7
    Beginning blends – Ending blends
    Quick Self-Check II 9
Consonant Digraphs 9
    The unique *h* digraphs: *ch, gh, ph, sh, th, wh*
    Quick Self-Check III 12
    Digraphs with a first silent letter: *gn* and *kn, wr, ck* – Special combinations: *dge* and *tch, ng*
    Quick Self-Check IV 14
Part 1, Section I, Review and Self-Check 15

Section II. Vowels 15
The Single Vowels, *a, e, i, o, u,* and the schwa 15
    The short vowel sound – The long vowel sound – Special vowel sounds – The schwa
    Quick Self-Check V 18
Final Unpronounced Letter *e* 18
    Quick Self-Check VI 20
Vowel Digraphs and Diphthongs 20
    Vowel digraphs and diphthongs with *a: ai* and *ay, au* and *aw*
    Quick Self-Check VII 21
    Vowel digraphs with *e: ee, ea, ie, ei, ey*
    Quick Self-Check VIII 24
    Vowel digraph with *i* – Vowel digraphs/diphthongs with *o: oa, oo, ou, ow, oi* and *oy*
    Quick Self-Check IX 29
    Vowel diphthongs encoding /oo/: *ui* and *ue, ew*
    Quick Self-Check X 30
Part 1, Section II, Review and Self-Check 30

Section III. The Letter Y 31
Y as a Consonant and Vowel 31

Other Considerations with *Y*   31
   Quick Self-Check XI   32

Section IV. R-Conditioned Vowels   32

With Single Letter Vowels   32
   er, ir, ur, and *wor – ar – or*
With Vowel Digraphs   34
   ea – ai – ee
   Quick Self-Check XII   36

Section V. Special Combinations that Decode as /sh/   37

Part 1, Sections III, IV, and V, Review and Self-Check   38
Part 1, Final Phonics Review   38

Section VI. Preparing to Read: Reading Readiness   40

Prereading Tasks   40
A Prereading Phonics Inventory   41
Other Readiness Factors   43

Section VII. Beginning to Teach Phonics   43

Procedures for Introducing a Beginning Sound–Symbol Relationship   43
   A strategy to teach beginning sound–symbol relationships – Dittos and workbook page examples in beginning reading
Blending: A Controversy   46
Vowel Sounds May Cause Difficulty   47
Synthetic/Analytic/"Linguistic"/Phonics: Differing Points of View   48
   The synthetic approach – The analytic approach – "Linguistic phonics," a third approach
Phonics Tutorial Programs   52
Implications for Teaching   52
Teaching, Extending, Reinforcing, and Reviewing Sound–Symbol Relationships   53
   Examples of game-like activities – Examples of puzzle-type activities – Manipulatives – Materials inundation!
Guidelines When Teaching Phonics   61
Questions Teachers Ask When Teaching Phonics   62
Summary   63
Part 1, Sections VI and VII, Review and Self-Check   64

PART 2
Additional Word Attack Skills   65

Section I. Sight Words   66

Sight Word Lists   66
Teaching Sight Words   66
Activities for Teaching Sight Words   69
When Sight Words Are Especially Troublesome   72
Phonics and Sight Words   73
Sight Word Storehouse: The Goal in Reading   73
Sight Words for the Computer Age: An Essential Word List   73
   Quick Self-Check XIII   75

Section II. Structural Analysis: An Increasingly Important Decoding Strategy   75

Compound Words   75
     Activities for teaching compound words
     Quick Self-Check XIV   77

Prefixes, Roots, and Suffixes   77
     Prefixes: definitions and dilemma – Suffixes and roots: more problems – Spelling and suffixes – Affix lists – Teaching affixed forms – Example lesson, younger children – Example lessons for more advanced students – Turning incorrect answers into learning experiences – Activities for teaching words with prefixes and suffixes – Questions teachers ask
     Quick Self-Check XV   94

Syllabication   94
     Syllabication, another debate – Teaching syllabication – Dividing words into syllables – Activities for teaching syllabication

Language Change   97
     American and British spelling
     Quick Self-Check XVI   98

Section III. Context Clues   99

Advantages and Disadvantages in Using Context Clues   100

Guidelines for Teaching about Context Clues   100

Sentence Context Clues May Be Limited   101

Activities to Help Students Become Aware of Context as an Aid to Decoding   101

Context and Cloze Technique   103
     Quick Self-Check XVII   104

Section IV. Using the Dictionary   104

Activities to Teach the Dictionary Skill Areas   106
     Alphabetizing skills – Guide words – Pronunciation key and accent marks – Phonics spelling and pronunciation – Word meaning

Creative Activities to Motivate Students in the Use of the Dictionary   107
     Quick Self-Check XVIII   109

The More Commonly Used Dictionaries and Thesauri   110
     Primary – Elementary/Junior High

Section V. More About Materials and Activities   111

Pros and Cons of Hand-Produced and Commercially Produced Materials   113

Summary   113

Part 2, Final Review   114

PART 3

Aids in Decoding   115

Section I. Toward an Improved Decoding Strategy   116

Finding the Right Combination   116

Presenting Vocabulary to Students   116
     Direct instruction – VLP – Word Wonder

Some Suggestions for Aids in Decoding Difficulties   118
     The short vowel sounds – The ECRI Method – Low level of accuracy in word attack

Reading and Evaluation   120
Helping Students Develop Flexibility   122
Fluency Is Necessary While Reading   122
    Imitative method – Impress – Repeated readings – Recalling word meaning
Basic Principles in Remediation   125
Summary   125
Part 3, Final Review   125

PART 4
The Expanding Role of the Computer in the Reading Classroom   127

Section I.   Advantages and Disadvantages   128
Computer Programs   129
Availability and Programs   130
Example Programs   130
Classroom Programs in Clinics   134
Evaluating Microcomputer Software for Reading Instruction   134
Research Needed to Answer Questions about the Efficacy of Computer Use   135
Summary   135
Part 4, Final Review   135

PART 5
Other Considerations   137

Section I.   Meeting Special Needs of Students   138
Parents and Reading   138
    Reading activities to share between parent and child
Children Who Speak with a Dialect or Who Use English as a Second Language   140
The Black Dialect   141
    Phonology – Grammar
Spanish-Speaking Children for Whom English is a Second Language   143
Teaching the Dialect Speaker   144
    Past and present proposed teaching methods – Reading transcripts, their implication – Reading tests and the dialect/ESL speaker – Methods of teaching
The Asian Student   147
Summary   148
Part 5, Final Review   148

PART 6
Appendixes   149
A. Answers to Quick Self-Checks and Reviews   150
B. Record Form for Informal Assessment of Code Consciousness   159
    A List of Basic Sight Words for Older Readers   160
    A Typical Scope and Sequence Chart   161

C. Example Word Lists 164
   Initial consonants, 164 – Consonant blends, 165 – Variant consonant sounds, 166 – Consonant digraphs, 166 – Consonant digraphs with first silent letters; also *tch, dge,* and *ng,* 167 – Short vowels, 168 – Long vowels and silent *e,* 168 – *Y* as a vowel, 169 – Vowel digraphs, 169 – Diphthongs, 170 – R-controlled vowels, 171 – Active prefixes, 172 – Absorbed prefixes, 175 – Derivational suffixes, 176 – Practice words for syllabication, 181

D. Tests
   A teacher's test of decoding skills, 186 – Answers to a teacher's test of decoding skills, 186 – Example text for the diagnosis of student word attack skills, 188

Resources for the Teacher 191
Manufacturers of Games—Some Names and Addresses 194
Manufacturers and Distributors of Reading Computer Software 195
Questions to Ask About Computer-Based Reading Programs 197
A Model Sheet for Evaluating Reading Games 199

Glossary Terms 200

References 201

PART

1

Understanding Phonics

"DENNIS THE MENACE® used by permission of Hank Ketcham and © Field Enterprises, Inc."

Each of the five basic word attack skills is presented separately in this book. The separation, however, is an arbitrary one. It is necessary to focus on a single skill at a time so that teachers, for whom this text is written, develop a thorough understanding of each one. Fluent reading is impeded when only one type of word attack skill is relied upon exclusively. Therefore, as students learn to read, teachers should show and encourage them to be flexible and use a variety of word attack skills. Most basal readers will suggest this in their series, although some stress one skill over another.

To emphasize, students need to learn that sometimes a single clue and sometimes combinations of clues work best to decode words, and that the effectiveness of any one word attack skill is often enhanced when used in combination with others.

Generally, five areas are considered in evaluating the word attack skill competency of students:

1. ability to use phonics clues
2. knowledge of basic sight words
3. ability to use structural clues
4. ability to use context clues
5. ability to use the dictionary

Look back to Appendix D, for a Teacher's Test of Decoding Skills to evaluate your own knowledge in these areas. After you have completed Parts I and II of this book, you should be able to have a perfect score on this test. (Answers to the questions follow the test.)

Support for the Use of Phonics

While phonics is not always the most important strategy students use in word attack, it is by far the most detailed, and it is this detail perhaps that causes difficulties for some students when learning to read. This is compounded by the fact that there is not always a one-to-one correspondence between letters and sounds. For this reason, some educators argue that teaching phonics should be minimized, but we suggest this conclusion is too simplistic. Phonics must be viewed as only one tool, but an important one, for giving students a foundation for understanding how most of our sound-symbol relationships work. Thus, the mystery between squiggles on paper and oral language becomes clearer. Further support for the use of phonics derives from one comprehensive survey of English that was based on a computerized study of 17,000 words, indicating English is about eighty-five percent phonetic (Hanna, Hodges and Hannna, 1971, pp. 79-83). Disagreement still persists about the actual percentage, some claiming it is much higher.

The controversy continues, however, over the reliability of phonics generalizations that are useful in decoding words.[1] During the last two decades, the trend in basal reading texts was toward a *greater* emphasis on phonics, introduced

(1) Since a lack of sound-symbol relationshps exists in some of our English words, you will always be able to think of word exceptions to the generalizations we present on the following pages. When you teach, your students will also notice these exceptions. Compliment them when they do, as it shows they are applying those generalizations under discussion.

earlier in the child's reading program, and due largely to the publication of the classic book, *Learning to Read: The Great Debate* by Jeanne Chall (1967). Her book compared the effects of varying amounts of phonics taught in the early grades and concluded that programs with systematic phonics resulted in higher pupil achievement in reading in primary grades than did programs with little or no phonics. Her book, revised in 1983, reiterated the earlier finding as does research from Johnson & Bauman (1984) and Williams (1985).

It is unclear from Chall's original study whether phonics alone resulted in improved achievement. The children exposed to phonics may have additionally spent more time in reading than the control groups, who learned to read chiefly through sight. Despite some early questions, the book revolutionized the way publishers organized their early reading programs. As a result a far greater number of words were learned earlier by competent readers, sometimes with a stress on phonetic patterning (*ran, tan, van*). The trend towards a strong early reading phonics program in most basal readers continues up to the present time.

The "New" Debate

Balmuth (1982), an assistant in the study that resulted in Chall's *Learning to Read: The Great Debate*, presented an historical perspective on the differing phonics viewpoints in her book. She showed the debate continuing with the anti-phonics group represented by such researchers as Frank Smith and Kenneth Goodman and the pro-phonics group represented by such researchers as Fries and Venezky. The anti-phonics group have what is referred to as a "top-down" model of reading while they refer to the pro-phonics model as being "bottom up" (Otto, 1982). The "top-down" view, based on psycholinguistic theory, postulates that when a reader decodes s/he thinks about what is meaningful and grammatically possible as well as about the visual stimuli (the letters), thereby using meaning, grammar, and the letters to hypothesize about what is on the page. The "top-down" model, therefore does not view decoding as the primary or first step in reading (Otto, p. 17). More recently Fox (1986) again presents opposing viewpoints calling the debate systematic phonics vs. whole language learning.

This so-called "new debate" appears to the author to be more of the same, only couched in different terminology or educanese. The problem is not, nor never has been, whether to be anti-phonics or pro-phonics but how much or how little phonics to use depending on students' needs. Certainly other word attack skills besides phonics must be considered, and good teachers have always considered them. After reviewing the reading research of the last several decades Roger Farr (1981) concluded what has been concluded many times before—that it is not method nor materials but that *the teacher is still the key*. That conclusion is still valid today!

Altogether, there are probably over 100 published phonics programs, each dealing with the same subject, but with slight variation. (Phonics is simply defined as the way that specific sounds, phonemes, are related to specific letters, graphemes, or combinations of letters.) The variations in programs arise because some strive to cover all the possible letter combinations while others classify only the most regular writing features of English. Additionally, certain programs organize and group their sound-symbol relationships differently. Most programs, however, place the basic division between the consonants and vowels, and these two basic groups may be further divided. In the consonant group are:

1. single consonant letters with a single sound.
2. single consonant letters with dual sounds.
3. blends—two or three consonant letters with the sounds blended rapidly together.
4. digraphs—two consonant letters with only a single sound/sounds.
5. special consonant combinations.

In the vowel group are:

1. single vowels (long, short, and special vowel sounds).
2. schwa—a "reduced" vowel sound, neither short nor long.
3. vowel digraphs—two vowels together with only a single vowel sound/sounds.
4. vowel diphthongs—two vowels with a "gliding" sound between them.

The letter *y* has a unique position, sometimes operating as a consonant, vowel, digraph, or diphthong. In addition, there is a special group of R-conditioned vowels. See Table 1 for a model overview.[2]

Writers of phonics programs often find themselves in a dilemma. If they try to give attention to all letter combinations, their classifications become too cumbersome. If they strive for simplicity, they often omit combinations that deserve explanation. Since it is our opinion that teachers need far more background in sound-symbol relationships than their students do, we will be presenting a rather extensive phonics program for the teacher. This does not mean, however, that *all* students will need this kind of background to master reading. When the occasion arises for letter-sound relationships to be discussed, it is important that teachers possess the knowledge to explain why a word decodes or encodes[3] as it does.

Table 1.1 Basic Division of a Phonics Program*

Consonant Group with Examples	Vowel Group with Examples	Y	The Letter *r*
Single: b, m, p	Single: a, e, i, o, u	May be a consonant and vowel: yes, cry	Conditions the preceding vowel sound: ar, ur
Variant Consonants: c, g	(long, short, special sound)		
Blends: cr, gl, st	Schwa: ə		
Digraphs: ch, th, ng	Digraphs: ai, oa, ee		
Special Combination: dge, tch	Diphthongs: ou, ow, oo		

*Detailed overview of an entire phonics program is included on page 39.

Such explanations show word groups and patterns, and not only satisfy the curiosity of students but help to reinforce learning. When explanations begin by showing a generalization for one example, such as the *dge* in the word *bridge*, and then include other words that "behave" in a similar fashion, such as *dodge, edge,* and *fudge,* difficult reading-writing combinations are clarified.

SECTION I

CONSONANTS

Most single consonant letters and their related sounds are introduced very early in reading. To indicate that we are discussing a letter, we will italicize it as follows: *b, d, f.* To indicate that we are discussing a sound, we will enclose it in slash lines as follows: /b/, /d/, /f/.

(2) Such terms as *blends, digraphs, diphthongs, the schwa,* and *R-conditioned vowels* will each be discussed in detail.
(3) *Encode* means to write the word or sound.

Single Consonant Letters

The single consonant letters *b, d, f, h, j, k, m, n, p, qu,*[4] *r, t, v, w, x, y,* and *z* are generally decoded as the following sounds:

b	/b/	bat	*l*	/l/	land	*t*	/t/	top
d	/d/	dent	*m*	/m/	mat	*v*	/v/	vane
f	/f/	fall	*n*	/n/	name	*w*	/w/	well
h	/h/	hit	*p*	/p/	pan	*x*	/ks/	box[5]
j	/j/	jam	*qu*	/kw/	quite	*y*	/y/	yellow
k	/k/	kite	*r*	/r/	road	*z*	/z/	zebra

Notice that we have excluded mention of the consonants *c, g,* and *s* at this point because they will be discussed thoroughly in the following sections.

Consonants With More Than One Sound

The letters *c, g,* and *s* are sometimes called "variant" consonants.

The letter *c*

Examine the words in lists *A* and *B*

A *c* as /k/			*B* *c* as /s/		
*c*at	*c*ot	*c*ut	*c*ell	*c*ity	*c*ycle
*c*ame	*c*old	*c*ub	*c*ent	*c*ircus	*c*yclone
*c*ab	*c*one	*c*url	*c*ement	*c*itrus	*c*ypress

Notice that when the vowel following *c* is an *a, o,* or *u,* the letter *c* decodes (reads as) the sound of the letter *k.* As mentioned, sounds are written like this with slash lines, /k/. The /k/ sound is called the hard sound of the letter *c.* See the examples of *cat, cot,* and *cut* in list *A.* Repeat these words to yourself and listen to the sound.

When the vowel following the letter *c* is *e, i,* or *y,* the letter *c* decodes as the sound of the letter *s* (the sound for *s* is written /s/). This is called the soft *c* sound. See the examples of *cell, city,* and *cycle* in list *B.* Repeat these words to yourself and listen to the sound.

The letter *g*

A *g* as /g/			*B* *g* as /j/		
*g*ang	*g*ot	*g*um	*g*em	*g*iant	*g*ym
*g*as	*g*oat	*g*ull	*g*entle	*g*inger	*g*ypsy
*g*ame	*g*old	*g*uppy	*g*enius	*g*iraffe	*g*yrate

(4) Since *q* is always written with *u,* both letters are included with the single consonants.
(5) The letter *x* decodes as /z/ in the beginning of words, such as in xylophone. Because there are very few words beginning with this letter, one sound, as in the word *box,* is usually taught although some basals today do include xylophone. Sometimes the sound /z/ as in *exit* is also included.

Notice in list *A* that the words begin with the most frequent sound that single *g* encodes.[6] As with the letter *c*, when the vowel following *g* is an *a, o,* or *u,* the letter *g* decodes as the hard sound, and this hard sound is written as /g/. Examples from the list are *g*ang, *g*ot, and *g*um. Repeat these words to yourself in order to hear the sound.

In list *B*, the words begin with a second sound that the letter *g* may encode. When the vowel following the letter *g* is an *e, i,* or *y,* the letter *g* may decode as the sound of the letter *j* and this sound is written as /j/. Examples from the list are *g*em, *g*iant, and *g*ym. Repeat these words to yourself to hear the sound. This sound is called the soft *g*.

There is, however, a difference between the two generalizations for *c* and *g*. Some simple but often used words such as *girl, get* and *give* have the hard *g* sound. There are a few other exceptions to the *g* generalization, but it "works" a substantial amount of the time, so it is worth learning. In contrast, the *c* generalization "works" almost all the time.

Stated simply, then, in regard to the two letters *c* and *g*:

1. **When *a, o,* and *u* follow *c* or *g*, these letters (*c* and *g*) encode the hard sound.**
2. **When *e, i,* and *y* follow *c* or *g*, these letters (*c* and *g*) encode the soft sound. *G* has several exceptions, such as *girl, get* and *give*.**

The letter *s*

The letter *s* encodes three sounds. Pronounce the following words and notice the sound of *s* in each one.

A s as /s/	B s as /z/	C s as /sh/
*s*ale	hi*s*	a*s*sure
*s*end	name*s*	*s*ugar
*s*it	rea*s*on	*s*ure
*s*ob	ro*s*e	
u*s*	u*s*e	

Notice the difference between the words in lists *A* and *B*. In list *A* the letter *s* encodes its most common sound written as /s/. As shown, examples are *s*ale, *s*end, and *s*it. Say the words to hear the sound. In list *B*, *s* encodes a second sound called the /z/ sound. Unlike *c* and *g*, the vowels following the *s* consonant do not always affect whether the sound is /s/ as in *s*et or /z/ as in u*s*e. (Often, when the *s* is followed at the end of the word by an *e* it may encode the sound /z/ as in the word ro*s*e.)

Some intensive phonics programs teach a third sound /sh/, such as in the words *s*ugar, *s*ure, and a*s*sure, shown in list *C*. There are, however, only a few such words.

Stated simply, we may generalize about the single letter *s*.

Single letter *s* can decode as three sounds:
1. /s/ as in *s*at
2. /z/ as in hi*s*
3. /sh/ as in *s*ugar

(6) Again, *encode* means the written sound or word.

Before proceeding further, you may want to make cards as shown here to assist you as you study.[7] Note again the various sounds encoded by each letter.

c	**g**	**s**
2 sounds	2 sounds	3 sounds
hard *c* /k/ before *a, o, u*, as in *c*at, *c*ot, *c*ut	hard *g* /g/ before *a, o, u*, as in *g*ate, *g*ot, *g*um	/s/ as in *s*un
soft *c* /s/ before *e, i, y*, as in *c*ent, *c*ity, *c*yclone	soft *g* /j/ before *e, i, y*, as in *g*em, *g*iant, *g*ym	/z/ as in hi*s*
		/sh/ as in *s*ugar

Quick Self-Check I*

1. The letters *c* and *g* are conditioned by the vowels that follow them.
   a. What vowel letters cause *c* and *g* to decode as hard sounds?
   b. What vowel letters cause *c* and *g* to decode as soft sounds?
   c. What is the difference between the two generalizations?
2. The letter *s* can vary in the sounds it encodes. Explain.

*Answers to this, and the following Quick Self-Checks may be found in Appendix A.

See Appendix C, page 166, for example words to use in teaching the variant consonants c, g, and s.

Consonant Blends

Beginning blends

English does not permit the blending of two or more consonant *sounds* at the beginning of words unless they are one of the four combinations listed below. These four blend groups combine at the beginning of words (and sometimes in the middle, or medially) to give us hundreds of words in English. They are of four major types: the *r* blends, the *l* blends, the *s* blends, and the *tw* blend. By definition, a consonant blend occurs when two or three consonant sounds (with their related letters) cluster together and are pronounced very rapidly. As you study the following lists of words, you will notice several things.

When *r* or *l* are part of a blend, such as *cr* or *cl*, the *r* and *l* are second. With the *s* blends, the letter *s* comes first in the consonant cluster. Also the *s* blends may combine three consonant letter/sounds as in the words *scr*ub, *spl*ash, and *str*eak.

A *r* blends	B *l* blends	C_1 *s* blends	C_2 *s* blends	D *tw* blend
*br*eak	*bl*onde	*sc*an	*scr*ap	*tw*eak
*cr*ate	*cl*ean	*sk*ate	*scr*ub	*tw*eed
*dr*eam	*fl*y	*sl*eet	*spl*ash	*tw*in
*fr*ight	*gl*eam	*sm*all	*spl*it	*tw*inkle
*gr*im	*pl*ease	*sn*atch	*str*aw	*tw*irl
*pr*unes	*pl*ate	*sp*urt	*str*eak	*tw*ist
*tr*ain		*squ*eak		
		*sw*im		

(7) This is one set of cards. If you make each succeeding set in a different color, it will be easier for you to study. Explanations may be written on the front or back of the cards with a black felt pen.

With the letter *t*, the *tw* consonant blend is the only beginning *t* blend permitted in English.[8]

We might generalize about consonant blends as follows:

There are four consonant blend groups found at the beginning (and sometimes in the middle) of words. These are the *r*, *l*, *s*, and *tw* blends.
1. **The *r* and *l* blends consist of two letters with the *r* and *l* coming second.**
2. **The *s* blend comes first and may consist of three beginning consonants.**
3. **There is also a *tw* blend.**

Before proceeding further, you may want to make cards as shown here and study the various sounds encoded by each.

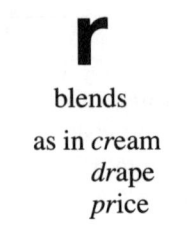
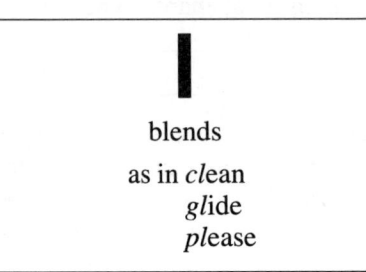
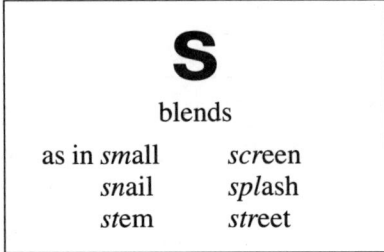

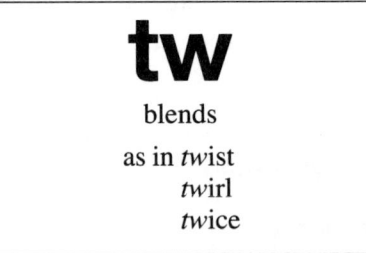

See Appendix C, page 165, for example words to use in teaching the consonant blends r, l, s, and tw.

Ending blends

In addition to the beginning consonant blends, many English words also have ending consonant blends. Examples of these combinations are *ld* as in bo*ld*, *nd* as in ba*nd*, *nt* as in se*nt*, *nk*[9] as in tha*nk*, and *lk* as in sta*lk*. Some phonics programs also include these blends. Others do not, because certain program writers believe that in decoding strategies the beginning letter/sounds are more important than the ending letter/sounds.

Another way of teaching ending blends is by combining a blend with a vowel. This cluster of vowel and blend is frequently referred to as a phonogram.[10] Some examples of these combinations are:

Phonogram	**Word**
old	sold
ind	find
ent	sent
ank	rank
alk[11]	walk

(8) There are three words beginning with *dw*: *dwarf*, *dwell*, and *dwindle*. Some phonics programs also include these.

(9) Some phonics programs classify this as a consonant digraph.

(10) See Appendix B for additional phonograms.

(11) In some areas, the sound encoded by the letter *l* is silent.

We might generalize about ending blends as follows:

Certain consonants combine at the ends of words. Some of the more common of these are *ld, nd, nt, nk,* and *lk*. To teach these ending blends, they are sometimes combined with a vowel.

You may want to make the following cards with final consonant blends to study and include with the *r, l, s,* and *tw* blends.

ld	**nd**	**nt**
as in o*ld*	as in fi*nd*	as in se*nt*

nk	**lk**
as in ra*nk*	as in wa*lk*

Quick Self-Check II

1. English contains four types of beginning consonant blends.
   a. Name the beginning blends.
   b. How are they similar?
   c. How are they different?
2. Some phonics programs include ending blends.
   a. Name some of the ending blends.
   b. How are they sometimes taught?

Consonant Digraphs

Two consonant letters together encoding only a single sound/sounds are called consonant digraphs. In the word *digraph*, the syllable *di* stands for "two" and the syllable *graph* stands for "any written symbol (letter)."

Digraph then means "two written symbols or letters that encode a single sound/sounds."

The unique *h* digraphs

Look at the following list of words and note the sound/sounds encoded by each digraph.

Words	**Digraphs and Sounds**
*ch*air, s*ch*ool, *ch*ef	ch /ch/ /k/ /sh/
*gh*ost, lau*gh*, thou*gh*	gh /g/ /f/ /-/
*ph*oto	ph /f/
*sh*ip	sh /sh/
*th*at, *th*in	th /t̶h̶/ /th/
*wh*at, *wh*o	wh /w/ /h/

You will notice that each digraph includes the letter *h*. Each digraph also has distinctive features:

ch   This consonant digraph encodes three sounds:

1. /ch/   as in *ch*air.
2. /k/   as in s*ch*ool.
3. /sh/   as in *ch*ef.

The most common sound *ch* encodes is the /ch/ as in *ch*air, *ch*amp, and *ch*op. Repeat these words to hear the sound.

A second sound, the /k/ sound, occurs in words such as *ch*aracter and s*ch*eme. These are frequently words of Greek origin. Repeat the words *ch*aracter and s*ch*eme to hear the /k/ sound.

The third sound of /sh/ as in *ch*ef is usually found in French words, such as *ch*ampagne, *ch*andelier, and *ch*aise. (There are only a few such words.)

gh   This digraph has three sounds:

1. /g/   as in *gh*ost
2. /f/   as in enou*gh*
3. /silent/ or /-/ as in thorou*gh*

The *gh* digraph causes a lot of problems because it derives from the former gutteral *gh*, a part of Old English. Through the years this gutteral sound has been replaced or modified so that today it appears as any of the three sounds in *gh*ost, enou*gh*, and thorou*gh*. Say these words with *gh* to remember the sounds. Actually, there are few words with the latter two sounds. These words are usually learned as sight words.

ph   This digraph does not include the sound of /p/ but encodes the sound of /f/ as in *ph*armacy. It often appears at the beginning of words but may also appear in the middle as in *ph*os*ph*orus, or at the end as in gra*ph*. Repeat these words to hear the sound.

sh   This digraph encodes only one sound as /sh/ in *sh*ip and da*sh*. Say the words to hear the sound.

th   This digraph has two sounds called voiced *th* and unvoiced *th*. Say the words *th*ere and *th*ink, while at the same time placing your hands on your throat. Notice that when you say the word *th*ere you feel the vibrations of your vocal chords on the /th/ sound. This sound is written /t̶h̶/. The /th/ sound that vibrates is called the voiced sound. When you say the word *th*ink, you do not feel these vibrations. Repeat several times. The /th/ sound that does not vibrate is called the voiceless sound.

Study the following additional examples. Say these words to yourself and again note the difference between the beginning sounds:

A voiced *th* as /t̶h̶/	B voiceless *th* as /th/
*th*an	*th*ank
*th*at	*th*atch
*th*em	*th*eater
*th*en	*th*ick
*th*ere	*th*ink

wh This digraph has two sounds: the sound of /w/ in *wh*at and the sound of /h/ in *wh*o. In Old English a word such as *what* was written as *hwat* and pronounced with the *h* initially (Liles, 1972, p. 236). Later the letters *hw* were reversed to become *wh*. In pronunciation, however, we were to differentiate between *wh*ich, and *w*itch by pronouncing the /h/ of *wh*ich first. Today with language still changing, most people pronounce such words as *wh*at, *wh*en, and *wh*ere with only the /w/ sound.

Notice the words below beginning with the digraph *wh* and followed by the letter *o*:

*wh*o
*wh*ole
*wh*olly

When *o* follows the *wh* digraph, this digraph decodes as /h/. (These words are generally taught as sight words.)

Insofar as the consonant digraphs with *h*, we might generalize as follows:

Digraphs are two consonant letters placed together that encode a single sound/sounds. The letter *h* combines to form six digraphs as follows: *ch, gh, ph, sh, th,* and *wh*. The digraph

1. *ch* encodes three sounds as the /ch/ in *ch*air, /k/ in s*ch*eme, and /sh/ in *ch*andelier.
2. *gh* encodes three sounds as the /g/ in *gh*ost, /f/ in rou*gh*, and /-/ in thorou*gh*.
3. *ph* encodes the /f/ sound as in *ph*oto.
4. *sh* encodes the /sh/ sound as in *sh*ip.
5. *th* encodes two sounds as the /t̶h̶/ in *th*ere and /th/ in *th*ick.
6. *wh* encodes two sounds as the /w/ in *wh*at and /h/ in *wh*o.

Before proceeding further, you may want to make cards with the unique h digraph and study the various sounds encoded by each.

ch	**gh**	**ph**
/ch/ as in *ch*air /k/ as in s*ch*eme /sh/ as in *ch*andelier	/g/ as in *gh*ost /f/ as in rou*gh* /silent/ or /-/ as in thorou*gh*	/f/ as in *ph*oto

sh	**th**	**wh**
/sh/ as in *sh*ip	/t̶h̶/ voiced as in *th*ese /th/ unvoiced as in *th*ick	/w/ as in *wh*at /h/ as in *wh*om

See Appendix C, page 166, for example words to use in teaching consonant digraphs with h.

Quick Self-Check III

1. The letter *h* combines with other consonants to encode unique sounds.
   a. Which combinations encode three sounds? List these with their respective sounds?
   b. Which combinations encode two sounds? List these with their respective sounds.
   c. Which combinations encode one sound? List these with their respective sounds.

Digraphs with a first silent letter

There is a second group of consonant digraphs, all of which have a silent letter. These digraphs are *gn, kn, wr,* and *ck*. Note the following:

A **gn as /n/**	B **kn as /n/**	C **wr as /r/**	D **ck as /k/**
*gn*arl	*kn*ack	*wr*ap	ta*ck*
*gn*at	*kn*ee	*wr*eck	che*ck*
rei*gn*	*kn*ife	*wr*inkle	sti*ck*
*gn*ome	*kn*ow	*wr*ist	tru*ck*

gn and kn Notice that when the letters *gn* or *kn* are used together, only the sound of /n/ is heard. The *g* is silent in the *gn* digraph as in *gn*arl, and the *k* is silent in the *kn* digraph as in *kn*ack.

wr In the *wr* digraph the *w* is silent. Interestingly enough, most words beginning with *wr*, such as *wr*ap and *wr*inkle, denote a twisting motion in their meanings.

ck The digraph *ck* also has a first silent letter when it appears at the end of a syllable or word (often with one syllable) and *follows a short vowel*. Notice the following two groups of words. In list *A* all the vowels are short and the ending /k/ sound is written as *ck*. In list *B* all the vowels are long and the ending /k/ sound is written as *ke*.

A **ck as /k/**	B **ke as /k/**
sa*ck*	ma*ke*
de*ck*	e*ke*[12]
ti*ck*	ti*ke*
do*ck*	po*ke*
lu*ck*	du*ke*

(12) Very few words end in *eke*.

We might generalize about these four digraphs, *gn, kn, wr,* and *ck* as follows:

1. **In the consonant digraphs, *gn, kn, wr* and *ck*, the first letter is always silent.**
2. **The digraph *ck* follows a short vowel.**

Special combinations: *dge* and *tch*

There is a third group of three-letter consonant combinations that behaves similarly to *ck*. Even though these combinations include three letters and not two, they are still often referred to as digraphs, principally because they encode a single sound. These two combinations are *dge* and *tch*. Note the following:

A *dge* as /j/	B *tch* as /ch/
ba*dge*	la*tch*
le*dge*	stre*tch*
ri*dge*	sti*tch*
do*dge*	blo*tch*
smu*dge*	clu*tch*

In every instance, the vowels preceding these combinations are short, just as with the *ck* digraph. Also, as with the *ck* digraph, these combinations are often found at the end of one syllable words. The reason for the combination *dge* goes back several hundred years when printers attempted to show whether vowel sounds were long or short. Often, an extra consonant letter was added to indicate that the previous vowel sound was short. The words in column A were written as *bagge, legge,* etc. The first *g* was eventually turned around and became the letter *d*.

We still see evidence of this printing device—doubling a consonant letter to keep the vowel short—in such words as la*dd*er, le*tt*er, li*tt*er, o*tt*er, and ru*dd*er. This is also the reason we usually only pronounce a single consonant letter in English even when it is doubled. (Other reasons for doubling consonant letters will be discussed later.)

We might generalize as follows for the special combinations *dge* and *tch*.

1. **The combination *dge* decodes as the sound of /j/, as in do*dge*.**
2. **The combination *tch* decodes as the sound of /ch/, as in sti*tch*.**
3. **These combinations follow a short vowel, often at the end of a one syllable word.**

ng

The two letters *n* and *g* blur to become one distinctive sound, or digraph. You can hear this unique nasal sound if you pronounce the following words: si*ng*, ra*ng*, lo*ng*.

14 PART 1 UNDERSTANDING PHONICS

You may want to make and study the following cards with these special digraphs and special combinations before proceeding further.

gn	**kn**	**wr**
/n/ as in *gn*ome	/n/ as in *kn*ee	/r/ as in *wr*ite

ck	**dge**	**tch**
/k/ as in che*ck* used after a short vowel	/j/ as in ri*dge* used after a short vowel	/ch/ as in ba*tch* used after a short vowel

ng

/ng/ as in ri*ng*

See Appendix C, page 167, for example words to use in teaching the consonant digraphs with a first silent letter, and the special combinations *dge* and *tch*.

Quick
Self-Check IV

1. What do the digraphs *gn*, *kn*, *wr*, and *ck* have in common?
2. Why are the special combinations of *dge* and *tch* referred to as digraphs?
3. What do the digraphs *ck*, *dge*, and *tch* have in common?

| PART 1, SECTION I: REVIEW AND SELF-CHECK | You have now completed what you should know about consonant letters and sounds. Before proceeding further, you may want to study your cards again. Group them into categories, such as consonants with more than one sound, blends, unique *h* digraphs, and digraphs with a silent first letter. Doing this will facilitate learning them. If you can answer the following questions, you are probably ready to proceed with the vowel sequence: |

1. List the consonant letters that encode more than one sound. Two of these consonants are conditioned by the vowels following them. Explain, using word examples. Do these generalizations work all the time?
2. Underline the unique *h* digraphs in the following words:
   graph
   chaise
   ghastly
   think
   airship
   while
   What sounds do each of these respective digraphs encode? Give word examples.
3. Four consonant digraphs contain a silent first letter. List these digraphs and indicate the sound encoded by each. Give word examples.
4. The digraphs *ck* and the clusters *dge* and *tch* decode as what sounds? Give word examples. What do these three combinations have in common?

SECTION II

VOWELS

The second major division in phonics analysis, and also the more difficult, includes the vowels.

The Single Vowels, *a, e, i, o, u,* and the schwa

Each vowel encodes a short and long sound, and also a schwa sound. While this latter sound has many regional variations, it is usually similar to short *u* as in *up* and is shown in texts as an upside down *e*, as ə. The vowels *a, o,* and *u* also encode an additional sound, sometimes called a special or third sound, to be discussed later.

Short Vowel Sound	Long Vowel Sound	Schwa Sound
*a*ct	*a*ble	b*a* na na /ə/
*e*lephant	*e*ven	tick *et* /ə/
*i*t	*i*vy	pen c*i*l /ə/
*o*live	*o*men	a pr*o*n /ə/
*u*ntil	*u*nit, r*u*de	

The short vowel sound

The short vowel sound is the most prominent in English. The breve mark (˘) is used in writing to indicate the short vowel. Examples: ăct, ĕlephant.

To aid in recalling vowel sounds, teachers with the help of their students often compose fun sentences beginning with these sounds as the two examples below:

An *e*lephant *i*s *o*ddly *u*npredictable.
S*a*d *E*mma *is* often *u*nhappy.

Another way to remember the short vowel sound is by thinking of key words that are similar:

băt
bĕt
bĭt
bŏp
bŭt

The long vowel sound

The macron (¯) is positioned above the vowel to indicate that it is long. Examples: ā*ble*, ē*ven*. The long vowel sound is identical to the name of the vowel as ā, ē, /ī/, ō, ū. In addition, sometimes the letter *u* has the "long" vowel sound o͞o as in the word *rūde*. The reason there are two long vowel sounds for *u* is the result of a change in language that has taken place during the last fifty years. An examination of the two word lists below will indicate the two long ū sounds.

A	*B*
u as /yū/	*u* as /o͞o/
cūte	brūte
fūture	dūke
hūman	Jūne
mūle	lūte
pūny	nūmeral
ūse	tūbe

Repeat these words to hear the difference between the two sounds. The words in list *A* have the traditional long /yū/ sound, while in list *B*, the long ū has the sound of /o͞o/, not /yū/. As indicated, this sound change began to take place in the 1930s. Prior to that time, the long ū appearing in words was generally pronounced as /yū/ (Rinsky, 1975). (The sound /yū/ or /o͞o/ is dependent on the preceding consonant sound.)

In sum, while the vowel letters ā, ē, /ī/, and ō may each decode as one long vowel sound the letter *u* may decode as two, /yū/ and /o͞o/.

Special vowel sound

Repeat the words listed below to hear the special or third vowel sounds of *a*, *o*, and *u*.

A as /ä/	*o* as /o͞o/	*u* as /o͝o/
c*a*ll	l*o*se	p*u*sh
w*a*nd	wh*o*m	b*u*llet
f*a*ther	pr*o*ve	b*u*shel

Many reading programs only teach short and long vowel sounds. Words such as those listed previously, representative of special vowel sounds, are sometimes treated as sight words and considered unphonetic.

A word of caution about these sounds. Except for the long vowels, it is extremely difficult to pronounce the vowel sounds in isolation. When learning or teaching the short vowels, place a consonant sound such as /t/ after each of them to make pronunciation easier. These combinations are often referred to as phonograms.[13] (Refer to page 160 and the appendix.) The short vowels would then be pronounced in a phonogram or word as follows:

/at/ as in săt
/et/ as in sĕt
/it/ as in sĭt
/ot/ as in tŏt
/ut/ as in hŭt

Key words are very important for remembering sounds, as we do not speak in sounds but in words! Capitalize on what is familiar.

The schwa

One of the changes occurring in the English language at the present time is the reduction of the short vowel to the schwa sound. What this means is that in *unaccented* syllables many of the short vowels have an /uh/ kind of sound, similar to short *u* as in *up*.[14]

Consider the following words as spoken in context:

*a*cróss He walked *a*cross the street.
tíck*e*t She waited for a tick*e*t.
pénc*i*l The penc*i*l needed sharpening.
séc*o*nd Just one second, please.

In each instance the vowel in the unaccented syllable has a schwa sound, written like an upside down *e*, /ə/. To indicate the sound you will often find words such as the above written in textbooks as follows:

ə cross
tick ət
pen səl
sec ənd

In view of what we have just mentioned in regard to short vowels, long vowels, third sound, and schwa, we might make the following generalizations about single vowels:

1. **Single vowel letters have a short and long sound.**
2. **The short vowel sounds are** ă (ăct); ĕ (ĕlephant); ĭ (ĭt); ŏ (ŏlive); and ŭ (ŭntil).

(13) Sometimes phonograms are referred to as a base.
(14) Regional variations must be considered when discussing the schwa.

3. The long vowel sounds are the same as the names of the vowel letters, ā, ē, ī, ō, ū. The letter *u* has a second additional long vowel sound of /o͞o/ (brute).
4. The letters *a* as /ä/ (call); *o* as /o͞o/ (prove); and *u* as /o͝o/ (push) have a special, or third sound. Sometimes words with these sounds are taught as sight words.
5. Unaccented syllables with a single vowel letter may have a schwa sound. The sound is written as /ə/ (tickət).

You may want to make and study the following cards showing the single vowel letter/sounds before proceeding further.

a
/ă/ as in *a*ct
/ā/ as in *a*ble
/ä/ as in *a*lways

e
/ĕ/ as in *e*lephant
/ē/ as in *e*ven

i
/ĭ/ as in *i*t
/ī/ as in *i*cy

o
/ŏ/ as in *o*live
/ō/ as in *o*men
/o͞o/ as in d*o*

u
/ŭ/ as in *u*pon
/ū/ as in *u*nit
/o͞o/ as in r*u*de
/o͝o/ as in p*u*sh

ə
/ə/ as in b*a*nana
/ə/ as in tick*e*t
/ə/ as in penc*i*l
/ə/ as in sec*o*nd

See Appendix C, page 168, for example words to use in teaching vowel sounds.

Quick Self-Check V

1. The vowel letters, *a, e, i, o,* and *u* may encode a long or short sound.
   a. In addition, what vowel letter has a second long sound? What is it?
   b. Which vowel letters may encode a third sound? Are words with these sounds taught phonetically or by sight?
   c. What is the schwa sound? In what part of a word is it usually heard?

Final Unpronounced Letter e

We sometimes use the single letter vowel and a final *e* to encode the long vowel sound. We do this to differentiate between words such as the following:

A	B
măd	māde
mĕt	mēte
rĭd	rīde
nŏt	nōte
cŭt	cūte

Therefore, we might generalize about final *e* changing the preceding vowel sound as follows:

The letter *e* at the end of a word may sometimes indicate that the preceding vowel is long. (Remember, too, that a final *e* may also indicate that the preceding *c* or *g* has a soft sound as in *stance* and *barge*.)[15]

The final *e* generalization needs a further word of explanation and we will have to digress for a moment to do so. You should now understand two reasons for the final unpronounced *e* at the end of certain words. Stated simply:

1. **Final *e* may indicate that the preceding vowel is long as shown by the contrasting words *mat* and *mate*.**
2. **Final *e* may indicate that the preceding *c* and *g* have a soft sound as in stan*ce* and bar*ge*.**[16]

There are other reasons for the unpronounced final *e*. Language is often arbitrary in decisions it makes about spelling. In English we have a particular rule to the effect that English words will not end in the letter *v*. With words such as *have, prove,* and *love,* the *e* does not make the preceding vowel long. It is simply there because English words do not end in *v*. Sometimes, however, the final *e* after *v* does make the preceding vowel long in such words as *shave* and *stove*. In these and other similar words, the *e* plays a dual role.

We now have three reasons for words ending in unpronounced final *e*. We might generalize as follows:

1. **Final *e* may indicate that the vowel before it is long, as in *mate*.**
2. **Final *e* may indicate that the preceding *c* and *g* are soft, as in *stance* and *barge*.**
3. **Final *e* is used after the letter *v*, as in *have* because English words do not end in *v*.**

Another reason an unpronounced final *e* appears after certain words, such as *house* and *awe*, is simply due to historical circumstance and the whims of early printers. When several words began to change during the Middle English period, the final *e*, formerly pronounced as an /ĕ/, became silent, but printers nonetheless retained the written letter. Second, during the earlier printing periods the letter *e* was added to fill up the line when words did not complete the required number of spaces. We still have to struggle with words such as these. Therefore, in addition to the preceding three reasons, we can generalize a fourth reason for the final unpronounced *e*.

4. **Final *e* may appear at the end of some words for historical reasons.**

The last reason for unpronounced final *e* can be found in such words as *table, maple,* and *noble*. The *e* follows an *l* and is needed to complete the second

---

(15) Refer to page 5 "Consonants With More Than One Sound," if you do not remember this generalization.
(16) Ibid.

syllable; otherwise the first vowel would be short, and the word would be unpronounceable. (For example try pronouncing tabl, mapl, and nobl.)

We now have five reasons why English words have a final unpronounced letter *e*.

You may want to make and study the following card:

FINAL UNPRONOUNCED *e*
1. Final *e* may indicate that the vowel before it is long.
2. Final *e* may indicate that the preceding *c* and *g* have a soft sound.
3. Final *e* is used after *v* because English words do not end in *v*.
4. Final *e* may be an historical leftover.
5. Final *e* follows *l* in a two-syllable word to complete the syllable.

A further note on final *e*. While this rule has about 93% predictability, most exceptions occur from some words that end in *ile* as *facile, ine* as *machine*, both derived from French spellings, and words ending in *Vre* as *mare*. See Louis and Heath "A Face Lift for the Silent *e*" (1983).

See Appendix C, page 168, for example words to use in teaching long vowels with final silent e.

Quick Self-Check VI

Next to each word indicate the final *e* generalization.
1. prove
2. stable
3. fence
4. stake
5. else

Vowel Digraphs and Diphthongs

We mentioned during our discussion of consonant letters that the word *digraph* means "two letters encoding only a single sound/sounds." In addition to consonant digraphs there are also vowel digraphs. There is also within the vowels a second category called diphthongs. The dictionary defines a diphthong[17] as "a gliding sound from one vowel to another."

Vowel digraphs and diphthongs that begin with *a*

Vowel Pair	Word
ai	m*ai*d /ā/
ay	st*ay* /ā/
au	v*au*lt /ä/
aw	dr*aw* /ä/

(17) Diphthongs will be discussed in more detail later.

ai* and *ay As you can see, we have, in addition to the silent *e* pattern, ways of writing the long *a* sound using two letters. Examples: m*ai*d and st*ay*. This is one of the difficulties in understanding the English writing-decoding system. We have too many different ways of representing the same sound!

The vowel digraph *ai* may decode as long *a* in the middle of a word while *ay* decodes as long *a* at the end.[18] The reason for this is that English words do not end in *i* except for the foreign words we have borrowed, such as *spaghetti* and *macaroni*.

au* and *aw In some phonic systems the combinations *au* and *aw* are considered digraphs and in others diphthongs. Both *au* and *aw* decode as the sound of /ä/. Since English words do not usually end in *u* (as in the case of *v*), *au* is used at the beginning and middle of a word as in *au*thor and f*au*lt, and *aw* is used at the end as in l*aw*.

These four pairs, *ai, ay, au,* and *aw,* are considered stable in that they almost always decode as these sounds.

We might generalize about these digraph/diphthongs beginning with the letter *a* as follows:

1. There are four vowel pairs beginning with *a: ai, ay, au,* and *aw.*
2. The digraphs *ai* and *ay* decode as the long /ā/ sound. *Ai* may be used at the beginning or in the middle of a word. *Ay* may be used at the end.
3. *Au* and *aw* decode as the /ä/ sound. *Au* may be used at the beginning or in the middle of a word. *Aw* may be used at the end.

You may want to make and study the following cards before proceeding further.

ai	**ay**	**au**	**aw**
/ā/ as in m*ai*d	/ā/ as in st*ay*	/ä/ as in v*au*lt	/ä/ as in dr*aw*

See Appendix C, page 169, for example words to use in teaching vowel digraphs and diphthongs beginning with a.

Quick Self-Check VII

1. Why do we have the two digraphs *ai* and *ay*? What sound do they encode?
2. Why do we have the two digraphs *au* and *aw*? What sound do they encode?
3. Why are these combinations considered stable?

---

(18) When a suffix has been added to the word, *ay* may be in the middle. Example: *playing*.

Vowel digraphs with e

Vowel digraphs that contain the letter *e* are as follows:

Digraph	Word		
ee	sl*ee*p /ē/		
ea	h*ea*t /ē/	spr*ea*d /ĕ/	st*ea*k /ā/
ie	bel*ie*f /ē/	t*ie* /ī/	
ei	rec*ei*ve /ē/	v*ei*n /ā/	
	(very irregular digraph)		
ey	donk*ey* /ē/	pr*ey* /ā/	

Since the *e* digraphs are more complicated than the *a* digraphs we will generalize about each one individually.

ee The vowel digraph *ee* is usually the first vowel digraph introduced in reading because of its stability. Since it usually decodes as long /ē/ (sl*ee*p, j*ee*p, st*ee*p), we may generalize as follows:

The vowel digraph *ee* decodes as /ē/.

ea The vowel digraph *ea* is more complicated because it decodes as three sounds. Look at the following lists of words:

A	B	C
ea as /ē/	*ea* as /ĕ/	*ea* as /ā/
cl*ea*n	l*ea*ther	st*ea*k
r*ea*ch	br*ea*th	br*ea*k
s*ea*l	r*ea*dy	gr*ea*t
p*ea*ch	pl*ea*sant	

The first and most common sound is long /ē/ as in cl*ea*n, r*ea*ch, and s*ea*l. About 25 percent of the time this digraph decodes as short /e/, as in l*ea*ther, br*ea*th, and r*ea*dy (Burmeister, 1968). A third sound this digraph decodes is long /ā/ although there are only a few such words. Examples are gr*ea*t and st*ea*k.

We might generalize about the *ea* digraph as follows:

1. **The *ea* digraph decodes as three sounds.**
2. **It most commonly decodes as long /ē/ as in h*ea*t.**
3. **It also decodes as short /ĕ/ as in br*ea*d.**
4. **In a few words *ea* decodes as /ā/ as in st*ea*k.**

ie The *ie* digraph decodes as two sounds, long /ē/ and long /ī/. Excluding suffixed words, the most common sound is long /ē/. Only a few base words with *ie* decode as long /ī/. These are words such as p*ie*, t*ie*, l*ie*, and d*ie*. Words with suffix endings, however, often do decode as /ī/ as in tr*ie*d (try + ed), dr*ie*d (dry + ed), and supplies (supply + s). This is because the *y* is dropped and changed to *i*. There are, as stated, many examples of base words with *ie* decoding as long /ē/ such as the following:

ie as /ē/

bel*ie*ve	p*ie*ce
br*ie*f	sh*ie*ld
gr*ie*f	th*ie*f
n*ie*ce	y*ie*ld

We might generalize about the *ie* digraph as follows:

The *ie* vowel digraph decodes as two sounds, long /ē/ as in br*ie*f and long /ī/ as in p*ie*. Excluding suffixed words, the most common sound is long /ē/.

ei The *ei* digraph is highly irregular and very difficult to classify except for its relationship to *c*. When *ei* follows a *c*, it always decodes as long /ē/. This digraph may also decode as long /ā/ in a few words. See the following:

A	B
ei as /ē/ after c	**ei as /ā/**
rec*ei*ve	v*ei*n
conc*ei*ve	r*ei*gn
rec*ei*pt	v*ei*l

However, in addition to long /ē/ after *c* and the long /ā/ sound, this digraph shows considerable variability as evidenced in the following words:

counterf*ei*t	/ī/	l*ei*sure	/ē/
*ei*ther	/ē/	s*ei*zed	/ĕ/
forf*ei*ted	/ĭ/	sover*ei*gn	/ĭ/
h*ei*fer	/ĕ/	prot*ei*n	/ē/

Teachers sometimes use nonsense sentences to help students recall these words: 'N*ei*ther counterf*ei*t s*ei*zed the sover*ei*gn. They wanted the h*ei*fer, prot*ei*n and l*ei*sure.'

We might generalize about the vowel digraph *ei* as follows:

The vowel digraph *ei* decodes as the sound of long /ē/ after *c*. It also decodes as the sound of /ā/ as in v*ei*n. Its vowel sound also varies in other words.

ey The vowel digraph *ey* usually decodes as the sound of long /ē/. In a few words it decodes as the sound of /ā/. See the following lists of words:

A	B
ey as /ē/	**ey as /ā/**
vall*ey*	th*ey*
k*ey*	pr*ey*
pull*ey*	conv*ey*
attorn*ey*	ob*ey*

We might generalize about the *ey* digraph as follows:

The *ey* digraph generally decodes as the long sound of /ē/. In a few words it decodes as /ā/.

We can now summarize all the generalizations of the *e* vowel digraphs as follows:

The digraph
1. *ee* decodes as /ē/, as in sl*ee*p.
2. *ea* decodes most often as long /ē/, as in h*ea*t; also as short /ĕ/, as in br*ea*d; and in a few words as long /ā/, as in st*ea*k.
3. *ie* usually decodes as /ē/, as in bel*ie*ve; and also as /ī/, as in t*ie*.
4. *ei* decodes as /ē/ after *c*, as in rec*ei*ve; as /ā/, as in v*ei*n; and varies in its sound.
5. *ey* decodes as /ē/, as in donk*ey*; as /ā/, as in ob*ey*.

You may want to make and study these cards before proceeding further.

---

ee
/ē/ as in sl*ee*p

ea
/ē/ as in h*ea*t
/ĕ/ as in br*ea*d
/ā/ as in st*ea*k

ie
/ē/ as in bel*ie*ve
/ī/ as in t*ie* and cr*ie*s

ei
/ē/ after *c* as in rec*ei*ve
/ā/ as in v*ei*n (highly variable)

ey
/ē/ as in donk*ey*
/ā/ as in pr*ey*

See Appendix C, page 169, for example words to use in teaching digraphs with *e*.

Quick Self-Check VIII

ee ea ie ei ey

1. Which digraph is fairly stable and encodes one sound?
2. Which digraph has the greatest variability?
3. Which digraph usually encodes /ē/ and /ĕ/ and /ā/?
4. Which digraph usually encodes /ē/ and /ā/?
5. Which digraph usually encodes /ē/ and /ī/?

Vowel digraph with *i*

The letter *i* as mentioned on page 21, combines with *a* to form the vowel digraph *ai* that decodes as long /ā/. The letter *i* also combines with *e* in the vowel digraphs *ie* and *ei* (see page 22).

The letter *i* will also combine with the consonant digraph *gh* mentioned under the unique *h* digraph on page 9. This three letter combination *igh*, called a digraph by some, decodes as long /ī/ after a beginning sound. (It is often referred to as "the three letter *i*".) See the following word group for examples:

igh as /ī/
bl*igh*t
fl*igh*t
r*igh*t
s*igh*

We might generalize about the letter *i* as follows:

The letter *i* combines with *gh* in the middle or end of some words and decodes as long /ī/.

Make and study this card before proceeding further.

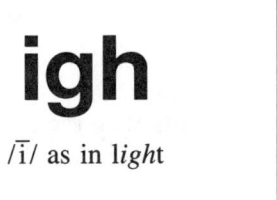

See Appendix C, page 169, for example words to use when teaching the three letter ī.

Vowel digraphs/diphthongs with *o*

As previously mentioned, there is not always agreement as to what is a digraph and what is a diphthong. By definition, a diphthong means a 'gliding sound from one vowel to another.' If you say the long *o* sound and watch your lips in a mirror, you will see that your mouth formation remains stationary. However, if you pronounce the diphthong /oy/ as in *oil*, your mouth moves or glides as it goes from one sound to the other.

This lack of agreement as to what is a digraph and what is a diphthong comes about because linguists and reading specialists, who define these terms, have different points of reference. Linguists are usually concerned with the nature of the sounds, and those who teach reading are concerned wtih decoding the letters that encode those sounds.

It is our opinion that learning such terminology as *digraph* and *diphthong* is not that important for children who are learning decoding strategies. What is important is that they see such vowel combinations as *oa* or *au* as units and do not try to read them as individual vowel sounds.

The following digraph/diphthong classification beginning with *o* is based on our examination of current basals.

oa The letter *o* combines with the letter *a* to form the *oa* vowel digraph and decodes as the long *o* sound rather consistently. See the following examples:

oa as /ō/
  coach
  coast
  float
  gloat

We might generalize about the *oa* digraph as follows:

The *oa* digraph decodes as the sound of long /ō/.

oo The letter *o* combines with a second letter *o* to form the combination *oo*, and this combination, together with *ou*, *ow*, *oi*, and *oy* are usually considered diphthongs. Examine the following two lists containing words with the *oo* diphthong.

A		B
oo as /o͞o/		**oo as /o͝o/**
bloom	soothe	brook
broom	spool	crook
croon	tooth	shook
shoot	troop	stood

There are many more words with the long /o͞o/ sound as in list A. Say the words in these two lists to yourself very slowly and hear the difference between the two sounds. Put a consonant such as *m* after the long /o͞o/ as in the word broom to hear the isolated long /o͞o/ sound. Put a consonant *k* after the /o͝o/ as in the words crook to hear the isolated short /o͝o/ sound.

We might generalize about the *oo* diphthong as follows:

The *oo* diphthong decodes as two sounds, long /o͞o/ as in broom and short /o͝o/ as in look. The long /o͞o/ sound is the more common of the two.

ou The letter *o* also combines with the letter *u* and encodes several sounds. It is a very complex combination. Its two most common sounds are /ow/ as in cloud and /ŭ/ as in touch. See the following lists for additional words:

A	B
ou as /ow/	**ou as /ŭ/**
about	cousin
crouch	double
hound	touch
proud	trouble
thousand	young

Say these words to hear the sounds.

Two additional sounds encoded by *ou* are /ō/ as in s*ou*l, and /o͞o/ as in gr*ou*p. Note these two lists:

A	B
ou as /ō/	**ou as /o͞o/**
s*ou*l	gr*ou*p
p*ou*ltry	r*ou*te
sh*ou*lder	w*ou*nd

Say these words to hear the sounds.

These last two sounds are not too common and are not always taught because together they represent only about 10 percent of the words containing *ou* (Burmeister, 1968).

We might generalize about the *ou* combination as follows:

1. **When *ou* is a diphthong, it most commonly decodes as /ow/ as in s*ou*nd.**
2. **Its second most common sound is /ŭ/ as in c*ou*sin.**
3. **In only a few words does it decode as /ō/ as in sh*ou*lder and /o͞o/ as in gr*ou*p.**

Now you can understand why it is so difficult to classify diphthongs and digraphs. Some vowel pairs as *ou* are diphthongs in one context, as in *about*, and digraphs in another, as in *touch*.

ow The letter *o* combines with *w* to form both the /ow/ diphthong and the long /ō/ vowel sound.[19] Examine the following two lists.

A	B
ow as /ow/	**ow as /ō/**
cl*ow*n	fl*ow*
dr*ow*n	gr*ow*
fr*ow*n	gr*ow*th
n*ow*	kn*ow*
pr*ow*l	sn*ow*
t*ow*el	

Repeat the words to hear these sounds.

In the first list *ow* decodes as the sound of /ow/ as in t*ow*el. In the second list *ow* decodes as the sound of long /ō/ in kn*ow*. Notice that most of the *B* list words are *ending* sounds.

We might generalize about the combination *ow* as follows:

The combination *ow* decodes as two sounds: /ow/ as in t*ow*el, and long /ō/ as in gl*ow*.

oi and *oy* The letter *o* combines with *i* and also with *y* to form the two diphthongs *oi* and *oy*. Both encode the same sound of /oy/. Note the following lists:

A	B
oi as /oy/	**oy as /oy/**
*oi*l	t*oy*
s*oi*l	empl*oy*
m*oi*st	destr*oy*

(19) Many linguists consider that all long vowels are diphthongs.

The *oi* is used at the beginning and in the middle of base words, and *oy* is used at the end. (This is similar to *ai* and *ay*.) English words, as mentioned, do not end with the letter *i* except for borrowed foreign words.

We might generalize about these two diphthongs as follows:

The two diphthongs *oi* and *oy* both decode as the /oy/ sound. *Oi* is used at the beginning and in the middle of base words, while *oy* is used at the end.

You may want to make these cards with the *o* digraphs and diphthongs and study them before proceeding further.

The letter *o* combines with other vowels to form digraphs and diphthongs. The combination(s)
1. *oa* decodes as /ō/ in c*oa*t.
2. *oo* decodes as /o͞o/ in m*oo*n, and as /o͝o/ in b*oo*k.
3. *ou* usually decodes as /ow/ in cl*ou*d, and as /ŭ/ in t*ou*ch, *ou* also decodes in a few words as /ō/ in sh*ou*lder and as /o͞o/ in gr*ou*p.
4. *ow* decodes as /ow/ in c*ow*, and as /ō/ in l*ow*.
5. *oi* and *oy* decode as /oy/. The *oi* diphthong comes at the beginning and middle of words while *oy* is used at the end.

You may want to make and study the following cards before proceeding further.

oa	**oo**	**ou**
/ō/ as in c*oa*t	/o͞o/ as in sp*oo*n /o͝o/ as in b*oo*k	/ow/ as in ab*ou*t /ŭ/ as in c*ou*sin /ō/ as in sh*ou*lder /o͞o/ as in gr*ou*p
ow	**oi**	**oy**
/ow/ as in t*ow*n /ō/ as in *ow*n	/oy/ as in *oi*l	/oy/ as in t*oy*

See Appendix C, page 169 and 170, for example words to use in teaching the *o* combinations.

Quick Self-Check IX	oa oo ou ow oi oy

1. Which combination may encode four different sounds? Identify the sounds and give key words.
2. Why do we have two diphthongs, *oi* and *oy*, encoding the same sound?
3. Which digraph encodes one sound? What is it?
4. List the two sounds encoded by *ow*. Write key words.
5. List the two sounds encoded by *oo*. Write key words.

Vowel diphthongs encoding /o͞o/

ui and ue The letter *u* combines with the letter *i* and also with the letter *e* to form diphthongs that decode as /o͞o/. Note the following two lists:

A *ui* as /o͞o/	B *ue* as /o͞o/
j*ui*ce	bl*ue*
j*ui*cy	d*ue*
sl*ui*ce	fl*ue*
s*ui*t	tr*ue*

Say the words to hear the sounds.

ew There is also another two-letter diphthong that begins with the letter *e* and decodes as /o͞o/. This combination *ew* could have been included under Section II with the vowel *e* combinations, but since it decodes as /o͞o/, it seemed more advantageous to place it here.

Examine this list of words:

ew as /o͞o/
bl*ew*
br*ew*
ch*ew*
cr*ew*
dr*ew*
fl*ew*
st*ew*
str*ew*n

We might generalize about these diphthongs as follows:[20]

The diphthongs *ui*, *ue*, and *ew* usually decode as the sound of /o͞o/ as in the words fr*ui*t, bl*ue*, and str*ew*.

---

(20) You will recall that during our discussion of the long vowel sound encoded by the letter *u*, we mentioned that there were actually two long vowel sounds, /yū/ and /o͞o/.

This is also true of the vowel diphthongs *ew* and *ui*. While they usually decode as /o͞o/, when particular consonant sounds precede them, the sound will be /yū/. Examples: *few, hue, cue, mew*. Some phonics programs teach two sounds for these combinations; others teach only the one most common sound /o͞o/. See page 170 for example words.

30 PART 1 UNDERSTANDING PHONICS

You may want to make and study these cards before proceeding further.[21]

ue	**ui**	**ew**
/o͞o/ as in bl*ue*	/o͞o/ as in s*ui*t	/o͞o/ as in st*ew*

See Appendix C, page 170, for example words to use in teaching these special diphthongs.

Quick Self-Check X

1. The special diphthongs *ui, ue,* and *ew* encode what sound?
2. Recall other grapheme possibilities for encoding this sound. What are they?

PART 1, SECTION II: REVIEW AND SELF-CHECK

Review the cards and questions for Section I. Study your cards for Section II again, grouping and studying them. If you understand the following you should be able to proceed to Section III.

1. List the single vowels and give a key word for the short sound of each.
2. What is the schwa sound? Why do we have it? Give word examples.
3. In addition to short and long vowels, *a, o,* and *u* encode a third sound. Give word examples for the third sound of *a, o,* and *u*.
4. What single vowel letter has two long vowel sounds? Why? What are these sounds? List some key words.
5. Two vowel digraphs beginning with *a* decode as long /ā/. What are they? Why are there two? List key words.
6. What vowel digraphs (some call them diphthongs) decode as the sound of broad /ä/? Why are there two? List key words.
7. The vowel digraph *ee* decodes as what sound? Give key words.
8. The vowel digraph *ea* decodes as three sounds. What are they? Which is most common? Least? Give key words.
9. What are the two most common sounds encoded by *ie*? Give word examples.
10. Why is the digraph *ei* so variable? What different sounds does *ei* encode?
11. The digraph *ey* generally decodes as what two sounds? Give word examples.
12. What three-letter combination decodes as long /ī/? Give word examples.
13. What is the difference between a diphthong and a digraph? Write the digraph and diphthong combinations with the letter *o* and give a word example of each.
14. The combined letters *ui, ue,* and *ew* decode as what sound? Give key words.
15. How many ways may the sound of /o͞o/ be encoded in English?

(21) Note again one of the difficulties encountered by children who are learning decoding strategies—too many ways of writing the same sound. For example, in addition to these three diphthongs that decode as /o͞o/, we also have *ou* as /o͞o/ in *group; oo* as /o͞o/ in *moon; o* as /o͞o/ in *prove; u* as /o͞o/ in *rude*.

SECTION III

THE LETTER Y

The letter *y* has a unique position in our language and may function as either a consonant or a vowel. Also *y* combines with other vowels to form digraphs as *ay* in pl*ay*, *ey* in vall*ey*, and additionally forms a diphthong as *oy* in empl*oy*.

Y as a Consonant and Vowel

At the beginning of words, *y* is always a consonant letter as in the words *yacht*, *yard*, and *yellow*. However, *y* in the middle and at the end of words has a variety of vowel sounds.[22]

A	B	C	D
y as /ĭ/	*y* as /ī/	*y* as final /ī/	*y* as final /ē/
cr*y*stal	c*y*cle	appl*y*	cand*y*
g*y*m	tr*y*ing	fl*y*	hill*y*
m*y*sterious		m*y*	penn*y*

Say these words to hear these sounds.

A word of caution. There are regional differences to be aware of with ending *y* words. Some people in various parts of our country would pronounce the words in column *D* with a short /ĭ/ sound instead of the long /ē/ sound.

We might generalize about *single letter y* as follows:

1. **When single letter *y* is first in a word it decodes as the consonant sound /y/ in words like *y*ard and *y*ellow.**
2. **When single letter *y* is in the middle or at the end of words it decodes as a vowel. The vowel can be short /ĭ/ as in g*y*m, long /ī/ as in c*y*cle or repl*y*, or long /ē/ as in prett*y*.**

Other Considerations with Y

As mentioned during our discussion of the vowels, the letter *y* also combines with vowel letters. Recall *ay* as in pl*ay*, *ey* as in vall*ey*, and *oy* as in empl*oy*. Putting all this together we see a variety of possibilities with the letter *y*.

y as a consonant at the beginning:	/y/ yard		
y as a vowel in the middle of words:	/ĭ/ gym,	/ī/ cycle	
y as a vowel at the end of words:	/ē/ pretty,	/ī/ apply	
y as part of the vowel digraph *ay*:	/ā/ may		
y as part of the vowel digraph *ey*:	/ē/ valley		
y as part of the diphthong *oy*:	/oy/ destroy		

(22) One reason for this is that the letters *i* and *y* were used rather interchangeably during the Middle Ages, and even later. Note this sentence from an early New England account. "The pylgrims were pyoneers in the land."

You may want to make and study the following card showing *y* in its entirety before proceeding further.

y as a consonant at the beginning of a word	*y*ellow
y as the vowel /ĭ/ /ī/ in the middle of words	g*y*m
or	c*y*cle
y as the vowel /ē/ /ī/ at the end of words	prett*y*
or	appl*y*
y as a digraph /ā/	m*ay*
y as a digraph /ē/	vall*ey*
y as a diphthong /oy/	b*oy*

See Appendix C, page 169, for example *y* words to use in teaching.

Quick Self-Check XI

1. When does the letter *y* function as a consonant?
2. How does *y* function in the following words: *yes, cry, play, royal?*

SECTION IV

R-CONDITIONED VOWELS

With Single Vowel Letters

er, ir, ur, and wor The letter *r*, often referred to as bossy *r*, combines with certain single vowels and may condition the *preceding* vowel sound. Look at the following four columns of words:

A *er* as /er/	B *ir* as /er/	C *ur* as /er/	D *wor* as /wer/
p*er*t	s*ir*	h*ur*t	*wor*se
f*er*n	f*ir*st	ch*ur*n	*wor*thy
h*er*d	squ*ir*m	c*ur*l	*wor*ld
	ch*ir*p		

Pronounce all of these words and note that in each instance the vowel letter and following letter combine to encode the same sound of /er/.

In list *D* you will note that the sound of /w/ precedes the sound of /er/ as in *w*orse, *w*orthy, and *w*orld. The letters *or* decode as /er/ when the letter *w* precedes them.

Several questions might arise in teaching these sounds. A student might ask, "How about words like *here, fire,* and *pure?*" In these words *er, ir,* and *ur* do not decode as /er/. Notice what these three words have in common:

her*e*
fir*e*
pur*e*

All of them end in a final *e*! Remember that we discussed several reasons for final *e*, one of which was to change the preceding vowel sound. In words that end in *re*, the final *e* also conditions the preceding vowel sound; therefore it will not have the /er/ sound.

We might make the following generalization about the above *r* combinations.

1. **The combinations *er*, *ir*, and *ur* decode as /er/ when not followed by final *e*.**
2. **When the letter *w* precedes *or*, it decodes as /wer/.**

A word of caution about the letter *r* and the /r/ sound. *No other sound in the English language is pronounced in such a variety of ways.* For example: Easterners tend to omit a final /r/ altogether and then add an /r/ where none exists! Midwesterners tend to give *r* its full pronunciation regardless of placement in a word. Black dialect speakers frequently omit final /r/ unless the following sound is a vowel (Wardhaugh, 1972, pp. 198-9). In certain areas, many unaccented syllables that end with an *r* have a preceding schwa sound instead of a full vowel sound (Fromkin and Rodman, 1974, p. 196). Therefore, as a teacher you must *take into consideration the regional pronunciation* of your area.

ar

The letter *r* with the single vowel *a*. See the following combinations:

A	B
ar as /är/	*are* as /âr/
f*ar*	f*are*
st*ar*	st*are*
m*ar*	m*are*

You will notice two different letter-sound combinations. In column *A*, the words, f*ar*, st*ar*, and m*ar* have the sound of /är/. In column *B* the words f*are*, st*are*, and m*are* have a different sound because of the final *e*. The sound is written /âr/. Say the words to hear the sounds.

We might make a second generalization.

The combination *ar* decodes as /är/ as in f*ar*. When *ar* is followed by an *e*, the sound changes to /âr/ as in f*are*.

or

The letter *r* combines with the letter *o* to encode the sound /or/ as in f*or*. Sometimes *or* encodes the schwa vowel sound /ər/ in final unaccented syllables. Again, this has to do with regional variation. Examine the following groups of words and note the difference:

A	B
or as /ôr/	*or* as /ər/
c*or*k	fáct*or*
f*or*th	dóct*or*
p*or*ch	flávo*or*
st*or*k	saíl*or*
th*or*n	vísit*or*

We might therefore make a third generalization about the letter *r*:

1. **The letter *r* combines with *o* to decode as the sound of /ôr/ as in st*or*k.**
2. **Sometimes it decodes as /ər/ in final unaccented syllables as in words like flav*or*.**

With Vowel Digraphs

The letter *r* combines with the digraphs *ea*, *ai*, and *ee*. We will consider the *ea* digraph initially.

ea

Note the following three columns:

A	B	C
ear as /ē-r/	*ear* as /er/[23]	*ear* as /âr/
cl*ear*	*ear*n	b*ear*
d*ear*	h*ear*d	p*ear*
f*ear*	l*ear*n	t*ear*
h*ear*	s*ear*ch	w*ear*
9%	6%	2%

In list *A* the *ear* combination decodes as /e-r/, its most common sound. In *B*, however, the *ear* combination decodes as /er/ while in *C*, *ear* decodes as /âr/. You will note from the percentages that only a very few *ear* words (2%) have the /âr/ sound; therefore words such as these are often taught as sight words. These percentages indicate the number of times such words are usually found in relation to the total number of words with the *ea* combination. About 83% of the time *ea* is followed by other consonants as in *mean*, *dread*, and *break*. See page 22 if you need to review the *ea* digraph (Burmeister, 1968).

ai

When *r* combines with the digraph *ai*, there is also a conditioning of the vowel sound to /âr/ as in st*air*. Note the following group of words:

air as /âr/
f*air*
p*air*
st*air*
pr*air*ie

About 15 percent of all *ai* words have a following *r* and therefore have this sound.

ee

The digraph *ee* is also conditioned by a following *r*. The sound becomes /ē-r/. See examples below:

eer as /ē-r/
p*eer*
st*eer*
qu*eer*
ch*eer*

---

(23) Sometimes the *ear* combination decoding as /er/ is included with *er*, *ir*, *ur*, and *wor*. See page 32.

Taking into consideration that there are regional differences, we might generalize about the letter *r* with vowel digraphs *ea, ai,* and *ee* as follows:

1. **When the letter *r* follows the vowel digraph *ea*, it usually decodes as /ē-r/ as in cl*ea*r. It may also decode as /er/ as in l*ea*rn. In only a few words does it decode as /âr/ as in b*ea*r.**
2. **The vowel digraph *ai* when followed by *r* decodes as /âr/ as in ch*ai*r.**
3. **The vowel digraph *ee* when followed by *r* decodes as /ē-r/ as in ch*ee*r.**

Examination of the following lists will show more clearly the relationship of *r* with single vowels and with vowel digraphs.[24]

/er/	/âr/	/ôr/	/ē-r/	/är/
p*er*t	c*are*	f*or*k	h*ear*	f*ar*
f*ir*st	b*ear*		ch*eer*	
p*ur*se	ch*air*			
w*or*se				
*ear*n				

We can now put together all of the generalizations with *r*.

The letter *r* conditions the *preceding* vowel sound in the same syllable.
1. **Combinations of *er* (p*er*t), *ir* (f*ir*st), and *ur* (h*ur*t) decode as /er/. When *w* precedes *or*, the cluster decodes as /wer/ as in w*or*th.**
2. **The combination *ar* decodes as /är/ as in f*ar*. When followed by an *e*, it decodes as /âr/ as in f*are*.**
3. **The combination *or* decodes as /ôr/ as in st*or*k. Sometimes it decodes as /ər/ as in visit*or*.**
4. **The combination *ear* decodes as /ē-r/ as in h*ear*; as /er/ as in l*ear*n; and as /âr/ as in b*ear*.**
5. **The combination *air* decodes as /âr/ as in p*air*.**
6. **The combination *eer* decodes as /ē-r/ as in ch*eer*.**
7. **Regional differences must be considered with the high variable sound of /r/.**

(24) The letter *r* controls the vowel when it appears *in the same syllable* and *follows that vowel*. In a word such as *arise* the *r* does not change the *a* to /ä/ because it is not in the same syllable. It does not affect the sound of /ī/ in any way since it *precedes i* in the syllable.

You may want to make and study the following cards before proceeding further.

er /er/ as in p*er*t	**ir** /er/ as in f*ir*	**ur** /er/ as in h*ur*t
wor /wer/ as in *wor*th	**ar** /är/ as in c*ar* /âr/ as in c*are*	**or** /ôr/ as in f*or* /ər/ as in act*or*
ear /ē-r/ as in f*ear* /er/ as in l*ear*n /âr/ as in b*ear*	**air** /âr/ as in p*air*	**eer** /ē-r/ as in p*eer*

See Appendix C, page 171, for example *r* words to use in teaching.

Quick Self-Check XII

1. What do these *r-combinations* have in common?
       her   fur   stir
2. How is *wor* like the three above words?
3. Examine the following words:
       fear   search   pear
   What conclusion can be drawn about the *ear* combination?
4. What other vowel digraphs combine with the letter *r*? What sounds do they encode?

SECTION V

SPECIAL COMBINATIONS THAT DECODE AS /SH/

Certain combinations in addition to *sh* as in *ship* decode as /sh/. In Section I, page 10, recall that the vowel digraph *ch* was shown to have three sounds, one of which was the /sh/ sound as in *ch*ampagne. There are three other common combinations that decode as /sh/ in addition to the two mentioned above.

Note the following words:

A *ci* as /sh/	B *ti* as /sh/	C *si* as /sh/
so*ci*al	cau*ti*ous	man*si*on
deli*ci*ous	men*ti*on	mi*ssi*on
spe*ci*al	sta*ti*on	ten*si*on
gra*ci*ous	fic*ti*on	permi*ssi*on

In each instance the *ci, ti,* and *si* all decode as the /sh/ sound. There was a period when these words were pronounced exactly as they are spelled, but this sound change took place several hundred years ago. The three combinations above are only found in the *middle* of words and are often taught as part of affixed endings.[25]

We might generalize as follows about these three combinations.

The letters *ci, ti,* and *si* often decode as /sh/ as in words like pre*ci*ous, fic*ti*on, and mi*ssi*on.

You may want to make and study these three cards before proceeding further.

ci	**ti**	**si**
/sh/ as in spe*ci*al	/sh/ as in sta*ti*on	/sh/ as in man*si*on

You have now completed what you should know about phonics generalizations. If you can pass the sectional review test and the final phonics review test, you may proceed with ways of teaching decoding strategies that use phonics principles.

---

(25) George Bernard Shaw, who disliked the English writing system and offered money to anyone who would improve upon it, once suggested that *ghoti* could be read as *fish*. This is not so, because the consonant digraph *gh* only decodes as /f/ at the *end* of some words, *never* at the beginning. The *o* in *ghoti*, he claimed, could decode as short /i/ as in *women*. The word "women" is the only instance where *o* has this sound, the word having gone through spelling changes. Also, the *ti*, which he claimed would decode as /sh/ as in *nation* is equally incorrect. The combination *ti* is *rarely* found at the end of words. A foreign adopted word such as *spaghetti* is pronounced differently.

PART 1 UNDERSTANDING PHONICS

PART 1, SECTIONS III, IV, AND V: REVIEW AND SELF-CHECK

First review your cards from Section I and II. Group cards in Section III, IV, and V and review them. Then try this short test for the last three sections.

1. The letter *y* may function in different ways. Group the following words according to that function, identifying each group: *gym, they, yam, dry, play, yellow, cycle, employ, key, royal*.
2. The following four vowels + r combinations can be classified similarly: b*er*th, m*ir*th, p*ur*se, w*or*th. Explain.
3. Three digraphs frequently precede *r* with accompanying sound changes. Explain.
4. What has happened to the sounds encoded by combinations such as *ti, si,* and *ci*? What other grapheme combinations encode the same sound?

PART 1: FINAL PHONICS REVIEW

Now apply what you should know. Place the words that contain related phonics features in the proper column. Some words may appear in more than one column. Underline the feature particular to that column. (You will be able to place all the words except one.)

scheme	flight	edge
world	now	coast
bridge	relative	chaise
receive	back	athlete
treat	surprise	hair
afraid	streamlined	earn
destroy	about	stitch
coaching	breath	physics
toil	spoon	fewer

Words with Consonant Digraphs[26]	**Words with Blends**	**Words with Vowel Digraphs**	**Words with Vowel Diphthongs**	**Vowels with R-Conditioning**

---

(26) Also include special consonant combinations.

Table 1.2 Overview of English Orthography for the Teacher

Consonants	Variant Consonants	Digraphs with H	Digraphs with First Silent Letter	Blends - Initial	Blends - Final	Special Combination of Consonant and Vowel
b bat	**c, g, s**	ch chair	ck deck	r break	ld sold	ci special
d dent	cat	scheme	gn gnome	l clean	lk walk	si mansion
f fall	city	chandelier	kn knife	s skate	nd send	ti station
h hit	got	gh ghost	wr write	scrap	nk thank	
j jam	giant	ph pharmacy		tw twirl	nt meant	
k kite	us	sh ship	Digraph Cluster Following a Short Vowel Like ck			
l land	his	th thick	dge bridge			
m mat	sugar	these	tch stitch			
n name		wh what				
p pan		who	Additional Digraph			
qu quite			ng			
r road						
t top						
v vane						
w well						
x box						
z zebra						

Vowels				
Single - Short	Schwa ə in Unaccented syllables	Digraphs/Diphthongs with *a*	Digraphs with *e*	Cluster with *i*
a ă act	a əbout	ai as /ā/ maid	ee as /ē/ sleep	igh as /ī/
e ĕ end	e tickət	ay as /ā/ stay	ea as /ē/ leaf /ĕ/ head /ā/ great	sight
i ĭ it	i pencəl	au as /aw/ vault	ie as /ē/ relief /ī/ lie	
o ŏ olive	o aprən	aw as /aw/ draw	ei as /ē/ (after c) receive /ā/ vein	
u ŭ upon			ey as /ē/ donkey /ā/ prey	
Single - Long				
a ā able				
e ē even				
i ī icy				
o ō omen ū unit				
u and ōō rude				
Single - 3rd Sound				
a ä always				
o ŏŏ do				
u ŏŏ push				

	Digraphs and Diphthongs with *o*		Diphthongs that encode /ōō/:	
	oa as /ō/ coat		ui fruit	
	oi as /oy/ oil		ue blue	
	oy as /oy/ boy		ew stew	
	oo as /ōō/ moon /ŏŏ/ look			
	ou as /ow/ around /ū/ young /ō/ soul /ōō/ group			
	ow as /ow/ cow /ō/ low			

	R-Conditioning with Single Vowels: her fir purse worse /er/ /er/ /er/ /er/	R-Conditioning with *a*: fär cāre	R-Conditioning with *o*: stôre doctər	R-Conditioning with Digraph *ea*: hear learn bear /ē-r/ /er/ /âr/	R-Conditioning with Digraphs: ai ee hair peer /âr/ /ē-r/
Y as a Consonant, Vowel, Digraph, Diphthong	Consonant at the Beginning: yellow Vowel: mystery, apply, carry Digraph: play, obey Diphthong: employ				

SECTION VI

PREPARING TO READ: READING READINESS

Parents play a tremendously important role in preparing their child for the school's formal reading program. During the preschool years, shared experiences with books lay the foundation for beginning instruction in the school and are invaluable in preparing children to read.

In schools, two areas of reading readiness have recently received attention. According to Sippola (1985) literature on reading readiness has changed drastically in the past two decades, with an important distinction noted between *learning readiness* and *reading readiness*. Learning readiness practices were based on the assumption that teaching very broad, general skills (such as visual discrimination of objects in the environment) were prerequisite skills for successful reading. Reading readiness, on the other hand, involves teaching reading—specific skills such as the sounds encoded by the letters of the alphabet. Research in this area has established the superiority of reading—specific training over learning readiness training, and materials used in readiness programs should reflect this orientation (Sippola 1985). The report from the 1985* Commission on Reading agrees that learning readiness activities have a negligible relationship to learning to read, but it does suggest that the child who is least ready for systematic reading instruction needs language activities with a light touch; opportunities to listen and to discuss stories that build vocabulary, and also to begin to write—"a balanced kindergarten, not an academic boot camp." With this, the author wholeheartedly concurs.

Another long-time controversy in readiness extends to letter names. In beginning reading, should these names be learned or not? Some researchers had positive opinions, recommending that letter names be taught "quite early in the beginning stages of reading" (Carnine and Silbert 1979, p. 206); others were neutral, and still others such as Venezky (1979, p. 281) had negative opinions about teaching letter names, believing that since there is not a perfect sound correlation, learning letter names creates confusion. Ehri's (1983) more recent and lengthy research indicates that if letter names are taught simultaneously with phonics, the integration of the two favorably affects reading acquisition. Since letter name knowledge and phonics knowledge are highly correlated, simultaneous teaching appears to be the best solution (Groff 1984). Additionally, Chall's research indicates "that a child's ability to identify letters by name . . . is an important predictor of reading achievement at various points in the first and second grades." (Chall 1983)

Prereading tasks

As schools introduce the formal reading program, activities are initiated that help children learn to discriminate among letters, both visually and auditorily, and help them develop a memory for some sound-symbol relationships. For example, children perform activities such as the following: they turn a spinner on a wheel, naming the picture where the spinner stops while subsequently finding pictures on charts that begin with the same sound. Songs are sung, poetry is read, and lots of language experience stories (children dictate stories that teachers write for a group or individual) are used to learn to discriminate among letters and sounds, to build vocabulary, to understand about capital letters and periods in sentences, and to begin a left to right eye sweep.

(*) Anderson, Richard, C. Elfrieda, H. Hiebert, Judith A. Scott, and Ian A. G. Wilkinson. *Becoming a Nation of Readers: The Report of the Commission on Reading*. Washington, D.C.: National Institute of Education, 1985.

A major consideration in readiness is whether children have the "linguistic" equipment to handle the technical vocabulary of beginning reading. Many children do not understand what the teacher is referring to when s/he uses *sentence, word, letter, sound, begins and ends with*. The following "tasks" were developed by Agnew (1982) to determine whether a child understands words used in learning to read. The children's recorded dictation is used with these procedures but no actual reading is done. The object is to discover whether reading instructions will be understood.

Task 1. *Word*
Ask the child to point to any word on the chart story, then to "cup" his/her hands around the word. Repeat the task with three or four other words.

Ask the child to match an individual word card with the same word in the chart story. If the word occurs more than once, ask the child to locate the word in another place in the story. Repeat the task with several other word cards.

Task 2. *Sentence*
Ask the child to match a sentence strip with its counterpart on the chart story. Repeat the task with three or four other sentence strips.

Task 3. *Letter*
Show the child an individual word card and provide him/her with individual letters that can be assembled to spell out the word on the card. Ask the child to "build" the word, using separate letters. Ask the child for the names of the letters. Probe understanding of the difference between letters and words. Repeat the exercise with two or three other word cards.

Task 4. *"Begins with" and "Ends with"*
Point to and identify a word in the chart story that begins with a single consonant. Ask the child to think of a word with the same beginning sound. Repeat the task with four or five different words.

Ask the child to point to the place in the chart story to answer such questions as:
1. Where is the *beginning* of the story:
2. Where is the *end* of the story?
3. This word is _____. Where is the beginning of the word? Where is the end of the word?
4. This word is _____. (Point to a word in the story and name it.) Here are two word cards from the story. One of them is *different* from _____. (Repeat the word that was just identified in the story.) Point to the word that is different from _____. (Repeat the word just identified.)

Task 5. *Knows "line"*
Run your finger under a line in the story. Ask the child to show you several other lines.

Task 6. *Knows "top" and "bottom"*
Ask the child to point to the top of the page. Ask the child to point to the bottom of the page. Ask the child to point to the top and bottom of letters.

A record form for these needed technical words called "code consciousness" by Agnew (1981, p. 452) may be found in the Appendix B, page 159.

A Prereading Phonics Inventory

Durrell and Murphy (1978), researchers for over fifty years in the area of reading readiness, developed a prereading phonics inventory that introduced two new measures in readiness: (1) awareness of *letter name sounds* in spoken words and (2) syntax matching. In addition to these two new items, the inventory includes other measures common to commercial readiness programs. A rationale for their total prereading phonics inventory follows:

1. Naming letters of the alphabet
   Children who know letters are more aware of differences between letters.
2. Writing letters from dictation
   Children who can do this have a very strong visual attachment of name to letter form.
3. Awareness of letter name sounds in spoken words
   Children with this ability show an earlier stage of phonics ability than awareness of *phonemes (sounds) in spoken words*. Letter name sounds refer to the fact that most consonant letters are syllables made up of basic phonemes plus a vowel. (Durrell and Murphy's explanation follows:) The names of most consonant letters are syllables made up of the basic phoneme plus a vowel. The "ee" vowel follows the phonemes in these consonants: /b/ ee, /d/ ee, /p/ ee, /t/ ee, /v/ ee, and /z/ ee while in the names of *c* and *g* are their less frequent phonemes, /s/ ee and /j/ ee. The "short e" vowel precedes these names: eh/f/, eh/l/, eh/m/, eh/n/, eh/s/, and in *x* we have eh/ks/. These names transfer easily to phonemes, since short vowel phonemes are continuant sounds and are dominant in the name.

   Letter names using the "long a" vowel are /j/ay and /k/ay; the name for *r* is ah/r/. Of the names of consonants, only *h, q, w,* and *y* do not contain their phonemes. The names of vowels are their "long sounds," easily noticed at the beginning of spoken words; they appear first in our inventory of letter name sounds.

   Twenty-two letter names contain their phonemes, counting the partial usefulness of the names of *c* and *g*. To say the letter name, the child *must* say the phoneme. (page 387)
4. *Syntax Matching*
   Children who can match words *in short spoken sentences* with the same word in printed sentences understand certain needed concepts.

See Figure 1.1 for the complete inventory.

Figure 1.1 Individual Prereading Phonics Inventory

1. Naming letters. How many of these letters can the child name?
   o s t a r e n i l u c p d
   m b h f y g v w x k z j q
2. Writing letters from dictation. Dictate the letters listed above. Score leniently; either a capital or lowercase letter will do; count reversed letters as correct.
3. Awareness of letter name sounds in spoken words. How many letters can the child name at the beginning of these spoken words? (Do not show the words.) Say, "Say *open*; say it again, *open*. What letter do you hear at the beginning of *open*?" Do the same for these words:
   open, even, iron, apron, useful, beaver, ceiling, deep, effort, genius, jail, Kate, elevator, emerald, enter, peach, army, Esther, teacher, veal, extra, zebra.
4. Syntax matching: awareness of separate words in spoken sentences and the ability to match them with words in print. How many of these words can the child identify in sentences? Put a marker under each sentence; do not point to the separate words while reading them. Say, "This says, *Come here;* Say it. Say it again, *Come here*. Now draw a circle around *Come*."
   Come here.   You have two thumbs.
   Don't fall.   These kittens are hungry.
   Clap your hands.   This girl has black hair.
   Catch the ball.   Can you climb a tree?
   Ride my new bike.   You can ride this horse.
   Words to circle: 1 - Come; 2 - fall; 3 - Clap; 4 - ball; 5 - new; 6 - two; 7 - hungry; 8 - girl; 9 - you; 10 - ride.

In testing more than 200 theses, these four areas yielded the most predictable results. Durrell and Murphy suggest that when children lack these skills they should be taught to them prior to more detailed reading instruction. While it does not ensure success, a lack of mastery of these prereading skills, they believe, will frequently signal failure in beginning reading. The test may be somewhat modified for group instruction.

Other readiness factors

While research in reading readiness continues, teachers use both formal and informal methods in determining students' readiness to read. Commercial tests like the Metropolitan screen for letter and sound discrimination and are very popular. Some schools, however, develop their own reading readiness tests based on the school's student body. Teachers, in addition to testing for discrimination abilities, consider many other areas such as the child's maturity, social responsibility, family background, language proficiency, and motivation to read. Eventually teachers plan definite instruction and introduce letters for identification visually and auditorily, and students write them. Some programs introduce a number of sight words and draw phonics generalizations from them. Other programs introduce definite sounds and directly teach a few sight words so children may begin reading sentences immediately. Research does not indicate that one approach is better than another.[27]

Beginning readers usually rely heavily on phonics clues to identify words, because of a more limited ability to use context. How are these beginning sound-symbol relationships introduced in the school instructional program?

SECTION VII

BEGINNING TO TEACH PHONICS

Procedures for Introducing a Beginning Sound-Symbol Relationship

In general each phoneme (sound) and its related symbol (letter/s) are introduced within the context of familiar short words. When the sound introduced is the first sound in the word, it is easier to hear. (Most difficult is the medial position.) Therefore, instruction usually proceeds from simple identification of beginning sounds in words, to ending sounds, and last to medial sounds.

A strategy to teach beginning sound-symbol relationships

1. Students identify the capital and small letter that encode a particular sound, presented by the teacher in a novel way that emphasizes the relationship (step 1).
2. Students next select words containing the specific sound from words containing related sounds. Students suggest words with the specific sound (step 2).
3. Students write the capital and lowercase letters that represent the specific sound (step 3).

---

(27) For a complete Scope and Sequence Chart of the Phonics strand of the 1987 Scott Foresman Reading Series, see Appendix B, page 161. Study the chart to note the progression of teaching sound-symbol relationships. Not all basals use the same sequence, but the phonics progression is quite similar.

4. Students participate in purposeful activities applying the knowledge of the relationship between the letter and sound (step 4).

Step 1   The teacher begins by having an activity in which students identify the sound-symbol under consideration as *l* /l/. For example s/he might ask them to watch his/her mouth because s/he is going to look like a singer. (Teacher sings the words *let, like, love, lend,* and *land,* exaggerating the /l/). At the same time s/he writes these words on the board, making one word a short sentence as *Let me go* to use a capital letter. (The words are written on the board so the written word will emphasize the symbol associated with the sound.)

Step 2   The teacher helps students notice how they open their mouths when they say this sound at the *beginning*[28] of words. Then s/he has them identify from words s/he says those that begin with /l/ such as *lion, lazy, maze, left, Brian, lift.* Sometimes pictures with distractors are used such as a picture of a lamp, a pencil, a lightbulb, a crayon, or a lemon. The teacher helps students think of words beginning with /l/ by asking riddles such as "What can you draw with a ruler?" (line).

Step 3   Prior to writing them without a clue students often trace the letter over dotted lines, with arrows indicating the direction of each stroke. This is so the lines and circles they make are drawn from left to right, or in the same direction as they read.

Step 4   The teacher passes out "little lollipops" for them to "lick," and enjoy. Students are to find and think of other words beginning with /l/. Meanwhile, words used by the teacher and students throughout the day that emphasize the /l/ sound are written on a list and displayed.

Dittos and workbook page example activities in beginning reading

Workbook activities and dittos proliferate in these beginning reading stages. Some of the more common types of these activities follow:

1. Circling the letter/word that is the same.

m	m	w	m	n
N	N	M	N	W

and	ran	and	and
Nan	Nat	Nan	Nan

2. Using rebus forms so children "read" more elaborate sentences.

---

(28) In actuality, the sound /l/ is not quite the same in other positions although most teachers are not concerned with this in beginning reading.

3. Circling those pictures on a page whose name begins with the phoneme under study.

M

4. Circling the correct word on a ditto from a matching list read by the teacher.

>   sun
>   run
>   fun

5. Using puzzle sentences such as:

    Which can you sit on, a tap or a lap?

    What keeps you cool, a fan or a pen?

6. Filling in the correct letter of the word that names the picture.

    (c)up

    (b)at

    (h)en

7. Making words grow by adding the appropriate letter.

b	c	r	m
—at		—an	
—at		—an	
—at		—an	
—at		—an	

8. Supplying the right word in the blank.
    cake   cane   race

    The man ran the _____.

Remember the first words children learn to read in most basal programs are chosen because they contain regular grapheme-phoneme correspondences, or because they occur frequently in adults' materials or occur in children's materials written by adults. Studies, however, point to the fact that when children are asked what words they want to learn to read, the words are much more imagery-loaded than the early basal ones. A recent study (Hiebert, 1983) concurs with these findings that go back to Ashton-Warner's (1963) work. Typical "reading" words selected by children included pizza, frisbee, Frankenstein, Valentine, gorilla, kiss, and Star Wars.

While we would never advocate a haphazard word attack approach to teaching word attack skills, it is nevertheless important to use some high interest vocabulary with personal meaningfulness to individual children.

Blending: A Controversy

Once sound-symbol relationships are introduced, students must learn to blend the sounds together, a crucial stage in beginning reading. The idea of letters representing sounds that must be glided together quickly represents an abstraction; this becomes a difficult concept for some children to understand. Once they have mastered blending together a few sound-symbol relationships and can apply the principle, they progress far more rapidly. This blending step, so important in the early reading stages, is often ignored in commercial reading programs (Haddock, 1978) and (Eeds-Kniep, 1979). Rosenshine and Stevens (1984) found that time spent in blending activities at the first and second grades resulted in higher scores on achievement tests. The Commission on Reading's report (1985) also collaborates this, "teachers who spend more than average amounts of time on blending produce larger than average gains on reading achievement tests."

A major disagreement exists in the area of blending, as to the presentation of the combined sounds that make up words. Many reading educators feel that sounds must never be presented in isolation; that is, to have the teacher say /c-c-c-a-a-a-t-t-t/ and then blend this to *cat* is tantamount to dooming children to lifelong remediation! They feel that children will blend combinations together by noting when words begin and end the same and noting that a one letter change in a word makes a very different word.

Part of this blending controversy lies in the fact that particular consonant phonemes known as "stops," /p/ /b/ /t/ /d/ /k/ /g/ /ch/ and /j/, cannot be said in isolation. An /uh/ sound always follows when saying these sounds alone. They argue that children would sound a word such as *ball* as /b-u-all/; and that blending isolated phonemes distorts the true sound of the word.

Other educators argue that this is the only way some children will learn to read new words in the early stages; i.e., the teacher saying the sounds in isolation as /c-c-c-a-a-t-t-t/, then blending them together, and showing students the combinations that "make" such a word. After sounding the isolated phonemes, teachers have students say them faster and faster until they approximate the spoken word.

Some educators adopt a middle of the road attitude about blending and suggest a procedure such as follows: With the word *mat*, they have students pronounce the vowel sound alone /ă/; add the consonant sound /m/, blended together as /mă/; and then add the /t/ to form /mat/. Others suggest that when blending, students identify the ending sounds /ăt/ first, and then add the /m/ to form /mat/. In these latter methods the movement is from right to left and can interfere with directional eye sweep, since reading is from left to right. Nevertheless these methods are still used quite successfully, as well as the two blending methods previously mentioned.

A summary of ways to blend sounds follows:

1. No sounds are isolated. Children reason that changing one phoneme changes the word.
2. Individual phonemes are pronounced, then blended together. Teacher pronounces each phoneme separately as m-m-m-a-a-a-t-t-t, repeating the sounds faster and faster until they approximate the word.
3. The vowel is pronounced first, followed by the first consonant sound, then the final sound.

    ă
    mă
    mat

4. The ending phonogram is pronounced first, then the beginning consonant sound.

    ăt
    mat

As with other reading issues, this one is far from settled. The author believes that children profit from some formal instruction in blending—the method used is not as important as the children's ability to apply the skill to new vocabulary. For children who have problems learning to blend some of the more difficult consonant combinations as digraphs, the following suggestions by Eeds (1981) may be helpful.

> Hold up a word card and say, "This word is tick," and pointing to a word card with *chick* say, "Now, let's see what this word is." Take a tab with *ch* printed on it, placing it over the *t* to show the segmentation, and to make the blending step very clear. Show several more word pairs as best/chest; hair/chair; lamp/champ. To reinforce, find a word containing a pattern children already know and use it in blending exercises. Logos are excellent, and for the initial digraph *ch*, a Cheerios box or a Chee-tos label works very well. Most children can read the names of these and other common products and often help the teacher accumulate other logos. To teach blending with the *ch*, first ask children to read these two labels. When they do, point out the *ch* and have children listen for the sound as you again pronounce the name. If they fail to see the connection between Cheerios and chick, point out they start exactly the same way, and show the phonics pattern in each word. When there is great difficulty try something like this: "Let's say the first sound of Cheerios /ch/ and put it with the last sound here—/ick/. Ch-ick—what word is this?" With patient repetition even students who experience difficulty with blending should understand that you can take apart sounds and letters and recombine them to make new words (Eeds, page 138).

Vowel Sounds May Cause Difficulty

Vowels cause many problems and two suggestions may help minimize some of these difficulties. One way is to use a mirror to reinforce the sounds under study, the student watching the teacher's mouth shape as words are pronounced. Next, students produce the sounds watching the shape of their own mouth in a mirror. In addition to the visual sensation, students develop an awareness of the kinesthetic sensation in the production of vowel sounds—how the mouth, tongue and cheeks feel while creating the sounds. Instead of a mirror, students may place their hands on their mouth to sense the difference as they pronounce the sounds.

Many vowels become more distinguishable through this visual or kinesthetic system. Long /ō/, /o͞o/, /ī/, /ē/, and /ā/ differ greatly in the mirror. Diphthongs *oi* and *ou* differ from each other, and other sounds, because visually the mouth changes shape during production. The visual distinction between short vowels is slight but the tongue position can be of help in discrimination ability here (Ahmann, 1982).

Another way to reinforce vowel sounds is by using the idea of a voice choir. Students join in the respective sounds being reviewed (as /o͞o/) while the teacher motions for a crescendo as his/her palms are lifted upwards. Palms are turned down, fall, and hands are crossed to motion a cessation of sound just as in any choir situation. The teacher asks for words with particular sounds, writes and discusses them, and employs the "choir" to reinforce the sound (Hoopman, 1982).

Synthetic/Analytic/"Linguistic"/Phonics: Differing Points of View

At this time we need to digress for a moment and discuss another phonics "battle" that still continues—the synthetic versus the analytic versus the "linguistic" phonics approach. When working with sound-symbol relationships or new vocabulary, the teacher may follow one of three procedures: (1) guiding the lesson so s/he *tells* the sound-symbol relationships, and students memorize certain rules (synthetic phonics); (2) guiding the lesson so students conclude what the sound-symbol relationship is after studying particular known words (analytic phonics); (3) presenting words with regular spelling patterns such as *man, tan, fan, ran, can* ("linguistic" phonics).

To complicate the issue further, a difference in terminology has existed since Jeanne Chall's book *Learning to Read: The Great Debate,* with some educators calling the synthetic approach, "code-emphasis," and the analytic approach, "meaning-emphasis." This is because they claim the synthetic approach is too concerned with breaking the English code, while the analytic approach uses words in meaning situations. For the teacher, these labels tend to confuse the issue still further. *Either* approach can certainly be used in meaning situations, *and all three approaches* are based on giving insights into how the English code system works. Some teachers use a combination of the three approaches: They use synthetic phonics initially, moving then to analytic phonics, and use "linguistic" phonics to teach the vowels instead of teaching them in isolation (Gillis, 1982).

As mentioned, teachers who use the synthetic approach usually tell sound-symbol relationships and teach phonics rules, with students being taught how to combine these sounds into words. Teaching the synthetic approach does not always follow identical procedures. For example, some reading programs that use this approach advocate teaching all the vowel sounds initially, and then some of the consonant sounds; others introduce some of the consonant sounds first and only one short vowel. Blending may be done, as outlined in the previous section, a sound or phoneme at a time, as with *rip*, /r-r-r-i-i-i-p-p-p/, /rip/; sometimes using the vowel first, /ĭ/, adding the first consonant sound /r/ to form /rĭ/, and then tacking on the final /p/ /rip/; or starting with the ending base /ĭp/, adding the initial /r/, for the total /rip/.

Critics of the synthetic approach cite the following:

1. Students rely on the letter-sound relationships too much, paying no attention to context and meaning; hence, the term *code-emphasis*.
2. Memorizing rules does not mean they will be applied.
3. Many readers discover the rules and relationships themselves, and class instruction with these rules and sounds can be wasteful.
4. Prolonged work with phonics diverts students from getting meaning.

On the other hand, advocates of the synthetic approach are adamant that:

1. Children see very early that there is a relationship between letters and sounds, and quickly decode words instead of depending on surrounding context.
2. Children become independent readers, decoding many difficult words on their own and taking great pride in doing so.
3. Beginning readers can attend to meaning since they are not frustrated by unknown words.
4. The method systematizes and teaches the needed sound-symbol relationships.

Therefore, their basic argument is that the synthetic approach—structured, sequential, and comprehensive—will eliminate the student's foundering with unknown words and will therefore actually enhance meaning. They believe their approach not only helps to break the code, but also ensures that meaning (comprehension) will take place.

Like the synthetic approach, the analytic approach also has a great deal of variety, but usually begins with words students are familiar with at sight. Sometimes consonant sounds are identified first in these words, and then the vowel sounds. Often, there is a combination approach. Note is made of parts of words that are similar and parts that are different. Then a phonics analysis (hence the term analytic) of the words is made, and phonics principles deduced. A point of difference exists even among those favoring the analytic approach; that is, whether it should be systematic or incidental. Advocates of the latter argue that since there is not agreement as to the order in which phonics elements should be taught, phonics instruction should take place only when the need arises, and be strictly incidental!

Following are two example lessons for students in perhaps a third grade reader that help to clarify some of the stated differences in the two approaches. In actual practice, they do not have to be, nor are they, mutually exclusive.

The synthetic approach

Teacher: Today, we are going to learn about a new letter combination (teacher holds up a card with *ph* printed on it). This letter combination is *ph* and it stands for the sound of /f/. Here are three words you have probably seen with this combination: *Phil, telephone,* and *graph*. (Teacher writes them on the board or has them on transparencies.) Note that this combination may come at the beginning (points to *Phil*); middle (points to *telephone*); or end of the word (points to *graph*). (Teacher stresses the /f/ sound in the words.) (With slower children the teacher might want to show only the combination in the initial position.)

Students: (Teacher calls on different students to read the three words.)

Teacher: I have another group of words here. (Words are as follows.)

dolphin   elephant
phonograph   Daphne
photograph   pictograph

Will someone underline in each word the two-letter combination that stands for the /f/ sound?

Students: (One or more may underline the *ph* combination.)

Teacher: Let's read these words together, and then see if there are any that you want to talk about. (Continues) Who thinks they know what a *pictograph* is? (Discusses the word parts.) Let's try these words in sentences to make certain they are in your meaning vocabulary.

Students: (Offer sentences using the words.)

Teacher: (May call attention for review to other known phonics elements as, What three words do you notice with the *gr* blend?) (Continues) Let's compare these words (points to words on the board) with words that have the consonant *p* alone. Let's read these words. (Stresses the difference between the two sounds as follows:)

*p*ill   *Ph*il
*p*ant   *ph*antom
*p*easant   *ph*easant

(If necessary, the teacher might decide to review the *ea* digraph as in p*ea*sant and ph*ea*sant.)

Students: (Read words and place them in sentences orally.)

Teacher: On a piece of paper number from one to twelve. I will read several words to you, all beginning with the letter *p*. Tell me whether the first sound should be written as just *p* or as *ph*. (Reads *pantry, posture, phonograph, phase, protest, phantom, photograph.* (Continues discussing words and sounds, assigning some follow-up work if needed.)

The analytic approach

Teacher: I noticed yesterday we had some difficulty reading words with the letter combination *ch*.[29] One of the words is in this sentence: *The scheme failed, and they left* (The sentence should not be read but may be either on the board or on a transparency.) Before we look at the sentence, let's look at these words that you do know. Teacher reads:

chair
inches
beach

emphasizing the known sound of /ch/ but not removing the sound from the word.

Teacher: (Continues) What sound does the *ch* stand for in these three words?

Jane: The sound of /ch/.

---

(29) As mentioned, some teachers tell children that the *ch* is a digraph, while others never use any terminology. Again, always think in terms of your students and their ability.

Teacher: Good. Give me some examples of other words with this sound.
Tim: *Chip, champ*
Mary: *Attach*
Teacher: Good. (Teacher writes next to the original three words /ch/ to show the sound and at the same time underlines each one of the *ch* combinations:

*c*hair   /ch/
in*ch*es   /ch/
bea*ch*   /ch/

Now, we'll read some other words that also have the letter combination *ch*, but in these words notice something different about the sound that *ch* stands for. (With brighter students, one of them may know the words and could read them.) (On the board or on a transparency the teacher displays another group of words:)

*ch*aracter
a*ch*e
stoma*ch*

What sound do you hear as we read these words together?
John: Is it the /k/ sound?
Teacher: That's right. Will you read the words for us again? (S/he may do this several times to enforce the concept.)
Teacher: Who wants to try to read the sentence on the board now? The word we had trouble with was this one. (She points to the word *scheme*.)
Sue: Their scheme failed, and they left.
Teacher: Right. What other word can you think of? It's one of your favorite holidays and it contains a *ch* that stands for the /k/ sound?
All: Christmas!
Teacher: Right. Where do you go every day to learn?
Students: School!
Teacher: Right. Most of the words with *ch* that stands for the /k/ sound come to us from the Greek language. Therefore, when we have such a word we know it is of Greek origin. Let's look at this exercise, and use our dictionaries if we need to, and try to find the *ch* word with the /k/ sound that could complete each sentence.

The _____ on the car has rusted. (chrome)
I like the _____ holiday the best. (Christmas)
The children sang in the _____. (chorus)

(Always apply what has just been learned.)

"Linguistic phonics," a third approach

Some educators consider the linguistic approach to teach reading to be language experience while others consider the linguistic approach to be patterned phonics. The latter patterned approach has been advocated for many years. Basal readers with this method of word attack employ a highly controlled and systematic method of introducing phonics patterns. The emphasis is on the recognition of minimal differences in words that follow similar patterns such as mat-met, rang-rung, and pat-bet. Beginning readers read sentences such as *Dan ran* to the *tan van*. Four popular linguistic readers include the *Let's Read Series,* the *Palo Alto Reading Series, Merrill Linguistic Readers,* and *SRA.**

A basic criticism of this approach is that linguistic readers use a stilted unnatural language because of the tight control of phonics patterns. In speech a variety of sentence patterns are used, and if reading is "talk written down" then controlling the pattern creates an artificial language. Nevertheless, some teachers are quite successful in using these linguistic readers, especially with students who seem unable to learn to decode in other ways. For example, Janicke (1981) used a program called MOD (massive oral decoding) based on a technique developed by Johnson, Johnson and Kerfoot (1972). The program emphasized large amounts of practice at the student's independent reading level. Materials used included the four separate series of linguistic readers mentioned above. In the MOD program the student read all the pages in one series that dealt with a particular phonics pattern, then read corresponding pages in the other three series with that pattern. Using the four series allowed the student to encounter each pattern many more times than would have been possible using only one series, and each encounter was meaningful because the words were always in context.

While this type of program could be used in a classroom situation, in this particular instance it was part of an intensive clinical program scheduled for two twenty-five minute practice sessions per day. Students were directed by an aide who worked with only two students at a time. Taking turns they read every other page aloud while the aide noted each error after which additional work was provided by the teacher (Janicke, p. 158).

Phonics Tutorial Programs

In addition to using linguistic readers, there are other types of phonics tutorial programs for both younger and older students, both commercial and teacher constructed. Basically these programs are quite similar in that an aide, tutor, or community volunteer works with one or two students at a time, usually on their phonics skills. The major reason these programs work is not because of the method or materials, but because students do a lot of actual reading, receiving immediate feedback on their errors.

After we have discussed other word attack skills in addition to phonics, we will offer some suggestions to help students with particular decoding difficulties.

Implications for Teaching

The preceding discussion has undoubtedly raised the question which phonics approach is best? The answer of course is what is best for the student. For

---

*Linguistic Reader Publishers
1. Clarence L. Barnhart, Inc., Box 250, Bronxville, N.Y. 10016
2. Harcourt Brace Jovanovich, 757 Third Avenue, New York, N.Y. 10017
3. Charles E. Merrill Publishing Co., 1300 Alum Creek Drive, Columbus, Ohio 43216
4. S.R.A. Science Research Associates, Inc., 259 East Erie Street, Chicago, IL 60611

example, a difference exists between beginning readers and more advanced readers. More abstract underlying phonics generalizations could probably be induced by most of the latter, and an analytic approach might therefore be most appropriate. On the other hand, beginning readers need far more guidance on the part of the teacher, and a synthetic approach as one part of the reading program might be better. Other teachers who use a lot of language experience in the classroom with beginning readers who read stories they have written individually or in groups with teacher assistance) are more comfortable even getting very young children to deduce the phonics principle as needed, and would prefer an analytic approach. Some children, however, will have difficulty understanding the abstractness of sound-symbol relationships, whether presented synthetically or analytically, and will need practice with a single pattern for a period of time. For these children perhaps a linguistic reader would work most advantageously.

Most basals today use a kind of combination phonics approach and perhaps this is best for most teachers. At times a teacher can use the so-called synthetic method and directly show needed sounds and principles. At other times s/he might use written work to get students to analyze where certain errors are and how to correct them. Word patterns with minimal differences can be incorporated into the phonics lesson. Meaning can always be attended to, and should be, regardless of approach. And remember, as much as possible, vocabulary used in phonics analysis should include fun words that children will delight in decoding. Has something interesting or different happened? Can you incorporate this language in your lesson? Are there particular words that students have been trying to read and spell that would lend themselves to some kind of analysis? Capitalize on what vocabulary they are directly involved or interested in.

Teaching, Extending, Reinforcing, and Reviewing Sound-Symbol Relationships

In addition to direct teacher instruction, discussion, and the student reading more extended language with these sound-symbol relationships (always the most important), there are many teacher-designed phonics materials and many commercial materials used in teaching these skills. A number of different formats are used, and variation of these formats make up the myriad number of activity books, workbooks, games, puzzles, and manipulatives that are used to extend and reinforce phonics principles. Following are listed some of these materials/activities in three very broad categories. Because there is a good deal of overlapping and combining, the lists are somewhat arbitrary.

Game-Type Activities	Puzzle-Type Activities	Manipulatives
Open gameboards	Matching shapes	Fold-overs with answers
Filling the correct slot/cup/box, etc.	Concentration-activities	Plastic pockets with inserts
Pinning/sticking/taping on the correct response	Solving riddles Cards	Wheels with spinners or windows
Line/group games	Bingo variations	Tachistoscopes, single and double
	Domino variations	Flip-books
	Solving anagrams/crossword puzzles	Mini-computers

Some abbreviated suggestions for carrying out these activities or for constructing these materials follow: (They may often be extended to include more than one skill area. For example, instead of having an activity to identify just beginning consonants, the activity could be extended to include ending consonants, medial consonants, blends, digraphs, and vowels.) Also these ideas should always be adapted to your own particular classroom situation and your own particular students.

Examples of Game-Type Activities

1. Objective: *To identify lowercase and capital letters in various type sets.* Display a letter such as *b*. Have pupils look at it. Then remove. Ask them to search for the same letter in the room. When located, pupils stand by the letter and say, "I Spy." After several turns, the original *b* is displayed. Students check to see if they are correct.

2. Objective: *To identify lowercase and capital letters rapidly. Place particular review letters on a table in random order.* Ask pupils to find a letter in response to verbal directions such as, "Find the capital *M*. Find the small *h*." Have pupils give the directions after awhile.

3. Objective: *To identify beginning sound-symbol relationships. Give pupils an index card.* Have them write the letter name you are introducing or reviewing (both capital and lowercase) on one side. The other side is to be blank. Call out words. If the word begins with the letter on the card, pupils turn the card toward you with the letter displayed. If the called word does not begin with the letter, pupils display the other side. Variations include (a) having pupils clap hands softly if the word is correct, (b) pretending they are jack-in-the-boxes and jumping up if the word is correct, and (c) showing a smiling or an unhappy face. (A smiling face denotes the word is correct.)

4. Objective: *To practice beginning and ending sounds or letters that encode that sound.* (Be certain to specify which one.) Throw die to determine how many letters are in the first word or simply start with a word. The word could be *goat*. Next player may begin a word with the last letter of the word used, such as *tennis*, or have a word end with the first letter of the word, such as *drag*. Write the words on the board and continue playing.
    drag   goat   tennis

5. Objective: *To build and expand vocabulary.* Set a timer. Students write as many rhyming words as they can from a given stimulus word. Starter words could be *man, pat,* or *tag*.

6. Objective: *Reinforcing the CVC (consonant-vowel-consonant) rule.* Make cards of five vowels for each player; one or two sets of cards of all the consonants. Have each player place the vowel cards in front of him/her faceup on the table. In the center of the table, scatter the consonant cards face down. Each player draws a consonant card and attempts to place it at the beginning or end of one of his/her vowels. The first player to make words with all his/her vowel cards is the winner.

7. Objective: *Changing phonetic elements.*

came	Add one letter and get a word for an animal.
close	Add one letter at the end and get a word for a place for clothes.
flow	Add two letters at the end and get something you put in a vase.
hear	Add one letter at the end and get a part of your body.
plane	Add one letter at the end and get another words for Mars.
tin	Add one letter at the end and get a word that means "very small."

8. Objective: *Review of any of the consonant blends, consonants that vary, consonant digraphs, and vowel digraphs.* Prior to the activity, write on the board sets of three words that reinforce the skill/skills being reviewed. Have six sets each time for the sound-symbol/symbols under study. Example:

   1. tried   trade   tree   (consonant blend)
   2. city   cake   cents   (consonants that vary)
   3. think   thin   thimble   (consonant digraph)
   4. sleep   slick   slur   (consonant blends)
   5. gate   gallop   germ   (consonants that vary)
   6. champ   chef   school   (consonant digraph)

   Use a die. Each student rolls the die. The number on the die is the number of the set the student is to read. If s/he reads the three words s/he receives one point.

9. Objective: *Practice with any needed skill.* Teacher stands in the center of a circle. As the ball is bounced s/he says a word. The student who receives the ball must name the letter that begins the word, ends the word, is the vowel; or indicates the number of syllables, etc.

10. Objective: *Practice with digraphs.* Teacher or students construct "Digraph-Show" cards by dividing a paper square into four sections, labeling each with a particular digraph as

    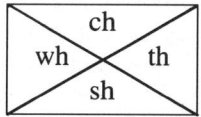

    The teacher reads a word from a list. Each player holds up the card with the correct digraph at the top. Points are awarded for correct answers. (For slower children, use four separate cards.)

11. Objective: *Review.* Construct word cards for review. The pupil in the first chair is the pilot. Show word cards. The pilot reads the words, continuing to do so until s/he misses one. S/he then goes to the rear of the "plane," and the next pupil becomes the pilot. If the pilot gets all the words correct s/he has reached destination and gets off. (Use a "pilot hat" for the first player.)

12. Objective: *Review and reinforcement.* Label each of several boxes with one of the phonetic elements being studied (for example *ch, sh, th,* and *wh*). Divide the class into two teams. Give the first student in each team a small bean bag. Students stand about four feet from the boxes. Pronounce a word and give a signal for the toss. Both students try to toss their bean bags into the box with the correct label. It may be the initial, medial, or final sound in the word. The first student to do so wins a point for the team. After all students have had a turn, the team with more points wins.

13. Objective: *Review and reinforcement.* Divide the class into four teams. Assign a different area of the room to each team. Give each team an equal number of blocks, toy logs, or other building materials. On the board write one or more letter combinations that represent a specific phonetic element (for example, *ou* and *ow*). Give Team A members fifteen seconds to name as many words that contain the element as they can. For each correct word, the team earns one building part with which to build a structure. Then write different letter combinations and have Team B follow the same procedure. Continue the game, alternating play between teams, until one team wins, having used all its building parts.

14. Objective: *Review and reinforcement*. Cover a bulletin board with white paper. Draw two downhill ski courses on the paper. On each course draw an equal number of flags. Cut two skiers from construction paper. Position one at the top of each hill. Divide the class into two teams. On the board write a word with the phonetic element being studied. The first student on Team A reads the word aloud. If correct, the student moves the team's skier to the first flag on the hill. The first player on Team B then takes a turn trying to read a word with a different phonetic element. The game continues in this manner with players from alternating teams taking turns. The first team to have its skier reach the bottom of the hill wins the race.

Examples of Puzzle-Type Activities

1. Objective: *Recognize letters of the alphabet*. Prepare an egg carton by writing a letter of the alphabet in each of the cups. The child places a marble or a penny in the carton, closes the lid, and shakes the carton. After opening the lid, the child names the letter upon which the marble or penny has landed.

2. Objective: *Recognize letters of the alphabet*. Pour glue on construction paper in the shape of a letter. Pour fruit gelatin over the glue. Shake to remove excess. When dry, have children touch and smell the letter. Proceed with other letters. When children know a certain number, have a "jello party."

3. Objective: *To identify beginning sounds of words*. Make a small chest from a box and cover it with paper. Place several items beginning with the same sounds, such as a nut, nail, necklace, nickel, and napkin, in a box. Also include items such as a ring and a crayon. Pupils remove objects one at a time, and tell whether or not they start with the /n/ sound.

4. Objective: *Recognizing beginning sounds*. Sing the song below, asking students whose names begin with B or another letter to come to the front of the room. Then have the class say each child's name while he or she takes a bow.*

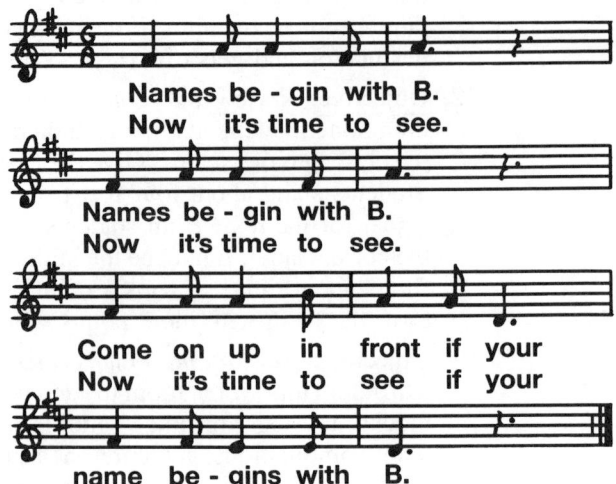

(*) Judy Meagher, *Instructor,* Sept. 1985, p. 148.

5. Objective: *Recognizing long and short vowel sounds*. Cover bulletin board with light-colored paper. Use thick felt-tipped pens to draw three or four short shelves on the left side of the paper and three or four longer shelves on the right side. Students flip through old magazines cutting out pictures of objects whose names contain long or short vowel sounds. The pictures should be of items that would actually fit on a shelf. Then have the students paste their chosen objects on the appropriately labeled shelf (longer shelves are for long vowels and shorter shelves for short vowels). Print the name of each object by the picture.

6. Objective: *Discriminating long- and short-vowel sounds*. Draw or cut out a picture of a popcorn wagon. Attach two small bags to the wagon and print "long vowels" on one and "short vowels" on the other. Cut out 20 fluffy popcorn shapes. Glue on each a picture of a familiar object or write a word on each. Students look at the picture or word, then decide whether it belongs in the long or short vowel bag.

7. Objective: *Adding consonants to make words*. Make four or five pictures of a clown carrying balloons. Print a common word part on each clown, such as *-ake, -et, -all*. Cut out colored circles the size of the balloon shapes; print a consonant on each. Students make words by combining the initial consonants on the balloons with the endings on the clowns.

8. Objective: *Recognizing final consonant sounds*. Prepare a colorful drawing of a roller coaster with 15 cars. Glue a small pocket on each car and print a consonant on each. Make 15 small picture cards, choosing objects that end with consonants printed on the cars; write the correct final consonant on the back of each card. Students match objects to cars, then check to see if they are correct.

9. Objective: *Practice in reading blends and digraphs*. Make flowers for the *r, l,* and *s* blends that the students have learned, such as *cr, gl,* and *sp*. Then make many bees with ending patterns on them, for example, _____*ad,* _____*ate,* and _____*ell*. Each child is instructed to place a bee and flower together, using a correct blend to form a word. If the word is incorrect, the child gets "stung" by the bee. (This puzzle match has many variations.)

10. Objective: *Review words*. Construct the necessary flower, turkey, tree, etc. Word cards are distributed to students. If they identify the word, they pin a petal on the flower, a feather on the turkey, a leaf on the tree, etc.

11. Objective: *Review words*. Sketch a large house on the board. Pupils draw "puzzle" word cards. If they can read the word, they draw a brick on the house and place their initials in it. Reshuffle the cards and continue.

12. Objective: *Practice and review of long vowel sounds using crossword puzzles*. Use any skill under study.

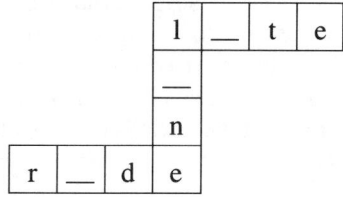

13. Objective: *Recognizing rhyming words*. Cut out 15 cone shapes and 15 cotton candy puffs from construction paper. On each pair of cones and puffs glue pictures of objects that rhyme. Mix up the cones and puffs. Students match cones to candy puffs by finding the objects that rhyme.

14. Objective: *Expanding vocabulary*. Create a grid similar to the one below. List various phonetic elements across the top of the grid. General categories are listed at the side of the grid. Duplicate a grid for each student. Have students fill in the grid with words that correspond to both categories. Allow students to consult books and dictionaries to find appropriate words. Have them share responses with the class. Students score one point for each word correctly completing a square. Play individually or in groups.

	ai	ay	ee	ea
things	train	*Clay*	*Cheese*	*lead*
action words	*Sail*	play	*freeze*	*Spread*

15. Objective: *Expanding vocabulary*. Provide large numbers of index cards or squares of paper. Students label items in the classroom by writing words that indicate possession on each card. For example, a pair of boots could be labeled "Tim's boots." The object is to label as many things as possible in a certain period of time. Encourage students to label items that belong to groups of people.

16. Objective: *Gain speed in rapid recognition*. Make two sets of several words. Individual pupils match words, trying to improve speed.

17. Objective: *Practice and review of words using anagrams*.

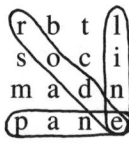

Manipulatives

1. Objective: *Reinforcing words through sensory experience*. Distribute individual letter cards to the students displaying such letters as *a, d, e, h, l, p, m, n, t, A, H, M, N*. Make word cards such as *am, man, mat, help, Nat, Ted,* and *Nan*. Place them face down in a stack. Choose and display word cards. Students with these letters are to stand next to each other to form the word. A student is then asked to read the word aloud. Continue until all the words are read.

2. Objective: *Practice with the final letter e*. Cut sixteen slips of paper into 6-by-3-inch strips. Fold over about 1½ inches of one end of each slip. Copy a word with one short vowel onto the larger portion of each slip of paper. Write an *e* on the back of the folded portion. When the *e* is flipped back only the short vowel word can be seen. When the *e* is flipped forward it changes the short vowel sound of these kinds of words to a long vowel sound. Suggested words: *cut, cap, tap, fat, hat, mat, past, rat, rod, tub, pan, man, sit, rob,* and *grip*.

| cut | e |

3. Objective: *Practice with letters or words using teacher-made or commercial flip books*.[30] On the back of letters place little pictures for self-checking. These flip books can also be made for CVC words with beginning blends and digraphs, and for final *e* words.

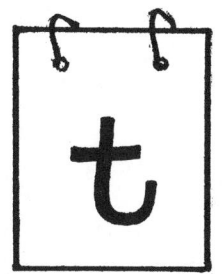    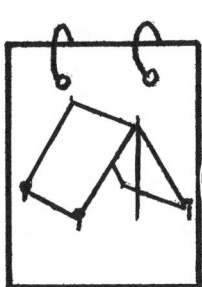

4. *Plastic pocket kits* (teacher-constructed or commerical).[31] These can be used for many skill activities such as learning beginning and ending sounds, compound words, contractions, etc. For example: The picture stimulis for compound words is in the center section. The sticks are "manipulated" or inserted in the proper position, with the answer key on the back of the sticks for self-checking. To construct, cut a piece of plastic into a 13-by-13 inch piece. Fold in half to form a 6½-by-13 inch piece. Stitch as per pattern. Size and number of slots may be altered.

Constructed Plastic Pocket Kit.

5. *Cut-out cards* (teacher-constructed or commercial.)[32] Students identify the correct vowel, etc., placing their pencil through the appropriate hole. The correct answer is on the other side.

(30) Commercial flip books may be purchased from Jane Ward Co. See Appendix D, "Resources for the Teacher."
(31) Commerical materials may be purchased from Reading Joy, Inc. See Appendix D, "Resources for the Teacher."
(32) Commercial materials may be purchased from Trend Enterprises. See Appendix D, "Resources for the Teacher."

6. *Flap answers* (teacher-constructed or commercial, many sources). The correct answer is under the short flap. The student writes answers on another sheet and checks inside the flap.

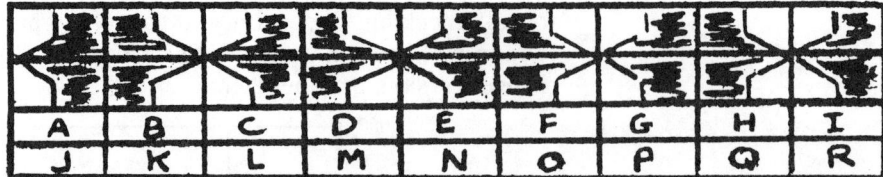

7. *Versa-Tiles* (commercial only).³³ Two components, a plastic answer case with plastic numbered tiles, and non-consumable problem-solving books. Work is self-corrective. Each set of correct answers results in a unique pattern formed on the tiles when the case is turned over.

8. *Tachistoscopes* (teacher-constructed of oaktag, or cardboard, or purchased commercially). For those that are teacher-constructed, a strip of paper is fed through the slits of a fun-type figure (see examples). The student reads each word as it appears. The object is to increase the rate of speed and to learn the words as sight words. Sometimes two slits of paper are used to teach such generalizations as the final *e* changing the preceding vowel.

Example Tachistoscopes

(33) May be purchased from Educational Teaching Aids. See Appendix D, "Resources for the Teacher," Publishers.

Materials inundation!

On the market are various types of hardware (expensive!) such as the *Language Master,* into which students insert cards with magnetic tape and the card "talks" back, reinforcing the correct response when given. There are *Controlled Readers,* something like an automatic fast filmstrip, for increasing the eye sweep, with the line of print adjustable for rate of speed and size of type. *Systems 80* is another type of hardware that allows students to sit before a TV-like screen, make correct responses by pushing various buttons, and program themselves through skills. In addition there are cassette phonics programs, some with filmstrips too; and a computer program called *Speak and Spell,* with a "voice" to test students on their ability to read and spell words. (In a later section we will discuss the computer in greater detail.)

Confronted with so many materials, activities, and ideas for teaching these sound-symbol associations (and many of these are useful in teaching other word-attack skills too), teachers often engage students in these activities to the exclusion of actual reading! Phonics or skill instruction becomes the end, instead of the means to an end. Because phonics skills, in varying degrees of intensity, are usually emphasized in early reading, it is important to stop a moment to consider some guidelines to help keep the teaching of phonics in proper perspective.

Guidelines When Teaching Phonics

1. The purpose of teaching phonics skills in reading is to help students develop the ability to recognize *at sight* large numbers of words.
2. *Periodic diagnosis must be used to identify students' skill needs,* and teaching/learning activities must be planned to meet those needs. *This is an important part of teaching any word-attack skill.*
3. Students must, after the beginning reading stages, apply what they have learned through followup activities/lessons that involve *actual reading.*
4. Students must be taught to rely on contextual and other visual clues, together with phonics.
5. A teacher must know the skills thoroughly so that what is taught is correct, appropriate, and necessary.

As a teacher ask yourself, "What is my objective in engaging in this activity? Is it necessary for all students? Would John, May, and Suzy, who seem to know and use these skills so effectively, need this exercise/activity?" Not only is it a waste of time for many students who already know and use the skill effectively, but many materials commonly used in class are confusing and have no real reading transfer value! For example, pictures that students must identify are frequently misleading. Shown a vague picture of a goat that could be identified as any animal, and then asking students to supply the beginning letter causes confusion. Often the directions for completing skill activities are so difficult that if the children could read them in the first place they wouldn't need the activity! Then too, as children become more mature readers, many activities can be completed without the child actually reading, but merely telling which word has a short *a* or a short *i*; the number of syllables; or the accent. (A test for diagnosing students' decoding skills may be found in Appendix D, page 182.)

For the reasons mentioned above and because phonics is such a controversial area, teachers frequently ask questions about it.

Questions Teachers Ask When Teaching Phonics

1. How much phonics do children need? Many educators flippantly say, "As little as possible." This answer is quite misleading. Initial reading can be frustrating and overwhelming if too many words are introduced too rapidly, and considerable phonics review is often necessary. On the other hand too much phonics for competent readers is a waste of time. *Periodic careful diagnosis,* coupled with teacher observation to determine who needs what, is the key.

2. Should the phonics lesson be taught before the reading lesson, after, or during a separate period? In beginning reading it must be part of the lesson, but after children begin reading more fluently by the second grade, the author would opt for a separate period. This is because group reading should be primarily concerned with comprehension and interpretation.

3. What do I say when a generalization doesn't work? Tell students that generalizations are merely starting points. Emphasize that they must remain flexible when decoding, and that when letters combine in different ways, they sometimes encode different sounds.

4. Should I try to induct generalizations? It depends. What must be kept in mind is that the goal of phonics instruction is teaching children to learn to decode quickly. Sometimes inducting generalizations takes a long time.

5. What is a reasonable skill sequence? Because there is greater consistency between consonant letters and their respective sounds than there is between vowels and their respective sounds, most instructional programs begin using the consonants to initiate learning some sound-symbol associations. In general, a few letters are introduced (no two programs agree!), together with the short *a*, followed by additional consonant letters, and some of the other short vowels. Gradually a few blends and consonant digraphs are introduced, followed by the long and special third sounds of certain vowels. The more difficult *R*-conditioned vowels, vowel diphthongs, and special combinations are taught later. (See Appendix B, page 160 for a basal skill sequence.)

6. Should I tell children to try the short vowel sound if they are undecided? Yes, especially with troublesome words, because short vowel sounds occur more frequently than do long vowel sounds except with the two sounds of /o͞o/ where the long sound predominates.

7. What correspondences are worthwhile teaching? It all depends. In order to learn to read, some children need intensive instruction in almost all the correspondences while others, through a kind of osmosis, seem to soak up these relationships without any explanation. Again the key is diagnosis.

8. Should children state the rule? The inability to state a phonics rule did not seem to hinder children's efforts to analyze unfamiliar words. They used the generalizations without being able to state them. (Rosso and Emans, 1981). The important thing therefore is their ability to *apply* the rule. The teacher, however, should be able to state a generalization *since s/he must verbalize it to the student.*

9. Should students use the term *blend* or *digraph*? As in the previous example, this is not essential but depends on the teacher's philosophy and the type of class. Students need to understand that blends are pronounced very rapidly, while digraphs encode only one sound. The teacher may use these terms as s/he is responsible for definitions.

10. What should I do when children who are *first learning* to read, continually ask for help in decoding words? Help them begin to develop a word-pronunciation strategy and suggest they do something similar to the following:
   a. Try the first sound of the word, noting whether it is a single consonant letter, a letter combination (blend or digraph), or a vowel.
   b. Continue reading the sentence to see if further clues are within the sentence to help decode the word.
   c. Reread the sentence to see if the word as they have decoded it makes sense.
   As children mature, their strategy must expand. Initially they will profit from using the sound pattern and context while later they will need to learn how to use the structure of words, context, and sound pattern.[34] They must also learn to use the dictionary.
11. Does peer tutoring work? Absolutely, but only with very careful organization and lots of preplanning by the teacher/teachers involved.[35]
12. What is meant by a skill-centered approach? Teachers agree on a set of skills important to reading ability, pretest students to determine which skills they have and which they need, and then provide instruction and opportunities to apply these skills. Students are subsequently posttested to see if they have learned these skills. There are many of these skill-centered commercial programs on the market, such as *The Wisconsin Design; Read: An Individual Pupil Monitoring System;* and *The Prescriptive Reading Inventory.*[36] These programs are frequently used with an individualized reading approach.

Summary

This first section has indicated the phonics debate still continues. The main focus of the section, however, has been on phonics, to show the relationship between sounds and symbols. Understanding the relationship provides a foundation for seeing how much of our written language decodes. The scope of this written language may be more easily understood by dividing it into categories that include within the consonant group, single consonants, consonants that vary, blends, and digraphs; and among the vowel group, short, long, and third vowel sounds, the schwa, vowel digraphs, and diphthongs. Additionally, the letter 'y' has a unique position, sometimes functioning as either a consonant or vowel. The letter 'r' may condition the preceding vowel sound when it is encoded by a single vowel or a vowel digraph. As with all word identification strategies, phonics works best when used in combination with other strategies that provide clues.

Reading readiness was briefly discussed, and a set of prereading "tasks" for children was presented. Additionally, a rationale for a prereading phonics inventory and the inventory itself was included.

A method to teach beginning sound-symbol relationships was suggested with some examples of the kinds of classroom materials and activities used. Also with beginning phonics instruction a very important part includes work with blending,

---

(34) Context and structure of words will be discussed in later sections and an expanded word-pronouncing strategy suggested.

(35) See article by Nancy Boraks and Amy Roseman Allen, "A Program to Enhance Peer Tutoring," *The Reading Teacher* 30, no. 6 (February 1977): 479-84.

(36) *The Wisconsin Design,* Educational Systems, 4401 W. 76th St., Minneapolis, Minnesota 55435; *Read: An Individual Pupil Monitoring System,* Houghton Mifflin Publishers, Boston, Massachusetts; and *The Prescriptive Reading Inventory,* McGraw-Hill Publishers, Del Monte Research Park, Monterey, California 93940.

and several methods were suggested. Disagreement still exists as to whether phonics instruction should be synthetic, analytic or linguistic, and as in the case of blending techniques, the method used depends on student maturity and ability, and on teacher preference. Example lessons of each type were included.

Ways of teaching, extending, reinforcing, and reviewing sound-symbol relationships were presented. As students, however, begin and continue to learn to read, it is only through periodic diagnosis that their skill strengths and weaknesses may be identified, and appropriate lessons planned.

Questions asked most frequently about teaching phonics with suggested answers were included. When phonics teaching is purposeful and helps children learn to decode words and read them at sight through meaningful activities, then teaching phonics has a definite place in today's elementary school classroom, and at higher levels where needed.

Tests to check phonics and other decoding skills of the teacher are included in Appendix D. A decoding skills test for students may also be found in the same Appendix.

PART 1, SECTIONS VI & VII REVIEW AND SELF-CHECK

1. What are some factors considered in reading readiness?
2. What are the purposes of prereading tasks?
3. Describe a strategy for introducing a beginning sound-symbol relationship.
4. (a) How many different ways may students be taught to blend sounds? (b) What are these ways? (c) Which would you use and why?
5. (a) What is the difference between synthetic, analytic, and linguistic phonics? (b) Why are these terms confusing?
6. Suggest some game-type activities, puzzle-type activities, and manipulatives that teachers may use in teaching, extending, reinforcing, and reviewing sound-symbol relationships.
7. Why is the "inundation" of phonics materials a problem in schools?
8. What should be the major goal in teaching phonics to children?
9. What should teachers say to students when generalizations about sound-symbol relationships do not work?
10. What is meant by a skill-centered approach to teaching phonics?

PART
2
Additional Word Attack Skills

SECTION I

SIGHT WORDS

In reading, a particular group of "heavy duty" words, such as *at, the, be, of,* are referred to as sight words. These words are encountered with great frequency, and it would be difficult to read any extended passage without meeting a large number of them. As they must be recognized at sight instantly, the term *sight words* is used when discussing them. Percentages for the frequency of these words are often given, and these range from 50 to 66 percent. The difference in occurrence is due to the nature of the text, with simpler reading materials usually containing a higher percentage.

A good number of these high-frequency words contain irregular spellings, therefore limiting the effectiveness of teaching them through phonics, and consequently providing another reason for teaching them as "sight" words. As students in early reading learn both sight words and sound-symbol relationships as part of word attack skills, they will see them in proper perspective and will avoid relying completely on either one.

Sight Word Lists

One of the most popular of these high-frequency sight word lists is the Dolch list, a total of 220 words. There are a number of others, including the Harris-Jacobson, the Dale Johnson, and the Durr. Two of these lists, the Dolch and the Harris-Jacobson, are included in Tables 2.1 and 2.2, respectively.

There are four levels to the Dolch list, with the words arranged in increasing levels of difficulty, although these divisions are somewhat arbitrary. There have been many attempts to update this list since Dolch first compiled it in 1936, but nevertheless it retains its original popularity. A later revision is a list by Johns (1978) in which 189 of the Dolch words have been retained, and changes made in the others.

In a more recent study Palmer (1985) checked the Dolch list against four newer series of basals: Ginn's Reading 720, Holt, Rinehart & Winston, Houghton Mifflin, and Scott Foresman. She found the Dolch words made up between 57% and 82% of the vocabulary in the passages and levels, with the average being 60%.

You will notice that there are no nouns in Table 2.1 because the nouns used in any passage are determined by the subject matter and vary enormously. In contrast, most of the words included in this list occur repeatedly in reading materials, regardless of reading level. The Harris-Jacobson core list (Table 2.2), which is quite a bit longer, does include some very common nouns.

Students who do not experience reading problems will have learned most of these words by the end of the second or third grade. However, problem readers, even some junior and senior high school students, have not mastered them. Appendix B includes a list of basic sight words for older readers that incorporates frequently used words at upper levels.

Teaching Sight Words

Mastery of a core vocabulary such as the Dolch list is necessary in order for children to become fluent readers. It is a good idea to test them individually on their ability to recognize these words, with mastery defined as the "instant"

Table 2.1   Dolch Basic Sight Word List

Preprimer	Primer	First Grade	Second Grade	Third Grade
1. a	1. all	1. after	1. always	1. about
2. and	2. am	2. again	2. around	2. better
3. away	3. are	3. an	3. because	3. bring
4. big	4. at	4. any	4. been	4. carry
5. blue	5. ate	5. as	5. before	5. clean
6. can	6. be	6. ask	6. best	6. cut
7. come	7. black	7. by	7. both	7. done
8. down	8. brown	8. could	8. buy	8. draw
9. find	9. but	9. every	9. call	9. drink
10. for	10. came	10. fly	10. cold	10. eight
11. funny	11. did	11. from	11. does	11. fall
12. go	12. do	12. give	12. don't	12. far
13. help	13. eat	13. going	13. fast	13. full
14. here	14. four	14. had	14. first	14. got
15. I	15. get	15. has	15. five	15. grow
16. in	16. good	16. her	16. found	16. hold
17. is	17. have	17. him	17. gave	17. hot
18. it	18. he	18. his	18. goes	18. hurt
19. jump	19. into	19. how	19. green	19. if
20. little	20. like	20. just	20. its	20. keep
21. look	21. must	21. know	21. made	21. kind
22. make	22. new	22. let	22. many	22. laugh
23. me	23. no	23. live	23. off	23. light
24. my	24. now	24. may	24. or	24. long
25. not	25. on	25. of	25. pull	25. much
26. one	26. our	26. old	26. read	26. myself
27. play	27. out	27. once	27. right	27. never
28. red	28. please	28. open	28. sing	28. only
29. run	29. pretty	29. over	29. sit	29. own
30. said	30. ran	30. put	30. sleep	30. pick
31. see	31. ride	31. round	31. tell	31. seven
32. the	32. saw	32. some	32. their	32. shall
33. three	33. say	33. stop	33. these	33. show
34. to	34. she	34. take	34. those	34. six
35. two	35. so	35. thank	35. upon	35. small
36. up	36. soon	36. them	36. us	36. start
37. we	37. that	37. then	37. use	37. ten
38. where	38. there	38. think	38. very	38. today
39. yellow	39. they	39. walk	39. wash	39. together
40. you	40. this	40. were	40. which	40. try
	41. too	41. when	41. why	41. warm
	42. under		42. wish	
	43. want		43. work	
	44. was		44. would	
	45. well		45. write	
	46. went		46. your	
	47. what			
	48. white			
	49. who			
	50. will			
	51. with			
	52. yes			

Copyright (c) 1952 by E.W. Dolch. Available in testing and teaching aids packages from Garrard Publishing Co., Champaign, Illinois.

Table 2.2   Harris-Jacobson Core Words for First Grade

Core Preprimer List

a	daddy*	green	look	ride	want
and	did	have	make	said	we
are	do	he	me	see	what
at	dog*	help	mother*	something*	who
ball*	down	here	my	stop	will
big	for	I	no	that	with
blue	fun*	in	not	the	work
call	funny	is	play	this	you
can	get	it	ran	to	
come	go	little	red	up	

Core Primer List

about	car*	home*	of	show	tree*
all	eat	house*	on	sit	two
around	fast	into	one	so	us
ask	father*	jump	out	some	want
away	fish*	know	paint*	soon	word*
bike*	from	let	pet*	take	yellow
birthday*	goat*	like	put	thank	yes
boat*	good	man*	run	then	your
book*	has	may	saw	they	
but	him	new	say	too	
cake*	his	now	she	train*	

Core First Reader

after	cat*	girl*	live	prize*	think
again	catch*	give	long	rabbit*	those
airplane*	children*	gone*	lost*	race*	three
along*	coat*	goodby*	made	rain*	time*
am	cold	got	many	read	told*
an	color*	grass*	maybe*	ready*	tomorrow*
animal*	could	guess*	men*	right	took*
another*	cow*	had	met*	road	town*
any	cry*	hair*	miss*	rocket*	toy*
as	cut	hand*	money*	sang*	truck*
baby*	dark*	happy*	more*	sat*	try
back*	day*	hard*	morning*	school*	turtle*
bag*	didn't*	hat*	must	seen*	TV*
balloon*	does	head*	name*	shoe*	under
bark*	don't	hear*	never	should*	very
barn*	dress*	hello*	next*	sing	wagon*
be	drop*	hen*	night*	sister*	walk
bear*	duck*	her	nothing*	sleep	was
bed*	fall	hill*	off	sound*	water*
bee*	far	hold	on	stay	way*
before	farm*	hop*	old	step*	were
began*	fat*	horse*	or	still*	wet*
behind*	feet*	how	other*	stopped*	when
better	fight*	hurry*	our	store*	where
bird*	find	I'll*	over	story*	which
black	fire*	ice*	own	street*	white
box*	first	if	pan*	sun*	why
boy*	five	it's*	party*	surprise*	window*
bring	fly	just	peanut*	talk*	wish
brown	food*	kind	penny*	tea	won't*
build*	found	kitten*	picnic*	than*	would
bus*	four	last*	picture*	their	zoo*
by	fox*	laugh	pig*	them	
cage*	friend*	leg*	please	there	
came	game*	letter*	pocket*	these	
can't*	gave	light	pony*	thing*	

For a rationale of the list, and the list itself see Albert J. Harris and Milton D. Jacobson, *Basic Elementary Reading Vocabularies*. (New York: The Macmillan Co. 1972) pp. 60-82. Also see Albert J. Harris and Edward R. Sipay, *How to Increase Reading Ability* (New York: David McKay Co., 1975, pp. 362-363.)

*Words that are not on the Dolch Basic Word List.

recognition of 90-95 percent of the words in any one test list. Reading words in such a list is more demanding for poor readers than reading these same words in context (Krieger, 1981).

To master many of these words, some bright students learn them in context by merely reading a variety of interesting stories and articles (the best way). Other students need simple introduction to the words followed by a little practice, engaging in some of the following activities for learning these words. There are others who need a more structured program. Each word must be very carefully introduced by perhaps placing it in a pocket chart and asking such questions as:

1. How many letters are in the word?
2. With what letter does the word begin?
3. What is/are the letter/s at the end of the word?
4. Read the word.
5. What is the difference between this word and _____?
   The focus here is on minimum contrasts such as *then* and *than*.

With a more structured program, the introduction of each word is followed by lots of review and practice as suggested in some of the following activities. Before describing these activities, it is important to sound a note of caution. When teaching any word attack strategy, children need to know that words spoken in isolation are frequently stressed differently than when they are spoken in sentences. Sight words are particularly vulnerable in this respect. For example, the word *an* would be pronounced and accented as /án/ in situations where it is spoken in isolation, but it would be unaccented as /ən/ when spoken in the context of a phrase as /ən áppl/. For this reason whenever possible, present these words as parts of phrases and sentences. Remember, too, that most of these words have a variety of meanings depending on the context in which they are used. For example, notice the various meanings of *up* in these phrases: *add up, shape up, dress up, eat up, clam up, slip up, fold up, mess up,* and *frame up*.

Activities for Teaching Sight Words

The objective for the following activities is to help students who experience difficulty with particular sight words:

1. When particular words are easily confused such as *on* and *one*, have children identify the letter that causes the difficulty. Place several children's names on the board with the particular letter such as *e* — *Jerry, Ted, Jane*. Ask the student to identify the "demon" letter in the names.
2. Trace words in sand that are repeatedly missed and point out the salient feature. Have the student repeat the tracing, verbalizing the difficult letters as s/he does so.
3. Construct a slotted stand-up frame to hold "My Word for the Day." Insert words needed for practice.

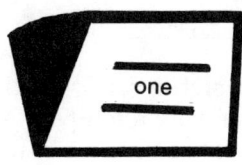

4. Note and draw the configuration of a word such as

The objectives for the following activities are review and extension:

1. Drill with phrase and sentence cards. (See Table 2.3)

Example: Phrase Card

Example: Sentence Card

2. Prepare pairs of phrase or sentence cards. Start with about five pairs, or ten cards, turning them upside down. Students must read the word or phrase card as they turn it over and attempt to find the matching pair.
3. Cards (phrase or sentences) may be passed out. The teacher says such things as "Whoever has the phrase *will do*, stand up, get in line, or whistle," etc.
4. Have about a dozen pairs of phrase cards ready. Take one set and distribute the remaining cards among a small group of students. Place one card in the pocket chart and say, "All those who have this same word or phrase card may place it in the pocket chart with mine." Continue with the rest of the cards.
5. Write some of the words or phrases on the blackboard, leaving off a beginning or ending letter. Ask the students to provide the missing letters. When possible relate them to sounds.
6. Write words on the blackboard. Read with students in unison. Erase the words one at a time, reading the remaining words on the list, and then "reading" the erased word when you point to the place where it had been written.
7. Have each student develop a "word bank" that includes a file of words known and a file of words that need to be learned. These may be kept in alphabetical order.
8. Write notes to learners with difficult decoding problems, using the words they are practicing, such as "Can you help me?" This proves highly motivating.
9. Words or phrases receive a monetary value of 25¢, 50¢, or $1.00. The value of the words read is added together. "Money" is owed to the teacher when a word cannot be read. The object is to "beat the teacher."
10. Use the ever-popular BINGO format with words or phrases as shown in these examples.

and	must	see
big	FREE	he
what	yes	play

I can	for me	is it
to run	FREE	what went
my new	to him	come down

11. Use a muffin pan or plastic egg carton. Write sight words on the bottom of each section with a felt pen. Make copies of these sight words on cards. Students sort and place them in the appropriate section, reading the word.

Table 2.3 Phrase Unit, Based on the Dolch Basic Sight Vocabulary

Phrase	Phrase	Phrase
about it	he went	of their own
are big now	help me	one or two
as I do	here is an	only one
ask him	his green one	our yellow one
at the	how much	out came three
ate his		out came two
	I am	
be good	I can	please let
be just right	I do	pretty white
before long	I have	pull us out
best of all	I like	
but I do	I want	ran fast
	I will	ran to stop
came because	if he goes	read and write
can always see	into the	run away
can buy	is cold	
can find	is full	saw her
can fly	is going	see how small
can laugh	is not black	see my green
can use	it came from	shall both talk
carry her	it is	shall know soon
come and play	it is going	she gave eight
could not grow		she has five
	jump up	sit down
did not	jump upon	so am I
do not	just then	
do you		take hold
does not	keep him	talk at once
don't you	know which	tell me
draw a green	know why	tell them
		thank you
for a walk	let me	that big yellow
four little yellow	let us	the first one
	like to ride	the funny one
get on	like to show	the hot
give up	live in	the kind of
go to	long, long drink	the light
go together	look after	their brown
	look at	there are
had not been	look for	there are ten
had to clean	look under	they called
have found	look up	they said
he could see		this is
he got	made a blue	to cut some
he looked around	made him white	to drink
he never saw	may I sing	to eat
he put new	must be warm	to keep those
he ran	my big	to make
he said	my red one	to play
he saw		to play with
	not very far	to sleep
		to work

12. Use well-known short nursery rhymes such as *Humpty Dumpty*, that contain lots of sight words. Write the words on the chalkboard. Read them aloud. Ask students to read them along with you several times until the words are well known. Then make word cards for each sight word you want them to retain from the rhyme. Shuffle the cards and spread them face down. Taking turns, the children choose a card and read the word. The card is then kept if read correctly. If a player misreads the card, s/he must keep it until the next round, and then read it correctly.
13. Write two columns of words or phrases on the board. There should be as many words or phrases as there are children in the relay. The first students of each team point to the first word or phrase in the column; read it; and if correct erase it, returning to the line. The side that erases all the words or phrases wins.

When Sight Words Are Especially Troublesome

Cunningham (1980) describes sight words as "four-letter" words because of the connotation of "bad" and the fact that many include four letters as *were, with* and *what*. For children who need remediation, she suggests a time-consuming method but reminds teachers that this "drastic" strategy should be used only for words which, year in and year out, are seemingly impossible for slow readers to learn. A rationale for her method follows:

> Since sight words have no tangible meaning and their function is to connect other words, children are often unaware of their existence as separate words. The word *what* is often used in "Whatcha doing?" *Them* is just pronounced "m". Some children do not even realize these are separate words such as *big, truck* and *elephant*, nor are they clear as to their function. (p. 160)

Using *what* as an example word, her method follows:

1. *Creating awareness of "what" as a separate entity and how it functions.*
   Tell a story with *what* in every line. Stop before the word to emphasize the pronunciation. Children hold up their *what* card every time they hear the word. Next children make up sentences and stories with *what* and other children hold up their cards when they hear it.
2. *Phoneme/Grapheme Awareness*
   (a) Each child in a group takes time to study his/her word card with *what*. Afterwards the teacher cuts the word apart, instructing the child to rearrange it. If the child is correct the teacher mixes the letters up again and has the child rearrange them several times. For those children who cannot do this initial step, the teacher points out what is wrong and corrects it with an explanation. She then tells the child to study the word again, mixing it up to be rearranged correctly.
   (b) The children place their letters in an envelope. The word is written by the teacher on the envelope's outside. In time each child has several envelopes on which are written all the sight words s/he has worked on, and in which can be found all the letters needed to reconstruct these words. This becomes a valuable seatwork activity for these children.
3. *Learning to Write the Word*
   The teacher writes the word on the board and asks each child to look closely at it and try to take a picture of it as a camera does. The children close their eyes to see if they can still see the word *what*. They check and repeat this

"open-your eyes, close your eyes" procedure several times. Next they try to write the word from memory after it has been erased. The teacher writes the word again and the children make a comparison with their own word. The child's first written word is covered and the experience repeated. The goal is to get the child to correctly write the word *what* three times.

4. *Learning to Read the Word*
   The teacher begins to write several sentences on the board that will contain *what*. When s/he comes to the place for *what*, s/he instructs a child to come to the board and write it since s/he has now learned to do so. The children are then provided with a mimeographed story sheet in which the target word *what* is used many times. They underline the word lightly in pencil every time they see it. Afterwards the teacher reads the story to them, stopping each time s/he comes to *what* so the students can read the word. Further practice for some children may still be necessary.

Phonics and Sight Words

Once a certain reading level is reached, the teacher can use these words to review certain phonics generalizations, building on the sight knowledge of the students. Any of the following could serve as a lesson:

Words with beginning consonants that are similar: *said, say, see*
Words with ending consonants that are similar: *get, it, must, not*
Words with the vowel digraph *ay: say, play, away*
Words with the consonant digraph *th* (voiced sound): *the, there, this*
Words with a final long vowel sound: *me, go, so, he, she, we*
Consonant substitution with the words find: *rind, mind, kind, bind,*
well: *sell, fell, tell, bell, dell, yell*
will: *bill, fill, hill, mill, sill, till,*
Dividing words between like consonants: *fun-ny, pret-ty*

Sight Word Storehouse: The Goal in Reading

The sight words listed and discussed previously differ from the sight words acquired weekly, monthly, and yearly by students as they progress through the grades. By repeatedly encountering words (the number of times varying for different students), words are recognized immediately without any form of analysis. *This should be the goal in reading,* that words read are all part of a growing expanding sight vocabulary. The vast storehouse of sight words accumulated by expert readers makes it possible for them not only to read rapidly, but also to pay full attention to thinking about what they are reading.

Sight Words for the Computer Age: An Essential Word List

Today's children need to familiarize themselves with words used in the computer environment. The following list represents a core of major procedural and feedback words in the samples of programs reviewed (Dreyer, Futtersak, and Boehm

1985). These words need to be introduced early in classroom instruction. They may be introduced in the context of phrases or sentences in which they actually occur in programs, such as:

> hold down
> sound effects
> video monitor
> Loading . . . please wait.
> Type your name.
> Do you want instructions?
> Press spacebar to continue.

While teaching these words, point out to students that the same terms may appear in different forms in different programs. Command key names, for example, are sometimes presented in capital letters such as RETURN, within angle brackets as in <RETURN>, abbreviated as in <esc> or <ESC> or ESC, or *highlighted* on the screen. Knowledge of the different visual representations of the words and their abbreviated forms is essential for the child.

Essential words for computer-assisted instruction in the elementary grades, based on a sample of 35 programs

activity	description	lesson	ready
adjust	different	letter	regular
again	directions	level	remove
another	disk	list	repeat
answer	diskette	load	*return
any	display	*loading	[rewind]
*arrow	document	match	rules
audio	down	memory	save
bar	drive	*menu	score
before	edit	[module]	screen
begin	effects	monitor	select
bold	end	move	selection
button	*enter	*name	*sound
[cartridge]	erase	need	*spacebar
[cassette]	*escape or <esc>	no	speed
catalog	exit	*number	start
change	find	off	team
choice	finished	on	text
*choose	follow	options	then
colors	format	paddle	try
column	*game	password	turn
compete	good	picture	*type
complete	help	play	up
command	hit	player	use
computer	hold	*please	video
*continue	incorrect	point	wait
control or <cntrl>	incorrectly	practice	want
copy	indicate	*press	which
correct	insert	print	win
correctly	instructions	problems	word
cursor	joystick	*program	work
delete	*key	quit	yes
demonstration	keyboard	rate	your

*Words present in at least 10 of the 35 programs
[ ] Additions—not in any of the 35 programs

Quick Self-Check XIII

1. Examine the following list and place a check mark next to the sight words:
   did   pepper
   from   for
   dragon   matching
   about   once
2. What is the name of the most popular sight word list?
3. What would be a structured approach to teaching sight words?
4. What is the best way for children to learn sight words?
5. What are some activities that may be used to teach sight words?

SECTION II

STRUCTURAL ANALYSIS: AN INCREASINGLY IMPORTANT DECODING STRATEGY

Two decoding strategies have been discussed, phonics analysis and instant recognition of high-frequency or sight words. Structural analysis, which entails identifying meaningful subunits within words, becomes increasingly important in decoding strategies as children move through the grades and on through high school. It consists of recognizing big word "chunks" such as compound words, prefixes, suffixes, and roots and understanding certain principles of syllabication, thereby having the ability to "break apart" words quickly.

Children begin learning about structural analysis as early as first grade when they are introduced to verb units such as *ing* and *ed* and plural endings such as *s* and *es*. Prefixes such as *re* and *un* are sometimes introduced as early as second grade, while work with more complex affixes and roots usually begins in the middle grades, and continues through high school.

The effectiveness of using structural analysis depends in large part on the extensiveness of a student's reading vocabulary. Those students who have internalized the phoneme-grapheme relationships of English, and have additionally a rich storehouse of sight words and word roots, are in the best position to profit from this kind of instruction. This is because these "chunks," simple words or roots, are discrete language units that can be identified and then readily combined with prefixes and suffixes to form new words.

Compound Words

Compound words are simply a combination of two base words and are fairly easy to decode. When words begin to be longer than one syllable, a quick check often indicates whether they are compound. English abounds with compound words and their number is increasing all the time (Ex.: *seatbelt*). As a matter of fact, about 60 percent of the new words that come into our language *(countdown, fallout)* are compound.

Students need to know that in most cases the meaning of the compound word is a combination of the two joined words. Sometimes, however, it is not, as in the word *redcap* meaning 'porter', or *blackboard* referring to a green chalkboard. Students should also know that because of wide usage, some actual compound words are thought of as single words. Example: *windshield* (shield from the wind) and *sidewalk* (walk by the side of the road).

Compounds are not restricted to structures of adjective plus noun like *blackbird* and *highchair*. Here are some other possibilities:

Noun + noun	doormat, soapsuds
Adverb + noun	downstroke, upstairs, onlooker
Verb + noun	scarecrow, watchman, daredevil
Preposition + verb	undertake, overdrawn

Activities for teaching compound words

1. Objective: To practice combining two base words. Write words on the board that can become part of a compound word, such as *dog, plane, thing, some, house, noon, man, air, after,* etc. Ask children to choose two of the words to form a compound, and write the word on a slip of paper, later sharing their word/words by using them in sentences.

2. Objective: Practice with known compound words. Construct or use matching exercises as shown in the following:

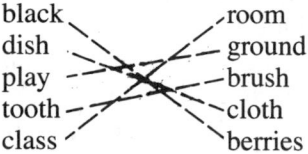

3. Objective: Practice and extension of roots that combine. Make word card "puzzles" (or purchase them commercially) that form compound words. Children match parts and read the words. Example:

4. Objective: Review and Extension. Use a folder with pockets. On one side place the first part of almost a dozen compound words. On the other side place the second part of these words. Students combine these pieces. Answers are on the back of the folder for self-checking.

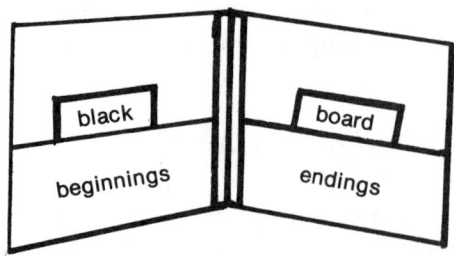

5. Objective: Review and Extension. Construct sentence cards as the following with students filling in the blanks.

Card 1   **Answers**
1. Sara flew to Texas on an _____.   1. airplane
2. The witch found her _____.   2. broomstick
3. They went to a _____ game.   3. basketball
4. John lived on a _____.   4. houseboat
5. Jane cleaned up her _____.   5. bedroom
6. Mark went to a _____ party.   6. birthday

6. Objective: Extending knowledge of compound words. Construct a large wall chart with five headings such as *People, Places, Things, Animal Life,* and *Time* at the top. Ask students to find compound words that fit under the headings. The list can be quite extensive as the following chart indicates:

People	**Places**	**Things**	**Animal Life**	**Time**
anybody	anywhere	airplane	butterfly	afternoon
chairman	barnyard	broomstick	goldfish	bedtime
everyone	bedroom	birdhouse	horseshoe	birthday
fisherman	doorway	boxcar	starfish	daylight
grandmother	downstairs	baseball	watchdog	lifetime
grownup	downtown	basketball	wildlife	playtime
housewife	driveway	cardboard		springtime
milkman	farmhouse	campfire		
nobody	farmland	dollhouse		
policeman	fireplace	doghouse		
postman	highway	doorbell		
runaway	outside	firewood		
salesman	playground	eyesight		
shoemaker	roadside	football		
	schoolyard	footsteps		
	sidewalk	flashlight		
	storeroom	greenhouse		
	upstairs	houseboat		
	workshop	moonlight		
		mousetrap		
		newspaper		
		raindrop		
		snowman		
		sunburn		
		sunlight		
		snowball		
		steamship		

Quick Self-Check XIV

1. What generalizations about compound words can be drawn from the words *carseat* and *blackball*?
2. List three words that are compound and have recently entered the English language.
3. Suggest two activities to teach compound words.

Prefixes, Roots, and Suffixes

Prefixes: definitions and dilemmas

The definition for a prefix has not been standardized for reasons that this text will clarify. Prefixes are often referred to as morphemes, and simply defined, a morpheme is a minimal unit of meaning. A morpheme must not be confused, however, with a syllable. (For example, the /t/ written as *ed* in *jumped* is a separate morpheme; therefore, the word *jumped* consists of one syllable, but two morphemes.) The definition of a prefix *(for teachers)* preferred by the author is an initial bound morpheme preposed to a free morpheme; i.e., prefixes, being bound, are *dependent meaning bearing elements* attached at the beginning of independent words. Therefore *un* as in *unable* is a prefix, but *un* as in *until* is not (because *til* is not an independent word). By definition, therefore, *pre* as in *presume, in* as in *insult,* and *dis* as in *disturb* are not prefixes, again because they are not attached to independent or base words. Words such as *presume, insult,* and *disturb* have historical roots, but as the language changed, these words changed or they were taken directly into English as whole words from Latin or French. Some educators refer to these kinds of related prefix syllables, attached to nonwords as "absorbed" prefixes.[1]

The above information and definition is, of course, for the teacher and older students. Certainly young children should not be burdened by such an explanation; instead, the teacher may proceed by instructing them with the lessons and activities suggested later.

Since true prefixes are active productive elements that change the meaning of the base word, elementary students should know the meaning of *frequently* used prefixes and be able to combine them with a variety of words. In educational jargon, these words are known as derived words; i.e., from two parts.

Three prefixes taught early are *un, re,* and *dis.* Generally exercises such as the following are used so that students can see the difference when the prefix is added. You will note that an independent base, a clearly recognizable whole English word, is used to minimize confusion.

re + pay	repay
re + state	restate
un + able	unable
un + sure	unsure
dis + like	dislike
dis + trust	distrust

What about words like *disdain, determine,* and *result,* in which there is a decodable common beginning syllable? Should students use their phonics/syllabication skills to help decode these words if they are unknown? Certainly! Clues are important. But students should be gradually introduced to read these absorbed "prefix" forms after first having exposure to the more traditional prefix plus whole word combination, as shown above. This does not mean that children cannot learn to read and understand words with absorbed prefixes while doing a lot of independent reading. It does mean, however, that in an instructional program, forms such as *repay, unable,* and *dislike* are introduced first.

To show there is variety in reading programs as they introduced each prefix or its variant, see Table 2.4.

Where blanks occur in Table 2.4 there is no mention of those prefixes in the publisher's Scope and Sequence Chart. Also each publisher introduces additional prefixes not included in this table. For example, Holt introduces *sub* while Ginn introduces *com.*

---

(1) While these absorbed prefixes do not change the word meaning, the prefix does affect the accent or stress pattern of the word. Absorbed prefixes are often unaccented syllables.

*Table 2.4 Prefix Table, Showing Basal Differences (Grade Level at Which Selected Prefixes and Their Variants Are Introduced or First Mentioned in Two Reading Series)**

Prefix	The Ginn Reading Program	Holt Basic Reading
anti	5	6
de	3	5
dis	3	3
ex	4	5
extra	5	6
in	4	3
im	4	3
inter	5	6
intra	5	6
mis	4	3
non	4	3
post	5	6
pre	5	4
pro	5	5
re	2	2
super		4
trans	5	6
un	2	2

*Holt, 1983; Ginn, 1984.

Suffixes and roots: more problems

Since suffixes are attached to roots (or bases), defining *root* at this point seems appropriate. A root is defined as a basic unit, having a semantic connection with other words. For example, in the words *lighted, lightning,* and *enlightening, light* is the root word. More specifically, the root is that part of a word, neither prefix nor suffix, that conveys the major portion of the word's meaning. (Linguists use the term *base*). Again, much of this information is provided for the benefit of the teacher and the older student.

As with prefixes, defining a suffix can also present difficulties. A suffix (again, not necessarily a syllable) is a "meaningful" language unit or morpheme, bound, as a prefix, and affixed to the end of a root or base word. While other aspects of meaning are involved, a primary function of a suffix is to indicate the part of speech of the word; i.e., how it functions in a sentence. Although there are some cases in which the suffix does not change the part of speech; i.e., *race* and *racist*, in general, there are four types of suffixes, and these may form nouns, verbs, adjectives, and adverbs. In addition to often changing the part of speech, some suffixes also change the lexical meaning of roots, such as *colorless* and *colorful* or *doubtless* and *doubtful*.

There is more than one kind of suffix; there are inflectional suffixes as defined in list *A* (the sum total) and derivational suffixes as exemplified in list *B* (only a few of the many that exist in the English language).

A
Total Inflectional Suffixes

s (es) Plural	boys, brushes
's (s') apostrophe	boy's, boys'
s third person singular	sings
ed past tense	grabbed
ing present participle	singing
en past participle	(has, have) eaten
er comparative	taller
est superlative	tallest

B
A Few Derivational Suffixes

Root Word	Part of Speech	Suffix	Affixed Word	Part of Speech
base	n	ic	bas*ic*	adj.
correct	adj.	ly	correct*ly*	adv.
fool	n	ish	fool*ish*	adj.
allow	v	ance	allow*ance*	n
person	n	al	person*al*	adj.
attract	v	ive	attract*ive*	adj.
clever	adj.	ness	clever*ness*	n
agree	v	ment	agree*ment*	n

The suffixes in list *A* (a closed group of only eight words) do not usually change the part of speech of the word. These suffixes also represent some of the first ones taught to primary children. It is much easier to understand the word changes in list *A* than it is to understand those in list *B*. (There are many, many derivational suffixes.) Not only are there alterations in the meanings of the words in list *B*, but in addition, the parts of speech change.

It is not difficult to decode a suffix, provided that the student recognizes the letters or syllables as a unit. The difficulty arises when the suffix has changed the part of speech or changed the word concept to such a degree that students do not recognize the meaning of the affixed word. Being familiar with the noun *person* and then having to shift to a phrase such as *a personal matter* may take some understanding. Studies show that students do not always make these shifts in meaning. While the root word is known, the affixed form may not be understood until much later. Table 2.5 provides pairs of related words with their grade level scores as found in the Dale nationwide study, *The Words We Know — A National Inventory*. (As with prefixes, suffixes are not always introduced in basals at the same time. See Table 2.6.)

*Table 2.5 Selected List from Dale's "The Words We Know"**

active (4) — activate (12)	nice (4) — nicety (10)
break (4) — breakage (10)	nominate (4) — nominee (8)
captive (6) — captivate (13-88%)	note (4) — notation (10)
college (4) — collegiate (12)	opportunity (6) — opportune (12)
competing (6) — competitive (10)	part (6) — partition (12)
decision (6) — decisive (12)	penalty (6) — penal (12)
demolish (6) — demolition (10)	persuade (6) — persuasive (10)
deprive (6) — deprivation (10)	pilgrim (4) — pilgrimage (10)
elephant (4) — elephantine (12)	plural (4) — plurality (10)
erase (4) — erasure (8)	pollen (6) — pollinate (10)
error (6) — erroneous (12)	population (6) — populace (12)
escape (4) — escapade (10)	pretend (4) — pretense (12)
evacuate (6) — evacuation (12)	real (4) — reality (8)
example (4) — exemplify (10)	recommend (6) — recommendation (10)
flirt (6) — flirtation (10)	response (6) — responsive (12)
globe (4) — globular (8)	result (6) — resultant (12)
habit (4) — habitual (10)	simple (4) — simplify (8)
infant (6) — infancy (10)	slavery (4) — slavish (10)
information (6) — informant (10)	true (8) — truism (12)
injury (4) — injurious (8)	type (4) — typical (10)
migrate (6) — migratory (10)	

*Edgar Dale and Joseph O'Rourke, *Techniques of Teaching Vocabulary* (Palo Alto, Calif.: Field Educational Pub., Inc., 1971), p. 183.

Table 2.6 Suffix Table (Derivational) Showing Basal Differences (Grade Level at Which Selected Suffixes Are Introduced or First Mentioned in Two Reading Series)*

Suffix	The Ginn Reading Program	Holt Basic Reading
able	4	3
ance	4	5
ant	4	6
er	3	3
ence	4	5
ful	2	3
hood	5	6
ible	4	
ic	4	4
ical	6	5
ion	3	5
ish	3	3
ist	4	5
ity	6	6
ive	6	6
less	2	3
ly	2	1
ment	3	5
ness	3	5
ous	3	3
ship	5	5
ure	6	6
ward	5	5

*Holt, 1983; Ginn, 1984.

Added to the problem of a shift in the part of speech of the word, which affects syntax and meaning, the suffixed word sometimes undergoes shifts in spelling as in *prescribe/prescription*. The same suffix is often spelled differently as *tion/ation/ition/sion; ant/ent; ance/ence; ar/er*. These differences are of historical origin, but have nothing to do with meaning or pronunciation. There are also shifts in some of the vowel pronunciations as *cave/cavity; crime/criminal; supreme/supremacy*. Even more puzzling, some suffixes denote words as either adjectives or adverbs: *kindly,* (adj.) and *quickly* (adv.). And then, there is a word like *hardly,* which has nothing to do with *hard!* Since oral language has far fewer derived words than does written language, many children have not had exposure to these affixed forms. TV programs, which monopolize much of children's time today, have a paucity of these kinds of words.

Added to these complexities is the difficulty of understanding the meaning of many of the bound roots. Therefore, it is necessary that the teacher guide discussion in the classroom to clarify the decoding, the meaning, and the related vocabulary of these affixed forms. This is certainly time well spent, and is *perhaps the most important aspects of teaching these words*. Some suggested activities will follow to reinforce teacher and student discussion.

Where a blank occurs in Table 2.6 there is no mention of that suffix in the publisher's Scope and Sequence Chart. Also each publisher introduces additional suffixes not included in Table 2.6. For example, Ginn introduces the suffix *ent* and Holt introduces the suffix *ize*.

Spelling and suffixes

A direct link exists between spelling generalizations about suffixes and the reader's ability to mentally separate suffixes from roots in order to identify the total derived or inflected word. The following generalizations are worth knowing:

1. When adding a suffix beginning with a vowel to a word that ends with an *e*, the *e* is usually dropped: *believe* + *able* = *believable*; *secure* + *ity* = *security.* In a word like *changeable,* the *e* is not dropped. To do so would "give" the *g* a "hard" sound.
2. When adding a suffix beginning with a vowel to a word that ends in one single consonant with a short vowel before it, the last consonant is usually doubled: *run* + *er* = *runner; knot* + *ing* = *knotting.* (This permits us to differentiate between words such as *sloping* and *slopping.*)
3. When adding a suffix to a word that ends with a *y* preceded by a consonant, the *y* is usually changed to an *i*; greedy + ness = *greediness;* fancy + full = *fanciful.* **Exception.** The letter *y* is never changed to an *i* when adding *ing; reply/replying; cry/crying.* This is because English does not permit two *i*'s together, and without the *y* the words would be pronounced as /repling/ and /cring/.
4. When adding a suffix to a word that ends with a *y* preceded by a vowel, the *y* is *not* changed; *employ* + *ment* = *employment; play* + *er* = *player.*

Affix lists

Although there is a difference of opinion as to which affix list best represents the most common prefixes and suffixes found in the elementary grades, the lists in Table 2.7 are given for your consideration. Some of the more common roots are also included.

A second list of affixes and roots is presented in Table 2.8.

A third list of affixes and roots, appropriate in science, indicates the importance of structural skills as students begin reading in the content areas. Refer to Table 2.9.

Teaching affixed forms

Stotsky (1978) suggests the following sequence for effectively teaching words with affixed forms:

1. Base words with common inflectional endings: *jumps, jumped, jumping.*
2. Simple compound words: *airplane.*
3. Prefixed and suffixed words containing a known base word: *untrue, careless.*
4. Words with well-known combining parts with meanings that are clear: *telegraph, microphone, tricycle.*
5. Complex noncomposite words containing roots and initial and final elements related to prefixes and suffixes already taught: *construct, expensive, intelligence.*

Because of research that emphasizes the importance of knowing how to decode and understand affixed words, especially as students move into more complex reading in the content areas of social studies and science, a proliferation of commercial materials to teach these skills has flooded the market. While some of them have a place in the classroom, we need to always remember the importance of teacher instruction, daily attention to vocabulary, motivating activities

Table 2.7 A List of Prefixes, Suffixes, and Roots for Elementary Grades

Common Prefixes

Prefix	Meaning	Word Example
anti	against	antiwar
ex	out of	exit
im	not	impossible
inter	between	intermission
ir	not	incapable
mis	not	misplace
non	not	nonfiction
out	beyond	outlaw
over	too much	overrate
post	after	postdated
re	again	replay
sub	under	submarine
super	above	superman
trans	across	transworld

Common Suffixes

Suffix	Part of Speech	Meaning	Word Example
able	adj.	can be	dependable
en	adj.	to make from	wooden
er	n.	one who does	farmer
ess	n.	woman	princess
ful	adj.	full of	cupful
hood	n.	the condition of	brotherhood
ify	v.	to make happen	beautify
ion, tion	n.	condition	rebellion
ish	adj.	like	selfish
ist	n.	one who does	racist
less	adj.	without	careless
ly	adv.	very	quickly
ment	n.	result	statement
ness	n.	state of	kindness
ology	n.	study of	biology
or	n.	one who does	sailor

Common Roots

Root	Meaning	Word Example
cap	head	captain
cycl	ring, circle	bicycle
dent	tooth	dentist
form	shape	uniform
geo	earth	geography
gram	letter	telegram
graph	write	autograph
move	move	movement
phone	sound	earphone
vis	see	television

Table 2.8 An Additional List of Prefixes, Suffixes, and Roots

Prefixes

Prefix	Meaning	Word Example
ante	before	anteroom
mono	one	monotone
peri	around	perimeter
semi	half	semimonthly
tri	three	trimester
ultra	beyond	ultrasuede

Suffixes

Suffix	Part of Speech	Meaning	Word Example
an, ean, ian	n.	relating to	artisan
ance, ence, ancy, ency	n.	quality, state of	resistance, dependence, constancy, emergency
ate	v.	to cause	populate
dom	n.	relating to	wisdom
ent	adj.	quality	competent, president
eur, eer	n.	one who does	amateur, volunteer
ette, let	n.	diminutive	statuette, booklet
ic	n.	relating to	dramatic
cle	n.	little	corpuscle
ism	n.	act of	ritualism
ize	v.	to make	oxidize
ive	v.	having the nature of	narrative
ity, ty	n.	quality of	hostility, fidgety
some	adj.	relating to	worrisome

Roots (For upper elementary and junior high)

Root	Meaning	Word Example
ambi, amphi	around	ambition, amphitheater
anthrop	man	anthropology
aster, astr	star	asterisk, astral
bio	life	biology
cav	hollow	cavity
chrom	color	chromosome
circum	around	circumstance
contra	against	contraband
corp	body	corpuscle
demo	people	demonstration
derm	skin	dermatologist
dict	to speak	diction
duc	to lead	induction
epi	upon	epidermis
fin	end, limit	refinish
gam	marriage	polygamy
hetero	different	heterogeneous
homo	same	homonym
loc	place	location
mal	bad	malformed
manu	hand	manual

Table 2.8 Continued

Roots	Meaning	Word Example
mar	sea	maritime
mort	death	mortician
port	to carry	porter
scrib, script	to write	transcribe
theo	god	theology
vid, vis	to see	vision
vinc, vict	to conquer	invincible, victim
vita	life	vitamins
viv	to live	vivacious
voc	to call	vocalize

Table 2.9 Affixes and Roots Used in Science

Root, or Affix	Meaning	Example
anti	against	antimissile
aero	air	aerobic
ambi-, amphi-	both	ambidextrous
aqua-	water	aquatic
astro-, aster-	star	astronomy
auto-	self	automatic
bio-	life	biology
cardi(o)	heart	cardiogram
chrono-	time	chronology
cyto-	cell, hollow	cytoplasm
dermato-, derm-	skin	epidermis
di-, dis-	two	dissect
epi-	upon, outer	epidermis
germ-	sprout	germinate
hemi-	half	hemisphere
hemo-	blood	hemoglobin
homo-	same, alike	homogeneous
kine-	movement	kinetic
-lysis, -lyze	break up	analysis
magni-	great, large	magnitude
micro-	small	microscope
oculo-	eye	oculist
psycho-	mind	psychology
-scope	view, examine	microscope
son(i)-	sound	supersonic
thermo-	heat	thermometer
zoo-	animal	zoology
ology	study of	pathology

that build interest in words, and most importantly, the benefits that accrue to students who do wide and varied reading, thus learning many of these words through the context of varied selections.

Following is an example of an abbreviated lesson for students who are in the early stages of learning structural skills. We will follow this with some example lessons for older students. Additional activities for teaching and extending skills in this area will follow and may be adapted according to grade level.

Example Lesson, Younger Children The teacher begins by drawing a simple picture of a house, telling children that some words can be compared to a house; that just as you can add on to a house, you can add on to a word. (S/he adds on to the house as in the example):

The teacher writes the words *happy* and *unhappy* on the board (under the house) and asks a student to underline the parts that are alike.

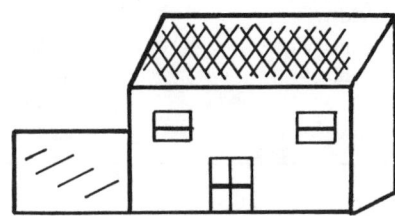

Teacher: What did we add to the beginning of the word happy? *(un)* We call this a prefix. Say prefix. A prefix is not a word by itself, but we add it to a word to make a new word.

Teacher: (writes the two parts under the house) What does happy mean?

Children: (respond)

Teacher: (Points out to children how *un* changed the meaning, or inducts the meaning from the children.)

Follow Up: Offers additional exercises with *un* for words such as *untrue, unfair, unlike, unreal,* and *unable*. Children dictate sentences with these words as the teacher writes them on the board or on a transparency. Children underline the root word, and draw a ring around the prefix. (The activity may be extended after sufficient practice, and an addition made to the house to introduce the idea of a suffix.)

Example lessons for more advanced students

I. Recognizing Prefixes

Purpose:

Students will recognize certain common prefixes and learn to read them as part of a larger word unit.

Procedure:

1. Write the following stems on the board explaining to students that each is a base word to which a prefix may be added. Also impress upon students that our stems are very selective and will only accept particular prefixes. A stem often carries the lexical meaning of the extended word. Read the stems with the students.

agree	sight	sense	war
claim	pay	circle	merge
place	play	world	port

2. Now write each prefix on the board. These are commonly found in reading materials. Have the students pronounce these prefixes. You may want to explain that we have several prefixes that mean "not" such as *dis, mis, non,* and *anti.* You may want to discuss some of the meanings of other prefixes although as mentioned some of these are absorbed prefixes and carry no meaning in and of themselves.

dis	in	non	anti
pro	pre	semi	sub
mis	re	trans	ex

3. Now attach the prefixes to the stems or base words and have the student read the new words:

disagree	insight	nonsense	antiwar
proclaim	prepay	semicircle	submerge
misplace	replay	transworld	export

4. This lesson should be followed by practice. Place prefixed words on the board or a ditto. Have students identify and pronounce the prefix, identify and pronounce the stem or base word, and blend the two together to pronounce the affixed word.

illegal	overbid	antifreeze	pro-American
degrade	redraw	preschool	supervisor
misbehave	transport	forewarn	subterranean

5. Students will, when asked to offer prefixed words, give examples such as 'pro/perty.' Tell them these are not prefixes in the true sense of the word but knowing prefixes can aid in pronunciation.

6. Have students verbalize that looking for a prefix can be a first step in decoding polysyllabic words and have them locate prefixed words in their reading materials, identifying prefix and the base word or stem.

II. Recognizing Suffixes

Purpose:

Students will recognize certain common suffixes and learn to read them as part of a larger word unit.

Procedure:

1. Write the following stems on the board explaining to students that each is a base word to which a suffix may be added. Again as with the first lesson on prefixes, impress upon students that our stems are very selective and will only accept certain suffixes. The suffix often changes the part of speech of a word whereas the prefix usually does not.

block	dance	music	wise
employ	wool	fear	simple
poet	act	fool	alarm

2. Now write each suffix on the board. These are commonly found in reading materials. Have the students pronounce these suffixes. You may want to explain that suffixes change the part of speech of the word and show them examples of these changes. Point out also that the spelling sometimes changes when words are suffixed, but does not usually change when words are prefixed.

ade	er	ian	dom
ee	en	ful	fy
ic	tion	ish	ist

3. Attach the suffixes to the stem and have the students read the new words.

blockade	dancer	musician	wisdom
employee	woolen	fearful	simplify
poetic	action	foolish	alarmist

4. Practice with other suffixed words. When students have confidence and show they understand the principle involved, have them locate suffixed words in their reading materials and identify the suffix and stem.

III. Recognizing Words with Prefixes and Suffixes

Purpose:

Students will recognize that certain words are composed of a prefix, a stem, and a suffix.

Procedure:

1. Write the following words on the board. Ask students to identify and pronounce the prefix and then to look at the rest of the word. If they cannot identify the stem, have them check the suffix first and pronounce it, then return to the stem, pronounce it, and then blend all three parts together. Some students will be able to identify the word parts in order after they have had practice and will not need to always locate prefix, suffix, and then stem.

repayment	exceeding	interchangeable	enrichment
enjoyment	unsinkable	unknowing	reboarded
undesirable	inaction	removable	preheated

2. Have students locate words in their materials with prefixes, suffixes, and stems. Practice with these word parts, trying to build other words with these structural parts.

Always remind students that after identifying the word parts of unfamiliar words as the prefix, suffix, and stem, and blending them together, the next step is to place the word in context to see if it makes sense.

Turning incorrect answers into learning experiences

Collins (1987) suggests some procedures to turn incorrect answers into learning experiences. While her suggestions were for comprehension questions, the same procedures can be adapted while working with affixes.

Think once again. If you believe a student has the background to answer correctly say something like "Take just a little more time. I believe you do know the answer." (You have asked the question, "Name two prefixes that mean 'not'?")

Paraphrase the question. By rephrasing the question to "Name two prefixes that mean 'not,' and that change the meaning of a word," you include a needed clue.

Help with a prompt. Offer a small piece of relevant information to help students such as, "If you understand something it is clear. If you do not it is unclear."

Expand the answer. Repeat the part of the answer that was correct as "Unclear, that's correct." Now add "Now, what is the prefix?"

Asking for clues. In some classrooms you might call on other students to give clue words or suggest some yourself such as 'unable, unbeaten, unusual.' You may also ask a student who missed the question to call upon a classmate to help with clues. The student could offer words such as misprint, misconduct, inaction, invalid.

Making students accountable. If students give two incorrect answers to the same question, tell them you will ask the question again to give them the incentive to remember. Return to the students before the period ends and ask the same question.

Nonexamples. If students don't raise their hands after a suitable time, tell them what the answer is not. This allows time for thinking and at times can introduce a little levity.

Types of activities When teachers believe students would profit from drill activities with affixes and roots, some of the types of exercises included in basals and teaching materials might prove useful. Examples of these types of activities follow:

1. Showing change of meaning when prefixes are added.
   dis   interest
   dis   agree
   dis   approve
2. Identifying the prefixes and suffixes in particular words.
   *un*desir*able*
   *trans*port*ation*
   *sub*scrip*tion*
3. Completing words with prefixes and suffixes as the result of a clue sentence.
   The students were not happy when their team lost.
   The students were ____ appoint ____ when their team lost.
4. Using roots to form new words.
   phone   phonograph, phonics, telephone
   graph   graphics, telegraph, photograph
   geo   geology, geologist, geography

Activities for teaching affixes

1. To decode words with the suffix *ful*:
   a. Write the following words on the board: *joy, pain, cheer, harm, hate, care, play, use, fear, wish, rest*.
   b. Ask pupils to read the words.
   c. Above the words write the suffix *ful*. Next to it write the meaning: full of or filled with.
   d. Now ask pupils to read each word, add the suffix, and use it in a sentence.
   e. Follow up with incomplete sentences in which students supply the reading word, as "I hurt myself and my leg was _____."
2. To decode words with the suffix *less:*
   a. Fold strips of tagboard in half. Write root word on one half and the suffix *less* on the other so that when the strip is unfolded the entire word appears. Display only the root word first. Ask pupils to read it. Then unfold the slip and have them read the affixed form.

   hopeless   fearless   countless
   endless   lifeless
   breathless   sleepless

b. Write this sentence.
   Sally spent a sleepless night because she was too excited to sleep.
c. Ask a student to read the sentence and explain the differences between the two words.
d. Help students determine the meaning of the suffix *less*. Remind them that a suffix is usually unaccented.

3. To decode words with the suffixes *able* and *ment*.
   a. Write two columns of words such as the following on the board. Teachers should extend this list.

movement	believable
payment	excitement
usable	portable
readable	agreement
equipment	lovable

   b. Divide students into two teams.
   c. A student from the first team selects a word from the first column, reads it, and uses it in a sentence.
   d. If the second team agrees that the word is correct, both in pronunciation and meaning, team one erases the word. The procedure continues and a member of the second team selects a word from the second column, reads it, and uses it in a sentence. The first team that erases all the words wins.

4. To note that an alteration in meaning occurs when the suffix *ment* is added, and that there is a change in the part of speech.

employment	government
replacement	amazement
improvement	settlement

   a. Have students circle the suffix.
   b. Have students note the root word.
   c. Have students identify that the root word is a verb, or action word.
   d. Have students tell what change in the part of speech occurs when the suffix *ment* is added.
   e. Have students use the root and the suffixed form in sentences.

5. To note the change in vowel sound and part of speech when certain suffixes are added. Write two columns of words:

sane	sanity
grave	gravity
extreme	extremity
serene	serenity
meter	metric
tone	tonic
proceed	procession
recede	recession

   a. A student reads the words in the first column while the group listens.
   b. Students conclude that the vowel sound in the word, or in the last syllable, is long.
   c. Follow the same procedure for the words in the second column.
   d. Students should note that there is a shift in the vowel sound, and also underline the suffixes in the second column.
   e. Draw the generalization that shifts in vowel sounds often occur when these suffixes are added.

6. To practice reading words with a particular prefix, use a tachistoscope with a strip of words.

7. To show how context can help explain suffix meaning. Bury the new affixed word so it is explained by context. Example: *ible*

   The wood Goldie's parents used in making dolls was easy to find. It was accessible.

8. To see the relationship between words with similar roots. Use word building whereby students begin with a word and build on this root to form as many new words as possible. With the root *graph,* a "tree" can be constructed with the word *graph* on the trunk, and the related words written on the leaves. Example words might include *geography, spectograph, telegraph, graphic, mimeograph, photograph, polygraph, phonograph, graphics*.

   Another method is to show the relatedness by drawing "bricks" of the meaningful word parts as:

respect				dis	respect		
respect	able			dis	respect	able	
*respect	ibil	ity		dis	respect	ful	
respect	able	ness		dis	respect	ful	ly
*respect	ab	ly		dis	respect	ful	ness

   *Note how the spelling of the suffix is sometimes altered.

9. To gain an overview of vocabulary in a new unit.
   a. The teacher places a list of words on the board, a transparency, or a ditto. The words are discussed and read. In pairs the students decide what words they will pantomime. These might be such words as *feudalism, nobleman, conquistadors* from a social studies unit about the Middle Ages. (Use about a dozen words.)
   b. In pairs they pantomime their word and then after a minute or so call on a classmate to spell the word, define it, and use it in a sentence.

10. To engage in overall practice.
    a. Mimeo bingo cards so that there is a total of twenty-five blocks. From a list of words on the board or a ditto sheet students make up their own card, placing the words in whatever block they wish. The teacher or a knowledgeable student) reads and gives the definition of the word.
    b. Students with limited vocabulary skills may sit with a buddy, and the two-member team then plays with two cards. The caller states whether the

winner must cover five spaces horizontally, vertically, or diagonally. An example card is shown below:

B	I	N	G	O
certainly	dependable	vocalize	autograph	appliance
disagree	biology	respectful	television	electricity
transportation	countless	free	carefully	intensity
subscribe	believable	replacement	selfish	impossible
phonograph	agreement	extremely	misplace	submarine

c. Further variations include covering the four corners, the *B* row, the *I* row, etc.

For more advanced students. Comparing and contrasting words is an effective technique in building knowledge of polysyllabic words (Cunningham, 1978). To engage in the following activity, students are divided into groups. Each group takes a turn and asks questions about a "mystery word." Points are given depending on how few questions are asked before the mystery word is determined.

To begin, the teacher or a student draws short lines to represent the number of letters in the mystery word, and then writes three "clue" words to help "unlock" the mystery word. Each of these three words has either the prefix (absorbed or bound), the root, or the suffix of the mystery word. Students pronounce the clue words, discuss meanings, and use them in sentences, which provide a lot of real practice. Students try to determine which part of the three clue words (prefix, root, or suffix) would be used in the mystery word. They ask such questions as "Does the mystery word begin like _____? End like? Have a middle like?" For example, if the mystery word were *contestant*, the teacher would write __ __ __ __ __ __ __ __ __ , the number of blanks equalling the number of letters in the word. Clue words could be *con*formity, pre*test*ing, and inform*ant*. The scenario would go something like this:

Teacher: John's team may begin.
John: Does the word begin like *pretesting*?
Teacher: No, it does not. Jan's team now.
Jan: Does it begin like *conformity*?
Teacher: Yes.
Mary: Does it end like *informant*?

The question-answer continues until the word is determined. An activity such as this involves reading and learning many words, costs nothing, and builds interest in vocabulary. Bright students can construct many of these sets themselves. Other examples that may be used include:[2]

1. *respectful*
   in*spect*or
   *re*member
   beauti*ful*

2. *refreshment*
   *re*evaluate
   astonish*ment*
   *fresh*ener

3. *removal*
   denial
   *re*assess
   im*mov*able

(2) For an extensive list of example sets, see Cunningham, "Decoding Polysyllabic Words."

Guidelines for Teaching Words with Prefixes and Suffixes

1. Teachers who use activity exercises to reinforce these skills should remember that difficult words with affixes encountered in reading should be *talked about*. Students should say the words aloud to one another and in groups. School language is more easily learned as it is learned initially, by frequently meeting and hearing words in meaningful context.
2. Try to encourage students to be "word collectors" with their own personalized list. Set aside a time to share and discuss these words. Have bulletin board displays with particular kinds of words. Bring in books about words. Build *word consciousness* through meaningful language activities.
3. Be certain to schedule time in the curriculum for working with affixed words. Don't assume students will learn to decode and understand them on their own.
4. Emphasize to students that base words are very selective as to which prefixes and suffixes they will accept. For example, *nation, national, nationhood,* but not *nationment*.

For extensive word lists of prefixes and suffixes, see Appendix, pp. 172–181.

Questions teachers ask

1. Should students be taught to search for "little" words in "big" words? Not really. This is a poor practice because it can lead to all kinds of misinformation. Example: In the word *father*, should it be *fat-her?* The only "little" words students should search for in "big" words are subunits of meaning. There is only one smaller word in *splashed: splash,* not *lash,* or *as,* since they do not represent a meaning unit within *the word*. Uncovering the root is therefore not the same as finding little words in big words.
2. Should students be aware of problems in definition? Should they be told why affixed words can present difficulty? It depends on many factors such as age and maturity. Teachers should know this so they are in a position to answer questions, but avoid burdening pupils with more information about affixes than they can utilize.
3. What should students focus on when they meet an unknown affixed word? They should be taught to isolate letter combinations resembling affixes in unfamiliar words, and to recognize what remains as a base word, subject to spelling changes *(debate/debatable)*. It is the underlying meaning units that should receive the focus. A strategy such as the following might be employed:
   a. Note the contextual clue. What kind of a word, (noun, verb, etc.) is it?
   b. Separate the prefix and suffix (depending on the word) from the root.
   c. Put the word together. Think about related roots and other affixes for clues to meaning.
4. Why is work with structural analysis considered so important? First, because it is particularly useful in identifying word forms not previously encountered in print, such as *dentist/dental*. Second, fluent reading depends on the ability to quickly decode unknown polysyllabic words, many of which are affixed. Third, many of the difficult words students meet in the content areas (social studies and science), beginning in the fourth grade, are often affixed words they have never met before.
5. Are phonics skills important in using structural analysis? Yes. This is because once the root is sorted out and recognized, sound-symbol relationships can help a reader arrive at the root's pronunciation. Of course, the ease with which students proceed through this structural reading skill stage depends as mentioned on their accumulated storehouse of a large sight vocabulary.

Quick Self-Check XV

1. State the differences between a prefix and a suffix.
2. Identify the two types of prefixes from the following list:
   recent   insist   dislike
   prepay   uncertain   impersonal
3. Identify the two types of suffixes from the following list:
   foolish   singing   called
   cleverness   jumps   safely
4. When suffixes are added to words, what are some of the generalizations students need to know?
5. What is one of the best ways for students to learn to read and understand affixed words?
6. When decoding, should students look for little words in big words?
7. Suggest some activities to teach affixed words.

For a more complete list of active and absorbed prefixes and example words and a more complete list of suffixes and example words see pp. 172–181.

Syllabication

Syllabication — another debate

As with other decoding skills, educators are not in agreement as to the usefulness of teaching syllabication principles. Cunningham, Cunningham, and Rystrom (1981) claim their studies show "there is currently no empirical support for teaching pupils to divide words into syllables . . . and call for a moratorium on syllabication instruction." (p. 213)

Groff (1981) has the opposite viewpoint and quotes extensive research, recommending "that teachers continue to instruct children to isolate syllables in unknown printed words as a means of word identification." (p. 690) Moreover, he states that "children have told researchers they recognize words by using syllables . . . and that 85% of the decoding done by successful readers in grades two and five was said by these children to be based on recognizing letter clusters, some of which were syllables." (p. 687)

From the author's extensive classroom experience both with younger and older readers she is in agreement with Groff's viewpoint. The question becomes what kind of syllabication instruction is best — a simple one or a more complicated version. As with Groff's viewpoint she would recommend a simpler one as having the most merit for decoding purposes. Furthermore, syllabication does not have to be like the dictionary as the rules used there are not based on linguistic research but on the arbitrary decisions of typesetters from early days. Dictionary syllabication rules sometimes have little to do with the actual sound patterns of syllables.

The division in the dictionary is simply a printing device to indicate the place at which a word may be broken by a hyphen in a line of print or writing.

Teaching syllabication

Good readers tend to learn to divide words into syllables intuitively and to capitalize on this skill to help them decode words. Some students do not have this ability and need considerable practice with syllabication, as an aid to both reading and spelling. They need to understand that a syllable is a *unit of speech* that always contains one vowel sound, and has nothing to do with the number of letters. (*Oleo* has three syllables, while *squashed* has one.) This is because the focal unit of language is the stress given to vowel sounds, with consonant sounds being subordinate to this stress. Therefore, in teaching students to syllabicate in order to decode multisyllabic words, it is necessary to help them understand that the vowel sound is the key unit (Waugh and Howell, 1975).

Young children do not have to know the precise rules of syllabication but after some reading instruction, they should have a general idea of how to break a word into smaller units, as aids to reading and spelling. Practice can take place by first working with words they do know to get the concept of a syllable. They may engage in such activities as

1. Saying words in syllables.
2. Clapping out the number of syllables.
3. Writing words in syllables.
4. Sensing the syllables by placing their hand under their chin and saying the word.

To begin instruction in syllabication, teachers do not always start with a definition such as "Every syllable contains a sounded vowel," but instead often begin in a gamelike format. Children are asked to note columns of words in which the vowel sound rather than the number of vowel letters is the key to the word parts or syllables. For example:

Teacher: We are going to play a game. Look at these three lists of words. Let's read these words together. How many parts, or syllables, do you hear? Listen carefully.

A	B	C
mat	same	can dy
talk	spray	rob in
short	mail	catch er
scrap	coat	but ter
duck	tease	may be

How may vowels do you see in column *A*?
How many vowel sounds do you hear in column *A*?
How many vowels do you see in column *B*?
How many vowel sounds do you hear in column *B*?
How many vowels do you see in column *C*?
How many vowel sounds do you hear in column *C*?

The teacher draws conclusions from the students about the three groups of words.

When introducing more formal syllabication instruction, many teachers begin with the concept of the open and closed syllable. By definition, an open syllable has a long vowel sound, and a closed syllable has a short vowel sound followed by a consonant.

A	B
Open Syllables	**Closed Syllables**
po ny	fin ish
pa per	hab it
la bel	mod el
mu sic	riv er
mo tor	sig nal

The idea is that in list *B* the second consonant sound has "closed" the syllable and the vowel is short. This is often referred to as the CVC rule: when you have one consonant, one vowel, and one final consonant (not *r*), you generally have a short vowel (m*a*t, b*e*d, f*i*g). In an unknown two-syllable word, however, there is no way for the student to tell whether the syllable division should be before or after the second consonant, and there really is no vowel "clue." Students must often try both vowel sounds to see which one "works," although many reading programs suggest that "if you do not find a double consonant in the middle of a word, divide after the first vowel, and it is long," Example: *sha/dy, me/ter*.

After practice and instruction in syllabication with older students, it is a good idea to place categories of words on the board and to draw from them generalizations about how these words are usually divided, as an aid in decoding. For example:

Compound Words		**Affixes**		**Double Consonants**	
birdhouse	bird/house	kindness	kind/ness	dollar	dol/lar
outside	out/side	lovely	love/ly	happen	hap/pen
seatbelt	seat/belt	return	re/turn	rabbit	rab/bit

Different Consonants		**le Preceded by a Consonant**	
envy	en/vy	icicle	ic/i/cle
picture	pic/ture	maple	ma/ple
silver	sil/ver	table	ta/ble

Dividing words into syllables

Something similar to the following may be realized and charted after the previous discussion. Remember that every syllable must have a vowel sound.

1. See if the word is compound. Examples: *birdhouse, outside, seatbelt*.
2. See if the word has affixes. Examples: *kindness, lovely, repeat*.
3. See if the word has a double consonant in the middle. Examples: *dollar, happen, rabbit*.
4. See if the word has two different consonants in the middle. Examples: *envy, picture, silver*. Do not divide a blend (*twisting, folding*) or a digraph (*mother, wishful*).
5. See if the word ends in *le*, preceded by a consonant. Place this consonant with the *le*. Examples: *ic/i/cle, ma/ple, ta/ble*.
6. Now try the word in context. Does it make sense? Then read on.
7. If it does not make sense, try the dictionary or ask a group leader.

Putting this all together, a simple syllabication generalization might be as follows:

Check to see if the word

1. is a compound or has affixes.
2. has double consonant letters or two unlike consonant letters. Do not divide blends or digraphs.
3. ends in *le;* if so, place the preceding consonant letter before it.
4. makes sense!

Activities for teaching syllabication

1. Objective: *To begin to recognize two syllable words.* Write words with one and two syllables on the board. Have them read. Then let one pupil read a word, while others clap hands softly to indicate how many parts they hear in the word.
2. Objective: *To teach syllabication of words with medial consonant digraphs.* Write these words on the board: *bucket, washer, cricket, gather, bother, nephew, bishop, leather.*
   a. Ask pupils what the words have in common.
   b. Divide words with a slash mark for students.
   c. Ask pupils what they can deduce from your division.
   d. Elicit from them that a digraph is not to be divided.
3. Objective: *To decode words based on syllabication generalizations (as many as they have learned thus far).* Pass out a worksheet with a number of words as follows:

pattern	department	equipment
shallow	oatmeal	subject
exposed	cardboard	pinhole
thickness	complete	darkroom
maple	thimble	staple

   On the board, write a word as below that typifies a specific example of each rule.

Compound Words	*Prefixes and Suffixes*	*Double Letters*	*le Words*
sidewalk	largely	butter	angle

   Pupils write each word under the generalization they used. Sometimes more than one generalization is appropriate.

Language Change

American and British spelling

In working with syllabication, students sometimes comment that they see words spelled in more than one way. This is because there are some minor differences in the spelling of American and British words. Some of these changes occurred over a hundred years ago when Noah Webster revised some of the spellings of American words in an attempt to regularize the lexicon, and have it more closely reflect American pronunciation. For the most part, the English have retained the original spellings of the Samuel Johnson dictionary, and examples of these alternate spellings are given here.

Preferred American English	Preferred British English
honor	honour
traveler	traveller
program	programme
veranda	verandah
story	storey (of a house)
catalog	catalogue
center	centre
jewelry	jewellery
pajamas	pyjamas
connection	connexion
theater	theatre

Language change today. As has been mentioned in the section dealing with phonics, language change, though difficult to notice, is always taking place. At present one of these changes affects what we say about syllabication and should be called to the attention of students. Many former three-syllable words are slowly losing the middle vowel sound even though the vowel letter appears in the written word (Burmeister, 1975). An examination of the following words—only a few of the many hundreds—will illustrate this point.

sep*a*rate	om*e*let	fam*i*ly	cath*o*lic
car*a*mel	cam*e*ra	card*i*nal	iv*o*ry
com*pa*ny	int*e*rest	eas*i*ly	mem*o*ry
marg*a*rine	bach*e*lor	cab*i*net	hist*o*ry
ins*u*lin	nat*u*ral		

In some locales and among some groups of people, these vowels will still be pronounced in varying degrees. In other areas of our country these sounds have practically disappeared.

The "formal" nature of English words. When working with students, comment that our words are written according to a more "formal" English code; i.e., as words tend to be pronounced in isolation, but not as they are pronounced in a sentence where stress patterns affect the sounds (minimizing some and doing away with others altogether). Additionally regional variation affects the pronunciation of words. For this reason, Samuel Johnson, the renowned lexicographer, concluded many years ago that only one pronunciation, a more "formal" one, should be "acceptable" and it should become the standard written form. This makes it possible for the millions of people who speak English, with a variety of pronunciations, to have a valid form of written communication among them.

Quick Self-Check XVI

1. What is the difference between an open and closed syllable?
2. State the simple syllabication generalization.
3. Suggest two procedures teachers use to teach syllabication.
4. What language change is occurring that affects the instruction of syllabication?
5. What should students know about the nature of our written words?

For a list of words to aid in teaching about syllables, see page 181.

SECTION III

CONTEXT CLUES

The words, phrases or sentences that appear on either side of a specific word are called the context. Clues may be obtained from the context around an unfamiliar word, provided the material is not too difficult for the student. This is one of the best ways to *attack unfamiliar words and gain meaning,* the result being a faster and more efficient word identification process than is available through any other single technique. It is important to remember, however, that word identification is usually most efficient when various techniques are used in conjunction with one another.

Two Broad Areas of Context Clues

There are two types of context clues, (1) semantic, which provides lexical or meaning information; and (2) syntactic, which provides grammatical information. When readers understand the meaning of other words in the surrounding context, they use their semantic knowledge to help decode the unknown word. Their syntactic understanding, or their sense of the English sentence, (and they must have this or they would be unable to speak!) can help them deduce what type of word (noun, verb, adjective, etc.) would fit in a particular slot.

Since these two types of clues, semantic and syntactic, are interdependent, readers tend to use the two together to anticipate and confirm what they believe the word will be. For this reason, most reading programs combine the two types under the umbrella term *context clues.*

Kinds of Context Clues

Many teachers claim that students do not use context to its full advantage (Cunningham, 1979). They need help in judging whether context can be an aid or whether the dictionary will have to be used. Sometimes there are extremes — some students consulting a dictionary at every instance and other students rarely bothering. Neither procedure is good and should be discouraged. Few students, however, are aware of the variety of ways context can help unlock unknown words and give meaning to them. The following are some examples of these many different ways.

Direct explanation clue. Often authors realize students will not know a word and place it in an explanation to help them. Example: *Lobbyists* got this name because they used to stand in a lobby or hall, outside the room where the laws were passed. They try to influence the laws that are made.

Experience clue. A student's own experience can help unlock an unknown word. Example: In any team, the members must *cooperate* by working together.

Words in a series. Often unknown words in a series can be decoded from clues. Example: There were marigolds, asters, and *chrysanthemums* among the flowers.

Restatement. To clarify, authors often repeat what they have stated. Example: In some places where fresh and salt water meet, as at the mouth of a river, the water is *brackish.* Brackish water is in between fresh water and salt water in saltiness.

Contrast and comparison. Words such as *but* often give clues to word meaning. Example: Jerry smiled at Tim, but looked *disapprovingly* at me.

Inference. Surrounding words or sentences provide clues. Example: It was necessary to make sure that the coin was as old as the date said it was. Any *artifact* with writing on it is very important to historians.

Advantages and Disadvantages in Using Context Clues

As with all types of word attack strategies, there are advantages and disadvantages to using context clues.

Advantages

1. Words can be identified in context that cannot be identified in isolation.
2. Readers who can use context clues become independent decoders more quickly. They learn to be good predictors of what the word will be, confirming or rejecting it, based on whether or not it makes sense in the context of what they are reading, and then they quickly read on.
3. Students who have difficulty with phonics skills that require closer attention to visual features may perceive unknown vocabulary more easily in this way.
4. Words that do not follow consistent sound-symbol relationships may be more easily generalized.

Disadvantages

1. Beginning readers have difficulty using context, as their reading vocabulary tends to be limited.
2. There are many similies in English and these could make sense in a given context; therefore, when context is used solely, apart from other word attack strategies, it does not result in exact word identification. When the exact word is required, readers must reinforce this clue with other word identification clues.
3. The surrounding context may be insufficient or provide misleading information about the word.

Guidelines for Teaching About Context Clues

1. Young readers are not always as successful in using context clues as older, more successful readers for two reasons: First, older readers have had more experience; they have heard, seen, and read more; they have accumulated larger vocabularies; and they have stored more information to draw upon. Second, because of maturation factors, they have developed greater reasoning skills. These enable them to put certain facts together, to become more successful at decoding unknown words through context.
2. Unfamiliar words that students are initially unable to decode in a selection are often decoded later as the student meets these words in varied contexts throughout the selection. Information in a selection is often accumulative; there is usually more semantic (meaning) information at the end of a sentence than there is at the beginning, and more information at the end of a paragraph than at the end of a sentence.

3. Materials that are too difficult present students with a disproportionate number of unknown words. This precludes the students' use of context because they cannot gather enough semantic information to bring the unknown word into focus.
4. Reading materials must be significant and interesting enough for readers to make use of context clues. They must be involved in what they are reading, because if they are not, they will be unaware of the semantic clues available, concentrating instead on individual words.

Sentence Context Clues May Be Limited

Note the following three groups of context clues. Some sentences provide all the clues needed; some limited clues; and some no clues whatever.

GROUP I. *Context does the work for the student.*
1. "It's cold in here. Shut the w _ _ _ _ _ ."
2. When I take an u_ _ _ _ _ _ _ _ , it never rains.
3. They have one d_ _ _ _ _ _ _ _ and two sons.
4. On the day David became ten, his Mom had a b_ _ _ _ _ _ _ party for him.
5. There is no e_ _ _ _ _ _ _ so you'll have to climb the stairs.

GROUP II. *Context clues are present here too, but they do not provide as much constraint as the former sentences. More reading than just the sentence is needed.*
1. How many p_____ are in the book? (pictures, pages)
2. Her coat was tan and bl_____ . (blue, black)
3. They like to play in the b_____ . (ballpark, basement, band)

GROUP III. *Some sentences provide no context clues.*
1. That is a s_____ statement.
2. The l_____ is here.
3. Have you ever p_____ ?

While a given sentence may lack context clues, the help needed may be in the sentence that precedes or follows it in a paragraph. Context is always more than just a single phrase or sentence.

Activities to Help Students Become Aware of Context as an Aid to Decoding

To help students become aware of context, the teacher may begin by writing a simple sentence containing one unknown word on the board.

She *ambled* slowly down the path.

Discuss with the students possible meanings that make sense in the sentence. Show them how the context limits the word choices they may have.
Suggest to students that when they come to an unknown word they continue reading the complete phrase, sentence, or paragraph. This may help infer the meaning of the new word. Then, see if they can supply the meaning of the word and find out if *it makes sense* to them.

Even when students use structural or phonetic analysis to unlock a new word, *the final check for accuracy must be the context* in which the word is originally found. This is of great help in correctly placing the proper accent and the vowel sound.

I *objéct* to the rule.   She will *condúct* the orchestra.
The *óbject* could not be seen.   Her *cónduct* in the class has improved.

There are other activities the teacher may use to create awareness of context:

1. a. Read a sentence aloud and omit an "unknown" word, but tell the students the beginning sound. Ask students what they think the word is and why they came to that conclusion.
   b. Discuss the "why" of the choices. Other students will be aided by the how-to-do-it of their peers.
2. Provide examples showing that context clues may precede or follow the unknown word.
   Preceding the unknown word
   People who write about famous persons, places, and events of the past are called *historians*.
   Following the unknown word
   Among them are *antibodies*. These fight germs.
3. Provide examples showing that context clues may be a phrase, sentence, or paragraph.
   a phrase
   The day was *sweltering,* too hot for any fun.
   a sentence
   She *announced* loudly to everyone that she was leaving.
   a paragraph
   He held the *questionnaire* in his hand. "I need your help," he stated. "I don't know how to fill out the answers to all these questions. Why are they asking so many?"
4. Have students search through some of their favorite books to see how skillfully authors provide many context clues.[3]
   a. But that quietness had been shattered by the coming of Mrs. Scallop, whose voice now *intruded* . . . every morning. (p. 5)
   b. People put out rat poison in their barns to kill the *vermin*. (p. 127)
   c. The old man's voice, its *exasperated* tone, showed Ned he was tired of the cat. (p. 137)
5. Have students write sentences to exchange with their classmates where the context explains the word, and where choices are provided.
   a. Mr. Barrows had a way of making the most difficult things seem easy. His *lucid* explanations lit up every subject and helped us understand it.
         interesting   relaxed   clear
   b. The *prototype* of the automobile was a clumsy three-wheeled carriage invented in 1770 in France. It was propelled by steam and produced to haul cannons. Though its speed was three miles an hour, it was the forerunner of the swift cars of today.
         original model   prospect   production
   c. The first task of a cub pilot on the Mississippi was to learn the *elusive* shape of the river since the shape of the river was constantly altering forever beyond the grasp of the cub pilot's mind and hand.
         complicated   basic   baffling

(3) Excerpted from Paula Fox, *One-Eyed Cat* (New York: Bradbury Press, Inc., 1984).

Context and Cloze Technique

One of the best ways to create awareness of context is through the cloze technique, although it is seldom used in primary grades with extended paragraphs.[4] It involves deleting every fifth, eighth, or tenth word in a 250-500 word selection. The *first and last lines are left intact* and the selection must be able to stand alone and be understood. Students quickly become aware of how much language is anticipated in reading, and how helpful context can be. Class discussion about why certain words were chosen by particular students gives insights into word attack strategies. In the following cloze example, note that every eighth word has been omitted. Note that the first and last lines are left intact.

My Dad

Outside the snow lay like a soft feather blanket. Tracks made by the animals made patterns _____ designs. The branches of the bare trees _____ , covered with ice. A bird appeared hunting _____ food, pecking at some spots on _____ ground where the snow had begun to _____ .

Mary looked through the moisture-covered window. _____ she wanted to be outdoors! But _____ had said "no."

"I don't know why _____ ten-year-old hasn't better sense than _____ go outside with a thin sweater in _____ cold weather," she had added. "You asked _____ that bad cold."

She still wasn't well _____ and she knew it. Perhaps tomorrow. She _____ of the new sled that hadn't been _____ yet, that Dad had bought her. In _____ of herself, she smiled picturing the Gibson _____ and how much fun it was going _____ be whizzing down at a dizzying speed.

_____ , enough of this day-dreaming. She had _____ to write a letter to Dad and _____ she was going to do right away. "_____ Dad," she began, "I miss you." After _____ five minutes of no thoughts and no _____ , she put the pen down and went _____ the window again. She thought of last _____ when her father and she had gone skating and followed it with mugs of _____ chocolate at home. Even though he had _____ been gone two months now, it seemed _____ two years. She went over and looked _____ his picture on her dresser, saying to herself, "Dad, Dad, I love you best. I always will."

Words

1. and
2. glistened
3. for
4. the
5. melt
6. How
7. Mom
8. a
9. to
10. this
11. for
12. enough
13. thought
14. used
15. spite
16. hill
17. to
18. Well
19. promised
20. that
21. Dear
22. about
23. writing
24. to
25. year
26. ice
27. hot
28. only
29. like
30. at

Variations of this kind of activity with short selections can be as follows:

1. Show the number of letters within the word by appropriate slashes. Example:
   A bird appeared hunting __ __ __ food. (for)

---

(4) Cloze is also used for diagnostic purposes, but it is beyond the scope of this text to discuss using it for that purpose.

2. Have multiple choice words by the blank with the correct choice included. Example:

   She $\begin{bmatrix} \text{thought} \\ \text{tried} \\ \text{trembled} \end{bmatrix}$ of the new sled. (thought)

3. Include only the first consonant, blend, digraph, or vowel sound in the blank. Example:
   She had to wr_____ a letter. (write)

After discussing context clues, a class chart such as the following might be constructed as a reference for students:

DOs and DON'Ts for Using Context

Do

1. try reading to the end of the sentence to try to figure out the unknown word.
2. search for clues and make certain the meaning "clicks" with what you have been reading.
3. use context when you need a general sense of what you are reading, such as in a story for pleasure reading or to get a general idea of a topic.

Don't depend completely on context

1. when you need an exact meaning of a word.
2. when clues suggest several meanings and you do not know which one is right.

Quick Self-Check XVII

1. Define the two broad areas of context clues.
2. What are some different types of context clues?
3. How many teachers help students learn to use context clues?
4. How is cloze used in teaching context clues?

SECTION IV

USING THE DICTIONARY

As the student moves toward becoming an independent reader s/he often meets words that cannot be decoded and understood according to the word attack skills s/he has learned. At these times the dictionary can be an aid, but only if the student is skilled in its use.

Some newer dictionaries include words from major subject areas and computer science. They also include a mini-thesaurus, vocabulary builders (showing students how to make new words out of prefixes and suffixes) and expand understanding by showing regional differences in pronunciation. For a typical page see below.

SECTION IV USING THE DICTIONARY

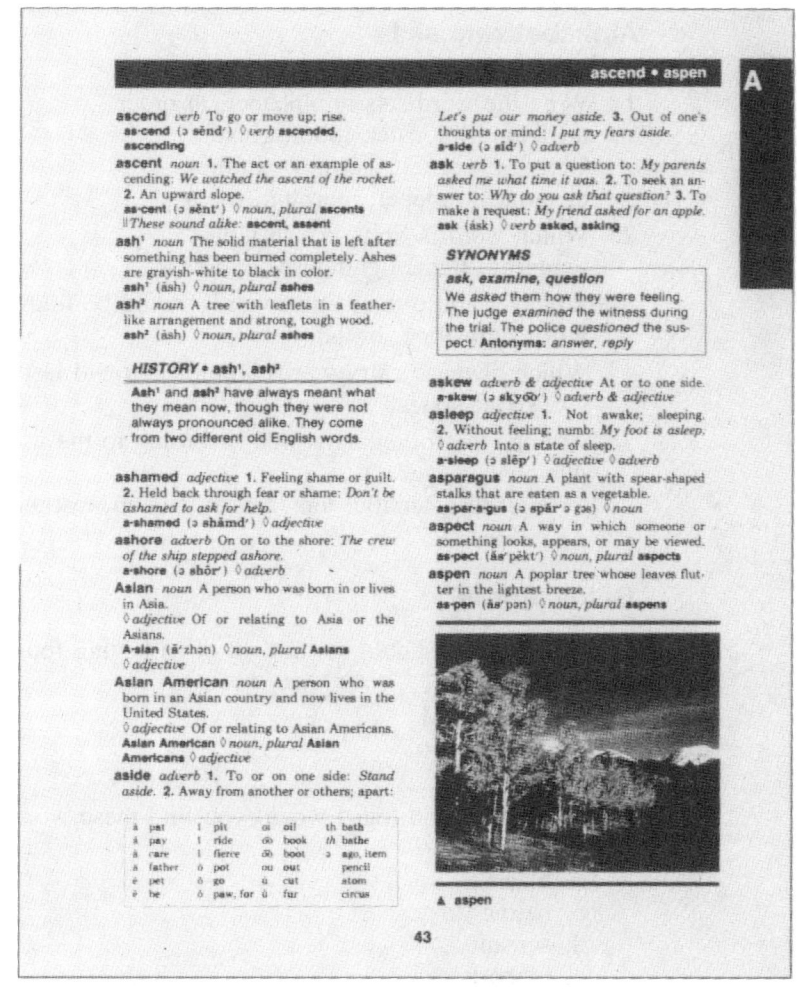

Copyright (c) 1986 by Houghton Mifflin Company. Reprinted by permission.

Houghton Mifflin Intermediate Dictionary 3-6 (1986)

A brief summary of needed dictionary skills include:

1. alphabetizing skills.
2. understanding the use of guide words.
3. ability to use the pronunciation key and interpret accent marks.
4. ability to use phonetic spellings for pronunciation.
5. ability to use the proper word meaning through the right definition, sentence example, and illustration.

Activities to Teach the Dictionary Skill Areas

Alphabetizing skills

1. Write the word sets in alphabetical order.
   a. demon, monster, robot, giant.
   b. mob, magnet, mermaid, million.
   c. money, moppet, morning, motor.
2. Which word is first? Which is last?
   lightning, light, lighthouse, lightyear
3. Which of these three entry words would be found first?
   birth, birthstone, birthday
4. Which of these entry words would be found last?
   six, sixth, sixteen
5. Arrange the following words according to the way they would appear on a dictionary page?
   termite, test, terrific, tent, tense, tension, testimony, terror, term

Guide words

1. A dictionary should be thought of as having four sections.
   Section 1 A-E
   Section 2 F-M
   Section 3 N-R
   Section 4 S-Z
   In what section (part) would you find these words?
   a. pepper
   b. black
   c. heroic
   d. scream
   e. kickoff
   f. window
2. Look at the following dictionary page. Write the first guide word. Write the second guide word.

can	canteen
candy	canvass
candle	canyon

3. The words *grown* and *gulf* are guide words at the top of one page in the dictionary. Select the words that would appear on that page.
   gull, guide, grumpy, guard, grab, gulf, guess
4. If you were looking for the entry word *honorable,* with what set of guide words would you find it?
   a. hobo   hog
   b. hole   home
   c. honor   hostess

Pronunciation key and accent marks

1. When you find the entry *extrovert* you want to know how the word is pronounced. The word is pronounced according to the code at the bottom. Check

the brief key there (bottom of the page) and the full key at the front of the dictionary. You will notice the following syllables and marks:

 ĕk′ short *e* and primary accent mark
 strə schwa
 vûrt′ light accent mark with *r*-conditioned vowels

Now try to say the word to yourself.

2. What part of speech is it? What is the abbreviation used for this part of speech?
3. What is the meaning of this word?

Phonics spelling and pronunciation

1. Write the correct word for the following phonetic spellings.
 ĕn sī klə pē′deə (encyclopedia)
 ĕg zoo′bər ənt (exuberant)
 rĭ bĕl yən (rebellion)

Word meaning

1. Look up these unusual words and write the dictionary definition.
 contankerous
 lionize
 greenback
 expatriate
2. Sometimes, dictionary words have more than one meaning, and you must decide from the context of the sentence the meaning that is appropriate. Read the dictionary entry below:
mesh (mesh) n. 1. Any of the open spaces in a cord, thread, or wire network. 2. A net or network. 3. The engagement of gear teeth. v. 1. To entangle or ensnare. 2. To engage or become engaged, as gear teeth. 3. To coordinate; harmonize (masche, maesche) mesh′y, adj.[5]
3. Examine these sentences. What meaning is intended in each?
 a. The mesh in the screen was in need of repair.
 b. The gear wheels do not mesh properly.
 c. The mesh of problems proved to be too difficult.
 d. The plans meshed and they proceeded accordingly.

Create Activities to Motivate Students in the Use of the Dictionary

1. Dictionary Background and Development
 a. A good brief refresher on the history of the dictionary is Robert Kraske's book, *The Story of the Dictionary*. Older students may read it independently, or teachers may share it with younger students in class. It is a fascinating book by which students learn, for example, that English dictionaries are really quite "young," dating back only about 400 years, and that listing words in alphabetical order was considered a brilliant, novel new idea at that time. Students are surprised to learn also that ordinary, commonly used words had to wait many years to win a place with uncommon words in the dictionary list. All the dictionary aids that we take for granted such as

(5) © 1980 by Houghton Mifflin Company. Reprinted by permission from *The American Heritage Dictionary of the English Language*.

word histories, illustrative sentences, pronunciation symbols, syllabication, accents, parts of speech, and usage notes very gradually developed as parts of a typical dictionary entry.

Sharing these insights with students, plus relating short stories about the controversial personalities of Noah Webster and Samuel Johnson, build an appreciation for the dictionary's use.[6]

    b. Teachers who have access to the compact two-volume edition of the Oxford English Dictionary can build lots of interest in this study by bringing these volumes into the classroom. The micrography, with thirteen volumes compressed in one, and the accompanying magnifying glass will not be easily forgotten by students.

2. The Word Factory, A Class Activity. Students are told they are to manufacture a "new" product using five words that are new to them according to these specifications: one must be a noun; one, a verb, a third, an adjective; a fourth, an adverb; and a fifth, any part of speech. All words must be previously unknown but which piqued their curiosity while browsing through the dictionary. After the students can read the words correctly (the teacher also determines the suitability and appropriateness of the words), and define them for the teacher, the words have passed the factory's "inspection." Now they are ready to trade with other students on the "open-market" for words and entries to help them manufacture and sell their new product. The final step involves using the five new words (some of their original ones plus those traded) to describe their new manufactured product. (This activity takes a week or so to complete.)

3. Creating Original Dictionary Entries
    a. Students create the sounds, syllables, and definitions for made-up words that reflect various dictionary entries. (This, of course, increases their familiarity with the different entry parts, and increases awareness that dictionaries differ in what they include.) These words with their respective entries are bound, and constitute the class's "Creative Dictionary."

> Example: stratmous (strat/moos) Eskimo stew made from venison, water, lichens, and moss. "This is the best stratmous I have ever tasted." Noun (Stratmous has different ingredients depending on the area.)

    b. Proceed as in the previous instance except this time students use their own names and write the appropriate entry. This also helps familiarize students with entries and pronunciation guides.

> Example: Jane Callaway. (Jān Căll ă wāy) 1. Third grade student at Hilltop School. 2. Also actress and musician. 3. Blue eyes, black hair, small and thin, Noun.

4. Dictionary Scavenger Hunts. Students engage in word quizzes. These are appropriate for middle-graders. Examples:
    a. Can a centaur be found in a zoo?
    b. Is a poetess a man who writes poems?

---

(6) See Robert Kraske, *Story of the Dictionary* (New York: Harcourt Brace Jovanovich, 1975). Also a book that contains a delightful fictionalized dictionary "happening" is Joseph Moses', *The Great Rain Robbery* (New York: Houghton Mifflin, 1975).

c. Does a lady prefer carrots, carats, or carets?
d. Is a grackle a kind of noise?
e. Was Ceres the same god as Demeter?
f. Can you wear a waste?
g. Is a limerick a kind of soft drink?
h. Is a puffin a small pillow?
i. Would you rather be a spelunker or a philatelist?
j. Is a statue a law?
k. Is an artichoke a disease of the lungs?
l. Is a goatee a baby goat?
m. Is a cherubim a delicious fruit?

5. Synonym Search. Students find synonyms for words beginning with particular letters. For example, all the synonyms for the words that follow begin with the letter F.

remote (far), panic (fear), trip (fall), elf (fairy), rapid (fast), savage (fierce), story (fable), end (finish), liberate (free). Also, strange (foreign, freakish, farfetched).

6. Mix and Match.

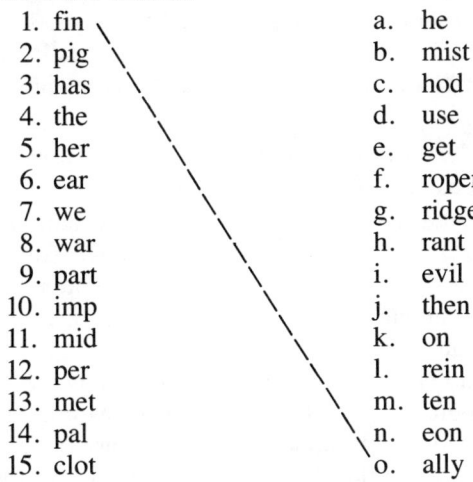

1. fin
2. pig
3. has
4. the
5. her
6. ear
7. we
8. war
9. part
10. imp
11. mid
12. per
13. met
14. pal
15. clot

a. he
b. mist
c. hod
d. use
e. get
f. roper
g. ridge
h. rant
i. evil
j. then
k. on
l. rein
m. ten
n. eon
o. ally

The activities suggested, while introducing students to some of the types of skills needed, and engaging students in some creative fun-type activities using the dictionary, do not ensure success in locating, pronouncing, and understanding the meaning of an unknown word. Skill in using the dictionary is acquired *through frequent and long time use and interest*. To motivate such use and interest, the teacher can serve as a good model, showing students that s/he too finds it often necessary to refer to it.

Quick Self-Check XVIII

1. Identify the five dictionary skills needed.
2. How might these skills be learned best?
3. What are some activities to motivate students to use the dictionary?

The More Commonly Used Dictionaries and Thesauri[7]

Primary

Daly, Kathleen N. *The Macmillan Picture Wordbook.* 80 pp. Macmillan, 1982. Grades K–2.
  Forty-four favorite categories of words colorfully and profusely illustrated and labeled to provide hours of enjoyment as children discover and identify familiar objects and concepts; includes such general topics as birds, dinosaurs, outer space, medical checkups, playtime, and manners; unit on manners illustrates parties, answering the telephone, greeting people; introductory chapter suggests ways in which parents or teacher can use book to help children build success in early stages of reading.

In Other Words: A Beginning Thesaurus. 240 pp. Scott Foresman, 1982. Grades 2–6.
  Valuable collection of over one hundred words used by children; each entry features word in boldface type, lengthy definitions and explanations of word and its synonyms, antonyms; colorful and appropriate pictures often help clarify shades of meaning; introduction offers sample entry, directions for use of text, practice exercises using words; contains separate illustrated section on groups of things with something in common, e.g., aircraft, kinds of boats, bodies of water, land shapes; accessible format; racially and sexually balanced; excellent for motivation and reinforcement of reading skills; ideal tool for helping students increase their vocabularies.

Macmillan Very First Dictionary: A Magic World of Words. 264 pp. Macmillan, 1983. Grades 1–4.
  Each of the nearly 1500 entries in this dictionary uses complete sentences to define a word or to present it in context; entry words stand out in bold print wherever used within the text, guide words are on every page, but there are neither pronunciation keys nor diacritical marks; some multiple verb forms are incorporated into the definitions, e.g., *lay* includes *laid* and *swim* includes *swam* and *swimmer*, but *lie* does not include *lay* or *lain*; entries do not include contemporary scientific meanings of words such as *space* or *engineer*, nor words with which modern youngsters are familiar such as *astronaut, computer,* and *robot;* five hundred large, colorful illustrations.

My First Dictionary. 340 pp. Houghton Mifflin, 1986. Grades 1–4.
  Paragraphs of two or three short sentences define 1700 entries, many of which are variants of and refer to other entry words. For example, in the separate entries for *did, do,* and *does,* each refers to at least one of the other forms; bold print accents each use of entry words and their variant forms; preface notes that five hundred of the entries are frequently used in early readers; other words are familiar to the average young student, e.g., *television, robot, astronaut;* most pages include large colorful illustrations—most often of nouns—which are fairly balanced racially and sexually.

The New Color-Picture Dictionary for Children. 252 pp. Childrens Press, 1981. Grades K–3.
  Sixteen hundred words suitably arranged for either informal perusal or easy reference; definitions rely on synonomous words or phrases and explanatory sentences; a few entries include past tense or plural forms; colorful pictures illustrate approximately one-half of the words defined; includes one hundred

---

(7) This information was excerpted from an Advisory List of Instructional Media, Dictionaries of the English Language, The Division of Educational Media, Materials Review and Evaluation Services, Department of Public Instruction, Raleigh, N.C. August 1983. For a more comprehensive overview of recommended dictionaries, write to them.

difficult words (e.g., *plumage, braggart, schedule*) to challenge competent readers; enjoyable opportunity to learn new words — if an adult is available for help in pronouncing them.

Elementary — Junior High

The American Heritage School Dictionary. 992 pp. American Heritage (available from Houghton Mifflin), 1977. Teacher's guide and student activity book. Also, teacher's edition. Grades 6–10.
Some 35,000 entries drawn from computer analysis of books used in grades 3–9; does not include many current slang terms; concise but not full definitions; useful homonym identifications; contains more sports-related words than the comparable Macmillan dictionary.

Houghton Mifflin Student Dictionary 1986. Grades 6–9.
Includes current computer and scientific terms, geographical and biographical information.

In Other Words: A Junior Thesaurus. 448 pp. Scott Foresman, 1982. Grades 5 up.
An adapted thesaurus of over three hundred words, plus more than two thousand synonyms, related words, and antonyms, designed for the middle grades; averages one word per page with illustrative sentences, synonyms, antonyms, definitions; specific use and connotation of each synonym explained; indexed; attractive format, much color, good graphics and photographs; excellent introduction thoroughly explains purpose of thesaurus and related terminology.

Macmillan School Dictionary. 1096 pp. Macmillan, 1977. Practice book. Teacher's guide free. Grades 6–10.
Definitions written specifically for junior high users; includes extensive gazetteer and biographic information; contains more religious and Biblical entries than the comparable American Heritage dictionary.

Scott, Foresman Beginning Dictionary. 768 pp. Scott Foresman, 1983. Grades 3–6.
Most attractive, authoritative, and current dictionary available for elementary and middle school students; based on excellent *Thorndike-Barnhart Beginning Dictionary;* clear, concise definitions, numerous illustrative sentences and phrases; well-placed, attention-getting, colorful photographs and prints illustrate obscure words, provide comic relief; designed to attract and hold student; appealing reference; a must for library and classroom.

Webster's Elementary Dictionary. 612 pp. G. & C. Merriam (available from American Book), 1980. Teacher's edition. Grades 3–8.
An authoritative Merriam-Webster dictionary with clear definitions, helpful illustrative phrases, and etymologies; pedestrian graphics.

Webster's Intermediate Dictionary. 910 pp. G. & C. Merriam (available from American Book), 1977. Teacher's edition. Grades 6–10.
Few illustrations; does not contain biographic or geographic information; full definitions; few illustrative examples, but many synonyms offset their lack.

SECTION V

MORE ABOUT MATERIALS AND ACTIVITIES

Just as with the teaching of phonics, the commercial market is also inundated with materials to teach basic sight words, structural analysis, and dictionary skills. A few guidelines about these materials (Cunningham, 1981) follow:

1. Will the materials help meet your reading goals?
   They should be an integral part of your reading program.

2. Are the materials flexible?
   Good materials should meet a variety of instructional goals.
3. Do they teach what they say they do?
   Close perusal often shows the skill is not what is purported.
4. Are the skills taught important to reading?
   Knowing a word is a noun or verb may be important to language instruction, but that knowledge does not help readers identify words or get meaning from them.
5. Are the skills taught appropriate for the level of the readers with whom you intend to use the material?
   Not all skills are important at all levels. Skill emphasis shifts from word identification to vocabulary and comprehension. If the skills are important, are they important to your particular level readers?
6. Are skills taught at the application level?
   Do students actually apply the skills or is it expected they will automatically transfer the knowledge to real reading? You may still purchase the materials but recognize you need to provide the application practice and assessment.
7. Are the materials intrinsically motivating?
   Avoid boredom. You may still have to use some extrinsic motivation to get students started working on a piece of material, but if it is interesting, worthwhile, and varied, students' intrinsic motivation system can take over.
8. What's the ratio of time spent actually reading?
   Material where students spend twice as much time doing other things as they do actual reading should get a very low rating.
9. Is the material worth the cost?
   How durable and sturdy is the material. How many children's needs will it help meet. Are there less expensive materials which meet the same instructional criteria?

For teachers who want to make their own reading activities for these additional word attack skills, a potpourri of game-making materials plus construction ideas is suggested by McCormick and Collins (1981):

Blank playing cards, resembling regular playing cards are useful for dozens of purposes. Coated with plastic, they are quite durable in the classroom. They may be used for words or word parts. Source: Sovereign Playing Card and Novelty Corporation, 200 Verdi Street, Farmingdale, New York 11735. Use pens designed for writing on overhead transparencies.

Gameboards, difficult to construct because of the tediousness of drawing little squares can be simplified by covering a commerical gameboard with a piece of tissue paper, securing it, and tracing the pattern of squares with a pencil. Remove the tissue paper, attach it to a piece of posterboard, and with a felt tip pen trace the pattern. Marks from the felt tip pen will soak through the tissue onto the posterboard, producing a neat pattern with minimum effort.

Markers can be buttons, small toys, and even poker chips. Small poker chips are often available in adult game stores in sets of 100 with 20 chips in each of five colors. For other types of game pieces write to Marie's Educational Materials, Inc., P. O. Box 60694, Sunnydale, CA 94088.

Decorating with themes such as space, cars, sports, or cartoon characters may be done with books of gummed stickers available in art supply stores or stores that carry educational materials. A publisher of educational stickers is Word Making Productions, Dept. C., P. O. Box 15038, Salt Lake City, Utah 84115.

Pizza Circles are especially useful for games or activities that require very sturdy materials.

A group of pre-service teachers (Snyder, 1981) experimented with producing reading games for 4th–6th grade children, evaluating whether or not the activities were worthwhile. They concluded that it was best to teach two to four children to play and allow them to teach others, and were pleasantly surprised to find that the children's inventions while playing were often quite intriguing and frequently superior to their own ideas. In considering the time and expense involved, they decided that at $6.00 an hour (quite low) for their time, an ordinary board game actually costs the teacher about $30 to make. See Figure 2.1 for a chart of some of their findings on the merits of hand produced versus commercially produced materials.

Figure 2.1 Pros and cons of hand-produced and commercially produced materials

Hand-Produced		Commercial	
Pros	*Cons*	*Pros*	*Cons*
1) Can be designed to meet specific needs and interests of target group.	1) Durability of the constructed material is sometimes questionable.	1) Material can be geared to specific needs of children.	1) May use a too difficult vocabulary or a different approach to skill development.
2) Use an appropriate vocabulary and level of difficulty.	2) Constant remaking or mending may be required.	2) Material is durable, legible, and colorful. Looks professional and may be long-lasting.	2) May be limited in usefulness.
3) Children can be actively involved in game production.	3) Construction *must* reflect high standards of neatness and legibility.	3) A wide variety already available on the marketplace.	3) Require much time to locate, evaluate, purchase.
4) Kits and activity game files can be expanded as needed.	4) Directions must be carefully thought out.	4) If teacher time is a factor, may be less expensive than "home made."	4) Lost items are expensive to replace.
5) Favorite "old" games can be easily adapted.	5) Construction sometimes require more time than is warranted.		5) Frequently considered too expensive.
6) Materials are sometimes more economical.	6) Easily available commercial materials are sometimes more economical.		

Their final consensus was that while purposeful games have a place in the school environment, *the "greatest game in town" is still book reading.* Hooray!

Summary

Part 2 has discussed additional important word attack skills as

1. knowing the basic sight words.
2. understanding principles of structural analysis that include compound words; prefixes/suffixes/roots; and syllabication.

3. using context clues.
4. using the dictionary.
4. using materials to teach these skills.

The importance of early mastery of the basic sight words cannot be overemphasized, as they represent a large part of the running vocabulary of any reading selection. A teaching method to employ when sight word learning is particularly difficult was presented. As students frequently encounter polysyllabic and affixed words in reading, structural analysis becomes increasingly important as *the* primary decoding strategy useful to students in and above the fourth grade. The differences between absorbed and active prefixes and inflectional and derivational affixes were discussed. Teachers need to actively involve students in discussions about affixed words, as they are most easily learned as language is initially learned, by actively hearing and using the words. More structured lessons for learning affixes for both younger and older readers were presented. Differences of opinion on the efficacy of syllabication principles were discussed, and a simple syllabication scheme was included. The use of context, both semantic (meaning) and syntactic (part of speech), continues to be one of the best ways to decode words, and for mature readers represents one of the first clues to use in attacking words. Finally, the use of the dictionary as an aid in decoding strategies was discussed. Throughout, lessons and activities to teach the above skills were presented, with some guidelines for teachers, and answers to some frequently asked questions. A rationale for selecting materials, a potpourri of game-making ideas, and the pros and cons of handmade vs. commercial materials were included.

PART 2: FINAL REVIEW

1. Sight words are sometimes referred to as high-frequency words. Explain.
2. What is meant by a sight word "storehouse"?
3. What are some activities to use with students to help them learn these words?
4. Evaluate this sentence: The meaning of a compound word is always a combination of its two parts.
5. Group the following words according to whether they contain active or absorbed prefixes: *contain, unsure, preclude, exceed, submarine, preview.* (What is the difference between these two types of prefixes?)
6. Group the following words according to whether they contain inflectional or derivational suffixes: *jumping, courageous, smallest, woman's, attention, merriment, draws.* What differences must teachers be aware of in teaching these two types of suffixes?
7. State several important generalizations for students to remember when adding suffixes to words.
8. What are the best ways to learn the meanings of roots and affixed words?
9. A simple syllabication generalization for students might consist of four steps. List these.
10. In teaching syllabication, a recent language change should be considered. Write three words that show this change.
11. What are two types of context clues? Suggest several ways teachers may help students see the value of context clues?
12. Proficiency in the use of the dictionary requires that students acquire certain skills. Identify what these are. How are they best learned?

PART
3
Aids in Decoding

SECTION I

TOWARD AN IMPROVED DECODING STRATEGY

Finding the Right Combination

Four decoding strategies are available to the student who meets an unknown word: context, structure, phonics, and the dictionary. For example, in the sentence "The fire burned down the house," the word *burned* may be deduced from the remainder of the sentence, or the context. Second, the root of a word or the affixes attached to it may be used as a key to unlock the rest of the word: *unhappy, dislike, hopeful*. Third, the arrangement of the letters in a word, or phonics, may suggest that clusters of letters may encode particular sounds as *igh* /ī/ in *mighty*, or *th* /th/ and *ir* /er/ in *thirst*. Last, the glossary or dictionary may help with the division of a word into syllables, and give clues to pronunciation. But this should only be used when previous clues have failed.

After a class discussion, a procedure could be charted, such as the one presented, with steps to follow when meeting an unknown word, and could expand the simple word attack strategy suggested earlier in the text.

To Unlock an Unknown Word
1. Try the context first.
2. Then look at the structure to see if the word is a compound and whether it has any roots or affixes.
3. Check for syllable or morphemic clues.*
4. Check for phonics clues.
5. If still unsure, try the dictionary.

Once students familiarize themselves with these procedural steps, however, they must be led to understand that often a word will necessitate a different sequence for identification. For example, context may be used *after* the word has been partially determined through the use of phonics to make certain the word makes sense in the sentence.

While a series of steps, such as those previously outlined, are useful, the rapid decoding of words including those met for the first time becomes essential so that meaning is not lost. The good reader sifts the options available when meeting an unknown word, selecting perhaps one, two, or all three in rapid succession. This is what all students must essentially learn to do: *understand the options available and make use of the best one/ones when decoding unrecognizable words*.

Presenting Vocabulary to Students

Direct instruction

Some students are able to zero in on the precise word attack skill needed for unknown words, while other students need direct instruction on how to proceed. With these students it is best to anticipate the difficult vocabulary that will be

---

(*) Morpheme (noun) morphemic (adj.) A morpheme is a minimal group of letters or sounds that carry meaning. For example, the *s* in boys, even though not a syllable is a morpheme since it carries the meaning of more than one. Likewise the prefix *un*, a syllable, is a morpheme because it carries the meaning of "not". Some syllables are morpheme; however, some are not.

encountered and place such vocabulary (in a phrase) on the board or ditto. Words are divided into syllables to teach structural analysis, followed by the teacher or student underlining the particular phonics features (such as consonants and vowel digraphs) that may present difficulties:

wi*th* dr*aw* (my plans)
la*unch*ed (the ship)
dis o b*ey* (the orders)
ple*dge* (to keep)
ple*dge* (to keep)
re b*ou*nd (the ball)
cam p*aig*n (every day)

This enables students to see the "why" of how to decode the word and includes both structure and phonics. The phrase also helps with the context. Vocabulary is then discussed from the standpoint of particular decoding strategies.

VLP

A teaching method referred to as VLP (Vocabulary, Language, and Prediction) (Wood and Robinson, 1983) involves the vocabulary part of a directed reading lesson and goes beyond decoding skills. In a typical lesson given the following vocabulary words to introduce, maintain or reinforce, the teacher engages in activities such as the following:

Words

typical	reservation	grazing	eighteen	spinning
woven	mesa	rough	pupils	weave
modern	cattle	supply	language	Navajo Indian

(Words are placed on separate cards with their respective page number to allow the teacher to emphasize the words from pages to be covered during the class period.)

1. Discuss the pertinent phonics and structural features of selected words as needed. Focus on a particular skill such as dividing words into syllables between like consonants. (cattle, spinning, supply)
2. Place the cards on a table in front of the students and explain they are to read the word that answers certain questions.
   Synonym   Which word means the same as student? (pupil)
   Antonym   Which word means the opposite of old-fashioned? (modern)
     I would rather feel a *soft* surface than a _____one.
   Categorization   Group all the words that may have something to do with animals. (cattle, grazing, spinning, weave, woven)
   Context   People in some parts of our country and in other countries speak a different _____ .
   Dictionary usage   Using your dictionary, find the definition of *supply* that fits in this sentence: "The Navajo brought a supply of food for our trip."
   Phonics and structural analysis   In which words do you find the same sound of *a* as in *play*? Which word ends like *examination*?

Once students can read and understand the vocabulary they use the words to predict what the passage will be about.

Word Wonder

Word Wonder is another teaching strategy useful with older children to help with a number of reading skills, among them word decoding and word-meaning. In its simplest form students tell what words they expect to find in a story and then read to find out if they are right. In a more complicated form, the teacher lists words and students decide after decoding the words whether each word is likely to appear in the story, giving a rationale for their decision. The teacher purposely includes words apt to be chosen incorrectly so post reading discussion can center around misconceptions. Post-reading discussion can determine whether wrong guesses where "bad" guesses or if the author just didn't choose to use those words. With this method, many students experience and learn to read many new words (Spiegel, 1981).

Some Suggestions for Aids in Decoding Difficulties

The short vowel sounds

When students have difficulty learning the sounds of the short vowels Azar (1985) has devised a clever technique to teach and reinforce them. She suggests teaching the vowels singly if they have not been introduced or all five if the students have already had exposure to them. After instructing or reminding students that each vowel has more than one sound, she places each vowel in a picture "because pictures are easy to remember." Procedures follow:

Teacher: If you can name the picture you can hear, see, and read its short vowel sound. (Write a large "a" on the board. Tell them to watch as you turn it into a picture that starts with its short sound. If the children fail to recognize your drawing—we're not all Rembrandts—give hints such as "What fruit for a day keeps the doctor away?")

Teacher: (after children say "apple") "What sound do you hear at the beginning of 'apple'? That's right, ă. Let's say it together— apple . . . ă–ă is correct."

Teacher: (cover the drawing showing only the symbol. Ask the key question several times.) "What is the picture? What is the sound?" (Continue reinforcing as needed.)

Pass out plain paper and crayons. Omit black. Go through the drawing step by step. Have the children draw it with you and then color it in. Have them outline only the short vowels in the picture with heavy black crayon. Reinforce the sound by asking the key questions. Children keep their drawing for reference. The next logical step would be to teach some of the vowel consonant patterns such as CVC.

The ECRI method

In situations where students have particular difficulties in decoding and fail to see clues, teachers may choose to place each vocabulary word on an individual card, and instruct students (in small groups) as to the decoding method that would work best with that particular word. They follow this instruction with lots of practice and discrimination exercises. They say something as follows:

Teacher: (has the word *concern* on a card) This word is *concern*. It is best decoded by syllables. Say *con/cern, concern*. S/he follows this by using the word in a sentence to make certain students understand the word: "The parents showed concern over the weather." (S/he asks students to orally offer sentences of their own and then s/he continues.) Write and say the word, *concern*, and then check it with this card to see if it is correct.

Students: (They write the word, read it, say the word, and then check it with the model.)

Teacher: (Shows them two words, one is *concern,* and the other is a word similar to it, *conceal*. S/he continues.) Look at these two words. Tell me what is the same and what is different about them.

Students: (They respond by identifying the letters and sounds that are similar and those that are different, somewhat as follows:) Well, the first syllables are the same, but the second syllables are different. In *concern*, the second syllable has the /er/ sound plus /n/; and in *conceal*, the second syllable has an *ea* with the sound of /ē/ plus /l/.

Teacher: Now look at these two partially written words. (Show the words *concern* and *conceal*, omitting key letters such as *con __ __ n* and *conc __ __ l*.) What sound is missing in the first word? Tell me how to write the letters that stand for that sound. What sound is missing in the second word? Tell me how to write the letters that stand for that sound.

By using this method the teacher encourages students to attend to the salient features that make the word decode as it does, showing students the particulars of one word by comparing it with another word. The method also includes *lots of timed practice with vocabulary* every day.

By initially saying, "This word is decoded best by its syllables," "This word is decoded best by using phonics clues," or "This word is decoded best by looking at the prefixes and suffixes," teachers illustrate for students which word attack method might be most appropriate. Also, they help show them that sometimes more than one type of word attack skill is used.[8]

Low level of accuracy in word attack

Students who exhibit a low level of accuracy in word attack during story reading may have a vision problem. This is usually not the case, however. More often it may be due to (1) the need to read a little slower; (2) a slight visual recall weakness due to noting only the outer configuration of words; or (3) constructing their version of the author's meaning based on context at a rapid rate, using whole word processing with not enough attention to detail. Their thinking processes run

---

(8) For more information on this very successful teaching method, write to ECRI Exemplary Center for Reading Instruction, 2888 Highland Drive, Salt Lake City, Utah, 84106.

faster than their perceptual and recognition processes for the letters and words. To remediate Moon and Scorpio (1984) suggest some of the following procedures:

Check to see if the student can read directions accurately and take tests. If so, the lack of accuracy in story reading may simply be an early stage in the development of a more flexible reading rate and the development of strategies for reading. When students fail to maintain high accuracy in situations that demand it, try some of the following procedures:

— Use a tachistoscope, increasing the span of materials.
— Use flash cards for similar words, such as *though, through,* and *thorough.*
— Read in unison with a partner. The goal is to increase the number of words read without error. Keep progress check.
— Record on cassette while reading. Recheck for errors while listening a second time.
— Ask the student where his/her eyes were when the error was made. Lead the student to see that the voice got ahead of the eyes which needed a little more time for a more careful look.

Also, be careful to see that the assignment quantity is not causing emphasis on hurrying to get through, versus quality. Keep a list of errors to be analyzed for patterns. Perhaps phonics rules and structure elements are weak. Review these skills in the context of the reading materials in which they are missed. Very often what seems to be needed is simply learning to allow enough time for the eye to stay ahead of the voice so it notices detail in words, and then gradually speed up.

Reading and Evaluation

In a speech over a decade ago, Wm. Glasser author of the classic book *Schools Without Failure* suggested that

> . . . it is not important for us to spend a great deal of time evaluating other people. That really isn't necessary. What's very very necessary is that we spend time evaluating ourselves and that we set up our schools so that children spend a great deal of time evaluating *themselves.*

There are indications even young students can use self-evaluation techniques effectively, often providing information that could not be discovered in any other way. Moreover, allowing students to evaluate themselves encourages them to take greater responsibility for their activities. Some useful techniques suggested by Coley (1983) follow:

Structured Techniques

An introduction to student self-evaluation can start on a small scale. With young children begin by asking them to put a happy or sad face at the top of their paper to indicate how well they feel they understand the story. With older students ask them to indicate on a 1–5 scale how difficult they felt the vocabulary was in a given selection or how well they felt they did on an activity involving syllabication. Once students get used to evaluating small bits of their reading behavior, move them to a task where they look at a more comprehensive picture of their reading. The skills checklist is a useful next step. A skills checklist may be as broad as the following:

☺ ☹   I can usually sound out words.

☺ ☹   I usually know what words mean.

☺ ☹   I usually understand the stories I read.

Checklists can also be specific to a given skill such as the partial checklist below on syllabication.

```
yes   no
____  ____  1. I know where to divide a v c c v word.
____  ____  2. I know how to pronounce the vowel in a syllable that ends with
               a vowel.
____  ____  3. I know . . . etc.
```

Another helpful self-evaluation format is the comparison checklist.

Student Name _____

	My Evaluation			Mr. Jones' Evaluation		
	Poor	Fair	Good	Poor	Fair	Good
1. vocabulary						
2. questions						
3. smooth reading						

Comments:

Open-Ended Evalutions

In addition to fairly structured evaluations, use some very open-ended sentences. Students may respond orally or in writing to stems such as:

The hardest thing about reading is . . .
When I come to a word I don't know I . . .
I like to read when . . .

Data gained from these statements give exceptional insights not only to the students' attitudes towards reading, but to the strategies they employ during reading, and provide many insights into their reading problems (Coley, p. 200).

Helping Students Develop Flexibility

Since no one word attack strategy is adequate, students who rely exclusively on one must be led to the use of other strategies (Frenzel, 1978). The teacher who wishes to help students become more flexible as they decode should

1. teach specific lessons in each skill and develop the skills in situations that *are truly reading oriented* rather than only in isolated drill.
2. encourage the student to try, to think, to reason, and to solve decoding "dilemmas." Determining words then becomes a personally satisfying encounter, done in a confident way.
3. encourage the expansion of sight vocabulary lists. These hold a significant spot in the strategies of all readers and help in the decoding of polysyllabic words.
4. get some insight into the student's sequence of word attack by having him/her tell precisely what s/he does when s/he meets an unfamiliar word.
5. help the student develop a procedure for unlocking words and understand there are alternative approaches, and that at times it is a case of trial and error.

Fluency Is Necessary While Reading

Imitative method

Some students appear to have decoding skills when tested on isolated words but seem unable to integrate these word identification abilities with any degree of fluency, in order to comprehend what they are reading. In many cases the reading is too slow and labored, lacking the automaticity of decoding that must take place if readers are to enjoy and comprehend what they read. (This *does not* apply to beginning readers who often read haltingly during the first year or so, as they learn decoding strategies.)

To improve fluency, Cunningham (1979) suggests several procedures from his own clinical experiences based on the work of reading researchers. These seem most appropriate for students in or above the fourth grade. One method is called the "Imitative Method," first suggested by Carol Chomsky (1976), a noted linguist.

Briefly, the teacher locates an interesting short story at the student's reading instruction level, and records it on a cassette in an appealing and dramatic form. While listening to the tape, the student follows along, reading the story from the book until the story is mastered. Patience is required of both teacher and student because it may take several weeks until true reading mastery of the story occurs, but when it does, the student is encouraged to read the story to parents, friends, and classmates. The story has not been memorized as the student will need the book, but elements of memorization are certainly present. Nevertheless, this approach to reading enables the student to have the real experience of successful, effective, fluent reading for perhaps the first time. An alternative method used by some teachers includes a filmstrip, a cassette, and an accompanying reading guide containing the cassette's text. Students view the filmstrip and listen to the cassette. After doing this several times, they follow the narrator with the reading guide, and eventually are able to read the story on their own.

This is followed by having the student show the filmstrip to the class and reading the text that goes along with it, just as the narrator would do on the cassette.

Impress

Cunningham suggests another method called "impress." A selection at the student's instruction level is located and given to the student to read silently. The student and teacher reread the material together orally, the teacher setting a moderate pace and moving his/her hand along under the lines being read. The teacher sits quite close to the student, practically reading into the student's ear, but adjusting the strength of his/her voice throughout the selection in accordance with the student's ability. This means allowing the student to take the lead when s/he is comfortable with the reading and the teacher moderating his/her voice to a whisper during that period, but then raising his/her voice to move the student along in the selection when the student appears uncertain or falters. The name of the procedure suggests what the teacher is attempting to do — to *impress* the words on the mind of the student through repeated practice. For a more complete detail of this method see the article by Heckelman (1969), who initially developed it.

A modified method is suggested by Eldredge and Butterfield (1986) whereby slower students can be assigned to read with a more skilled student. Students sit side by side reading aloud from one book. The faster student touches each word as s/he reads it and the slower student repeats each word after her/him. The faster reader reads at her/his normal rate with the slower student instructed to follow and repeat the words as quickly as possible. As the slower reader gains skill the more rapid reader reads silently, supplying words only when needed.

Repeated readings

A third procedure used by Cunningham involves a method called "Repeated Readings" based on the work of Dahl (1974). Students are given a selection of about a hundred words and asked to read and reread it, each time increasing their speed. Initially the passage should be read by the student with no more than five errors (95% word recognition), or else it will prove too difficult. The teacher may use this method in a group, listening to one student while others are practicing. Again, the idea is to improve the rate and give the student the feeling of fluency for perhaps the first time.

Two modifications to the procedure of repeated readings for group instruction with young children are suggested by Lauritzen (1982). These lie in the choice of materials and in the initial method of presentation. Materials chosen should have a singing quality loved by children with a definite rhyme, strong rhythm, identifiable sequence and oral literature patterns. These are all prevalent in folk literature as *Henny Penny,* the *Gingerbread Boy,* and the *Old Woman and Her Shoe*. The teacher first reads the entire selection, and the children follow the print, either from a book or from a copy on a chart or board. Then the children echo-read a line, a sentence, or a paragraph with length determined by the structure of the poem or story. Eventually the teacher and children read the entire selection in unison. The children may read individually, in pairs, or in small groups as many times as they wish. Because the teacher models fluent reading from the beginning, the children imitate it. Difficult material is mastered, and children can be motivated to improve their reading because of success (Lauritzen, p. 456).

Another modification of repeated readings is suggested by Swaby (1982) in what is called an *Instructional* Repeated Reading Program. Here a teacher, aide, or other adult works individually with a child. A short passage written on the student's instructional level is chosen. The passage is divided into three or four paragraphs or short segments. If the student has previously "read the material (best)," s/he should be reminded of the major concepts. If the material is new, the major concepts are briefly discussed. A segment of a passage is done at a time, and word errors made by the student are recorded. The segment is read back to the student to see if errors are recognized. Word choices that were errors are analyzed to determine whether they were errors of phonics, structure, or context. Often the word choice is poor, a student reading for example *chain* for *chair*. The semantic clues that make *chain* a poor choice are pointed out so the student learns to recognize the type of errors made — phonetic, structural, or contextual — to avoid them in the future.

After reading and analyzing all the segments, the student rereads the entire passage as fluently as possible, aiming for shorter reading time, fewer errors, more self-correction, and greater expression.

Recalling word meaning

Casale (1985) suggests motor imaging as a learning strategy for new vocabulary basing it upon psychomotor associations using the hands only. She claims motor imaging provides "intentional and systematic development of the psychomotor dimension of word learning." Modeling and practice are needed. The method encourages students to connect a new word with a pantomimed psychomotor meaning as well as a language meaning. The language meaning of the word is given immediately in Step 1, then translated into a motor meaning, using the hands, and subsequently reinforced. The procedure follows:

1. The teacher writes a word on the board, pronounces it, and states the meaning.
2. The teacher asks students to imagine a simple hands pantomime.
3. At a signal students do their "hands" pantomime.
4. The teacher selects the most common pantomime of the group.
5. This pantomime is shown to the students, who repeat the word while doing the pantomime. Words can be translated into a simpler synonym form and then pantomimed.
6. Each word is repeated, doing the pantomime, then the meaning or synonym is stated.
7. The student then reads the selection with the new vocabulary.

Casale claims the consistency of student pantomimes for a given new word suggests that fairly common psychomotor meanings do exist. This author, who frequently uses pantomiming new words for which students act out the meaning in a short play form (each one lasting about 30 seconds) can attest to the efficacy of this method. Casale's method would be much less time-consuming and done as part of seatwork. It would lack the more visual imagery that a short playlet offers, however. In any event, it would be a welcome break for students from some of the more conventional sedentary classroom procedures. Below is an example of motor imaging as suggested by Casale (1985).

Examples of motor imaging

New word	Language meaning	Motor meaning
appropriate	right or fit for a certain purpose	both palms together, matching perfectly
convey	take or carry from one place to another	both hands together, palms upward, moving from one side to the other
woe	great sadness or trouble	one or both hands over the eyes, head slanted forward
dazzle	shine or reflect brightly	palms close together, facing outward, fingers spread
utmost	the very highest or most	one or both hands reaching up as high as possible
abode	place where you live	hands meeting above the head in a triangular "roof" shape

Basic Principles In Remediation

Harris (1981) looked at what was new in reading remediation with particular attention to treatment. After his survey he concluded that certain basic principles of successful remediation instruction had not changed. The same holds true at the present time.

1. Begin at a low enough level and take small enough steps to ensure initial success.
2. Develop a pleasant rapport with each pupil.
3. Be flexible in choosing both method and materials, paying attention to the child's feelings as well as aptitudes.
4. Use ample review and repetition.
5. Use materials that combine high interest appeal with low difficulty.
6. Use progress charts to record progress towards important objectives.
7. Celebrate the child's successes.
8. Apply in connected reading those skills developed in isolation.

Summary

Part 3 has discussed additional aids in teaching word attack skills:

1. Procedures to follow when meeting an unknown word to find the right combination.
2. Presenting vocabulary to students.
3. Some suggestions to remediate certain difficulties.
4. Methods for student self-evaluation.
5. Ways to gain reading fluency.
6. A method to recall word meanings.

Students must view word attack skills as something to manipulate to their advantage when meeting unknown words so that minimum clues, but the right clues, are used as quickly as possible. Procedures to follow when meeting an unknown word were suggested. The ECRI method was outlined, and suggestions made for improving the level of accuracy for some students in using word attack skills. Student self-evaluation is a very important facet of the process, and to that end checklists for the self-evaluation have been provided. Suggestions were offered for helping students learn to decode words more easily and to become more fluent as they read. Finally, a method for recalling word meaning by using motor-imaging was described.

PART 3: FINAL REVIEW

1. Suggest a procedure for students to follow when meeting an unknown word.
2. Briefly describe the ECRI method.
3. What are the major reasons students decode words with a low level of accuracy?
4. Describe checklists that may be used for student self-evaluation.
5. What are some procedures to use that may enable students to read more rapidly?
6. What is meant by motor-imaging?

PART
4
The Expanding Role of the Computer in the Reading Classroom

SECTION I

ADVANTAGES AND DISADVANTAGES

Under a federal grant more than twenty-five years ago the first well-documented attempt to teach reading with the computer took place at Stanford University. Programs and publishers followed, and the role of the computer in the reading classroom expanded, with research, innovations, and pilot programs continuing. Advantages and disadvantages to teaching reading with CAI (computer assisted instructions) were frequently cited (Mason, 1980) (Rupley and Chevrette, 1983).

Advantages	*Disadvantages*
1. individualized instruction with immediate feedback	1. high cost of initial installation and programs
2. a pleasurable learning experience	2. failure of computers to listen to someone read
3. students actively engaged on task	3. teacher reluctance and needed training

More recently some of these same concerns were voiced and others also noted in a poll conducted by the editors of *Learning* (March 1986). Roughly five hundred teachers gave their opinions on computer use with about 70% responding positively. The key problems seemed to be with time spent on the computer and again with the limited training provided for the teacher. Most respondents said their students spent less than half an hour per week at the computer. To find enough time something else in the curriculum needed to be dropped, presenting a new set of problems. There seemed to be uncertainty as to "how much time was just right." Even among teachers whose students spent 60 minutes per week, there was disagreement as to whether it was sufficient. Teachers cited other concerns:

Improper Planning
— too much time spent watching
— lack of thinking activities
— slower students do not get as much opportunity
— software is not integrated with the program

Limited Application
— programs are enormously expensive workbook clones
— overemphasis on dull mechanical dittos
— computer becomes the 'subject' instead of a tool for subjects

Lack of Training
— teacher-release-time is needed for computer training program
— lack of good instructors to train teachers

Negative Attitudes
— instructor's negativism rubs off on student
— elitism develops among proficient teacher users and non-users

In spite of concerns most of the respondents in the survey were committed to using computers, citing improvement in schoolwork, student motivation, and teacher satisfaction. Most respondents believe computers will increase their influence in elementary education in the next five years and are facing that prospect with cautious optimism. Some additional poll results follow:

Computer Poll Results

1. How many computers does your school have?
   - None–1%
   - 1 to 4–14%
   - 5 to 9–27%
   - 10 to 14–19%
   - 15 or more–38%
   - No answer–1%

2. Where are the computers located?
   - Classrooms–59%
   - Computer lab–48%
   - Library–34%
   - Other (†)–21%
   - No answer–1%

   (†)Including: office, reading room, resource room.

3. Do your students use these computers?
   - Yes–87%
   - No–11%
   - No answer–2%

4. On average, approximately how much time each *week* do each of your students spend at the computer?
   - Under 15 minutes–25%
   - 15 to 29 minutes–35%
   - 30 to 59 minutes–25%
   - 60 minutes or more–13%
   - No answer–2%

5. What types of work do your students generally do on the computer?
   - Drill and practice–79%
   - Word processing–31%
   - Programming–31%
   - Simulations–30%
   - Other (†)–22%
   - No answer–1%

   (†)Including: Logo, games, keyboarding.

6. In what curriculum areas are your students using computers?
   - Math–80%
   - Language arts–72%
   - Social studies–34%
   - Science–27%
   - Art or music–7%
   - Other (†)–26%
   - No answer–2%

   (†)Including: computer literacy, Logo, critical thinking.

7. How do you feel about the amount of time your students spend at the computer?
   - It's too little time–63%
   - It's too much time–2%
   - It's just enough time–30%
   - No answer–5%

For an in-depth questionnaire useful prior to purchasing reading software, see Appendix D, p. 197. For the names of reading software publishers, also see Appendix D, p. 195.

Computer Programs

There are several types of computer programs. Some are designed to move in short, repetitive steps if the student seems to be having difficulty. Others switch to longer, faster steps if materials are grasped easily. The majority of programs require that materials at each level be mastered before proceeding farther. The student is often rewarded with such things as stars, pluses, or a printed or audio recognition with each response.

Many educational publishers are involved in providing software in the area of reading. Among some of the larger ones are Borg Warner, Houghton Mifflin,

Milliken Press, Random House, Scholastic, SRA, Texas Instruments, Davidson, and Sunburst. Computer companies like Atari and Apple are also providing reading software for the home and classroom.*

Availability and Programs

Wedman (1983) has categorized the number of available software programs from nineteen publishers in the major word attack areas:

Number of Word Attack Skills Based on Nineteen Publishers

Phonics
Alphabet	17
Consonants	18
Consonant Digraphs	5
Blends	11
Silent Consonants	1
Vowels	16
Vowel Digraphs	6
Diphthongs	2
Controlled Vowels	2
Vowel Rules	1

Sight Vocabulary	6
Context Clues	8
Syllabication Rules	5

Structural Analysis
Inflectional Endings	9
Compound Words	3
Contractions	12
Root Words	7
Affix Meaning	24

Using Dictionary Skills	6

As with much currently available reading materials, software today seems to be concentrated on specific reading skills, especially in the word attack area. The software publishers do have materials for comprehension, study skills, and interpretation but on a small scale.

Example Programs

Examples of some typical software programs follow:

Instant Zoo (ages 7–10) by Apple Computer. A set of four games plus a word list editor. Two of the games concern reading words. In *Quick Match* pairs of words appear on the screen. The student decides if they match and presses the correct key. If the student guesses wrong or too slowly, the computer gets a point. In *Scramble*, letters jog in wearing animated tennis shoes and must be unscrambled

---

(*) For other publisher names and addresses and specific skill titles and cost, see *Swift's Educational Software Directory,* Sterling Swift Publishing Co., 7901 South I H-35, Austin, Texas 78744.

before they jog to the bottom of the screen. Individual word lists to be used with *Scramble* may be created by the teacher.

Phonics for Grades 1–3 by SRA. The program includes nine levels, and can be used along with any basal. Tape cassettes with a human voice are the audio component. See Figure 4.1a for an example of the computer graphics in the program.

Wordskill for the Microcomputer by SRA. Levels 1–6 correspond to reading levels for grades 7–12. The program includes four games to improve knowledge of synonyms, definitions, antonyms, and analogies. In the game *Know It*, the definition is provided and students type in the correct word from their word list. Figure 4.1b has an example computer frame.

Texas Instruments is one of the largest publishers of educational software. See Figure 4.1c for a listing of the course offerings in word attack skills. Much of their emphasis is on structural analysis.

Figure 4.1a

 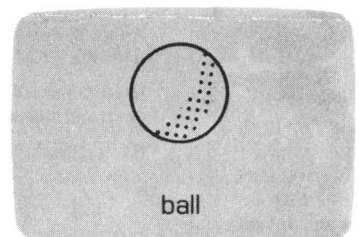

Figure 4.1b

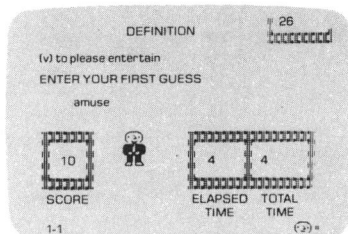

KnowIt Computer displays a definition of an unnamed word. Players must locate the word (in their lists) and type it into the computer. The same word may be defined in multiple meanings and as various parts of speech.

All of the following programs are recommended for classroom use in the guide *Technology in the Curriculum, Language Arts Resource Guide,* California State Department of Education (1986).*

Discrimination of letters, auditorially and visually

Alphabet Circus by D. L. M. K–1. Allows user to practice letter identification, letter matching, and alphabetical order.

(*) To order the guide write to: Publisher Sales, CA State Dept., P. O. Box 271, Sacramento, CA 95802-0271.

Figure 4.1c

Basic Skills 3-8
Reading

Subject	Program Packages	Programs	Grades	1	2	3	4	5	6	7	8	9	10	11	12
MAKING NEW WORDS	Basic Word Building	Simple Verb Endings			●	●	●	●							
		Basic Contractions with Pronouns			●	●	●	●							
		Abbreviations			●	●	●	●							
		Easy Compound Words			●	●	●	●							
		Basic Word Building: Review			●	●	●	●							
	More Basic Word Building	More Compound Words			●	●	●	●							
		Verbs Ending in E			●	●	●	●							
		Contractions of Not			●	●	●								
		More Basic Word Building: Review			●	●	●								
	Complex Word Building	Verb Endings After Consonants				●	●	●	●	●					
		Verbs Ending in Y				●	●	●	●	●					
		Word Endings for Comparisons				●	●	●	●						
		Compound Words: New Meanings				●	●	●	●	●					
		More Contractions				●	●	●	●	●					
		Complex Word Building: Review				●	●	●	●	●					
	Prefixes, Suffixes, and Compound Words	Noun Endings -er, -or, -ist, -ian					●	●	●	●	●				
		Suffixes -y, -ly, -less					●	●	●	●	●				
		Special Compound Words					●	●	●	●	●				
		Prefixes That Make Opposites					●	●	●	●	●				
		Prefix, Suffix, and Compound Words: Review					●	●	●	●	●				
	More Prefixes and Suffixes	Noun Suffixes -ness, -ship, -ment, -tion					●	●	●	●	●				
		Suffixes -ous, -al, -ance, -able					●	●	●	●	●				
		Prefixes mis-, pre-, post-					●	●	●	●	●	●			
		Using Prefixes ir-, il-						●	●	●	●	●			
		More Prefixes and Suffixes: Review						●	●	●	●	●			
	Prefixes and Suffixes in Context	Suffixes -ful, -ous, -less						●	●	●	●	●			
		Suffixes -ible, -able						●	●	●	●	●			
		Prefixes That Show Number						●	●	●	●	●			
		Prefixes and Suffixes In Context: Review						●	●	●	●	●			

Program Offerings in Word Attack Skills from Texas Instruments.

Customized Alphabet Drill by Random House. K–1. Students fill in letters in various sequence.

Ernie's Quiz by Apple. K–3. Four games to help students discriminate letters, to use context clues, and to recognize high frequency words.

Letters and Words by Learning Well. K–3. Three individual games with animated graphics to help in discriminating letters, develop a sight vocabulary, and use context clues.

Recognition of high frequency sight words

Kermit's Electronic Storymaker by Simon and Schuster. K–2. Children create animal stories using the muppets as characters. Delightful drills on sight words, also drill on using different kinds of sentence patterns.

Keygame—Word Works by Teacher Support. K–6. Children participate in exciting game activities while practicing locating keys in a timed setting. They learn to recognize high frequency words while acquiring key boarding skills.

Word Memory-Word Works by Teacher Support. 1–3. Uses a game format to improve memory sequencing within a time limit. Includes an authoring system and database for several basal reading series. Good graphics to help in recognizing high frequency words.

Letter sounds

Building Reading Skills by Jostens Learning System. K–3. The program features 2 disks that use graphics and a voice synthesizer to present and review initial consonant letters and sounds. Games for practice and rewards are provided. A third disk presents the short and long vowels.

Word Spinner by Learning Company. K–4. Provides practice in recognizing 3 and 4 letter words with a consonant letter pattern. A computer-based dictionary for 500 3-letter and 1000 4-letter words is included.

Structure

Beamer by Data Command. 4–6. Game format to teach students to recognize prefixes, suffixes, and roots. The computer randomly selects words from a list of over 400. Words reappear until the student correctly identifies the specific word part.

Classifying—Prefixes and Suffixes by Random House. 4–6. Teaches recognition of prefixes and suffixes. Also includes root words and compound words. Students add and change prefixes and suffixes. Game format and graphics for reward.

Micro-Read by American Educational Computer. 3–6. Students learn to recognize root words, compound words. Prefixes and suffixes are added or changed. Six levels of practice also cover other skills. Branching depends on student achievement.

Additional programs to teach word attack skills

Stickybear Reading by Weekly Reader. K–3. Designed to reinforce word recognition and comprehension. Students create sentences by combining nouns, verbs, and objects. The Stickybear then acts out the sentence. Appealing graphics and useful repetition for reinforcement.

Sequencing Dictionary Skills by Random House. 4–6. Students place words in alphabetical order. Incorrect choices generate step-by-step assistance. Creation disk allows teachers to create additional lessons. Good format and ease of use.

Word Pairs by Microcomputer Workshop. 5 and up. Word Pairs offers instruction and practice on homonyms and synonyms by presenting definitions, models, explanations, and appropriate exercises. Users may select either a brief or extensive tutorial and practice.

Word Quest by Sunburst. 1–6. Two games utilize alphabetizing skills. In one, students try to find a word that fits between two given words. In another (competition mode), one student picks a mystery word, and another is challenged to guess what the mystery word is by getting clues as to which words it fits between.

Wizard of Words by Advanced Ideas. 1–6. Five word games reinforce vocabulary and spelling skills. Game characters include a juggler, knight, princess, fire-breathing dragon, and two heralds. Eight different learning levels within each game. A management system reports scores and allows teachers to enter new word lists.

Classroom Programs in Clinics

Mason (1983) describes several new uses of the computer in reading clinics based on school produced materials. While diagnostic tests using microcomputers are still uncommon, a computer program that writes prescriptions (but does not diagnose), has been developed by the Buckingham, Virginia County Schools. Materials prescribed are those entered by the teacher who will use the prescription.*

A second type of program is used for those readers who have difficulty in seeing small differences between words. They copy a program listing from a printout, then run their copy to see if it works. The computer cannot guess what is meant when letters are substituted, omitted, or reversed, and any error prevents the program printout. The student must then find the errors (program debugging) which requires careful proofreading and usually some recopying. Teachers report high student motivation when errors are found and corrected, and programs finally run as they should.

Evaluating Microcomputer Software for Reading Instruction

Devall (1983) and Blanchard (1985) offer the following guidelines when considering the selection of reading software for the classroom:

Overall
1. Does the program do something that a workbook or whole class instruction can't do as well, better, or cheaper?
2. Is it clear for whom this software is designed?
3. Are goals clear? Learner outcomes stated?

Program Specifics
1. Can students use it without prior computer training?
2. Must the student always begin the program at the beginning. Is it possible to begin in the middle?
3. Are correct answers confirmed? Incorrect remediated?
4. Are positive responses rewarded with more interesting graphic displays than incorrect answers?
5. Can the teacher intervene?
6. Are pre- and posttests available?

Teacher Resources
1. Is a teacher's guide provided?
2. Are there support materials, and are they clearly written?
3. What type of evaluations has been done or is the program experimental?

Mechanics of Use
1. If the hardware is already in place, is the software compatible?
2. If the program is purged accidentally, will replacement be available free or at reduced cost?
3. Has experience shown the dealer to be prompt and reliable and willing to provide service when required?

---

*Disseminated by the National Diffusion Network. Descriptive brochures are available from Debra Glowinski, CADPP, P. O. Box 292, Dillwyn, Va. 23936.

Research Needed to Answer Questions about the Efficacy of Computer Use

There still remains a paucity of research on using the microcomputer to aid reading instruction. Answers to the following questions are still needed (Devall, 1983, p. 553).

1. What types of students will benefit most from using micros?
2. How much time on task is useful?
3. What types of activities help students most: tutorial, drill and practice, simulation, games, or some combination of these?
4. What skills can best be taught using a microcomputer?
5. What size print is best suited at particular levels?

Summary

Part 4 has discussed the role of the computer in the classroom.

1. The advantages and disadvantages.
2. Recommended software programs.
3. Guidelines in using the computer and in purchasing software.

The role of the computer in the reading classroom has expanded. While this expansion poses many advantages, certain disadvantages require a careful monitoring. Many of the software reading programs are in the area of word attack skills. Classroom computer reading programs were described, all recommended for classroom use by the guide *Technology in the Classroom*. Guidelines for using the computer were listed and a more extensive list of questions to ask when purchasing software was offered.

PART 4:
FINAL REVIEW

1. List 3 advantages in using the computer in the reading classroom.
2. List 3 disadvantages.
3. What is the predominant kind of reading software?
4. List several guidelines when considering software selection.

PART
5
Other Considerations

SECTION 1

MEETING SPECIAL NEEDS OF STUDENTS

Parents and Reading

In the last few years there has been increasing support for the concept of parent involvement in reading. This can be attributed partly to the voluminous research that shows the important role the preschool years play in building experiences children can relate to as they read. Moreover, the economic climate plus the massive school budget cuts have made "parents as partners in education" more than a catch-all phrase. Not only are they involved in ameliorating reading problems, but there are even parent programs aimed at preventing them. Studies and projects (Newman 1982 and Shuck, Ulsh and Platt 1983) show how supportive home environments can make a substantial difference.

Parent programs involving reading are of several types: In one type parents receive direct instruction in reading skills (Vukelich, 1978), while in others parents simply cooperate by providing extra instruction in the home (Criscuolo, 1974, 1983). Another facet of this involvement is having parents have direct access to school materials provided for them in a special room. These materials may include reading games and learning devices, especially in the decoding skills.

Two interesting projects carried out with parental support follow: In one project, PEP (Parents Encourage Pupils), Shuck, Ulsh and Platt (1983) report on an innercity parent involvement reading project for remedial students from third and fifth grades. Parents were encouraged to tutor their children with individualized homework activities by the teacher and to report back monthly to the school via special calendars. See Figure 5.1 that shows part of a typical calendar used for reporting.

Figure 5.1 PEP Calendar

You can help your children become better readers by listening and helping them to do at least one of the following:

A. Read a book (10 points)
B. Homework (assigned by lab) (10 points)
C. Word list (from lab) (10 points)
D. Games (from lab) (10 points)

After work is completed, circle A, B, C, or D on the calendar to show the work done by your child. As a reward for doing at least one of the above activities, fill in the "Happy Face" with a pen or pencil. Please return this calendar to the lab at the end of the month.

Sunday	Monday	Tuesday	Wednesday	Thursday	Friday	Saturday
			Ⓐ 1 B C D ☺	A 2 B C Ⓓ ☺	A 3 B Ⓒ D ☺	A 4 Ⓑ C D ☺
A 5 B C D ☺	A 6 B Ⓒ Ⓓ ☺	A 7 Ⓑ C Ⓓ ☺	Ⓐ 8 B C Ⓓ ☺	A 9 B Ⓒ D ☺	A 10 Ⓑ C Ⓓ ☺	A 11 B C Ⓓ ☺

Each month the student either saved the accrued points or purchased a prize from the reading lab store from the donated items of parents and local merchants. Points were given as part of the behavior modification program.

In still another experiment involving not only parents but the community as well Sittig (1982) coordinated a project called "Reading in a Rainbow" (because of all the promises a rainbow holds). Here, families, merchants, and even local celebrities and the schools worked together to improve children's reading and to show them that reading is an enjoyable pastime. Parents received packets of ideas for sharing reading activities in the home and a list of recommended books (always the most important). Parents were to complete a minimum of eight activities (of the suggested sixteen) during two weeks. The goal was for children to see that books at home are a natural happy part of everyday life.

The following list for parents suggests some word attack reading activities.

Reading activities to share: parent and child

1. Cut out appropriate comic strips from newspapers after they have been shared with your child. Cut the sections apart. Have the children arrange the pictures in order and "read back" those words remembered.

2. When you take your child shopping with you at the grocery, let younger children find as many compound words in the store as they can (example – cranapple and oatmeal). For older children have them read the nutrition labels on some of the packages to discover what the main ingredients are. They will learn to decode some scientific terminology.

3. When driving, see how many signs your child can read. Teach him/her the signs they cannot recognize.

4. Hold an alphabet night. Let a primary child choose a letter of the alphabet. Together plan a menu with foods all beginning with that letter. The letter *p* might include pasta, pears, and punch. Older children can read the recipes.

5. Read to your child out loud and then let him/her read out loud to you and share feelings about what has been read.

6. Write a letter to your child, telling him/her why you think s/he is so special, using words in his/her reading vocabulary. Have your child write a letter back to you.

7. Make a scrap book with "special words" your child has cut out from magazines and newspapers, more difficult words he or she wants to learn.

8. Build vocabulary by elaborating on your child's sentences. For example, if your child says, "I brought you some flower," respond by adding, "Oh, you brought me these lovely chrysanthemums."

9. With young children read books with strong and "contagious" language such as the Dr. Seuss books and Bill Martin's *Brown Bear Brown Bear*. Hearing these books with a singing quality over and over soon has a child chiming in and reading the words.

10. Show a love of reading by being a reader yourself.

Remember to keep learning varied, fun, and enjoyable.

Additional illustrated suggestions (Cook, 1982) for parents follow:

Seasonal Task Cards. Use a 7" X 9" piece of cardboard. Over it place a sheet of paper. The children write (or say) words that tell of sights, sounds and smells that begin with the letters in the word "winter" or any word you choose.

Letter Laces. Provide colorful seals and small pictures for your child. The child sorts through them looking for specific beginning, medial or ending sounds. Paste these pictures on 2″ X 2″ squares of cardboard and then punch two holes through each card. These squares are then strung on a shoelace with knotted ends.

Vocabulary Strips. Cut a slot in the lid of a potato chips can. Animated strips can be used for vocabulary words, opposites, and word sounds. The child raises the strip out of the slot one word at a time. The strips can be reused if they are covered with clear pressure-sensitive plastic. Children can be active participants in this learning activity.

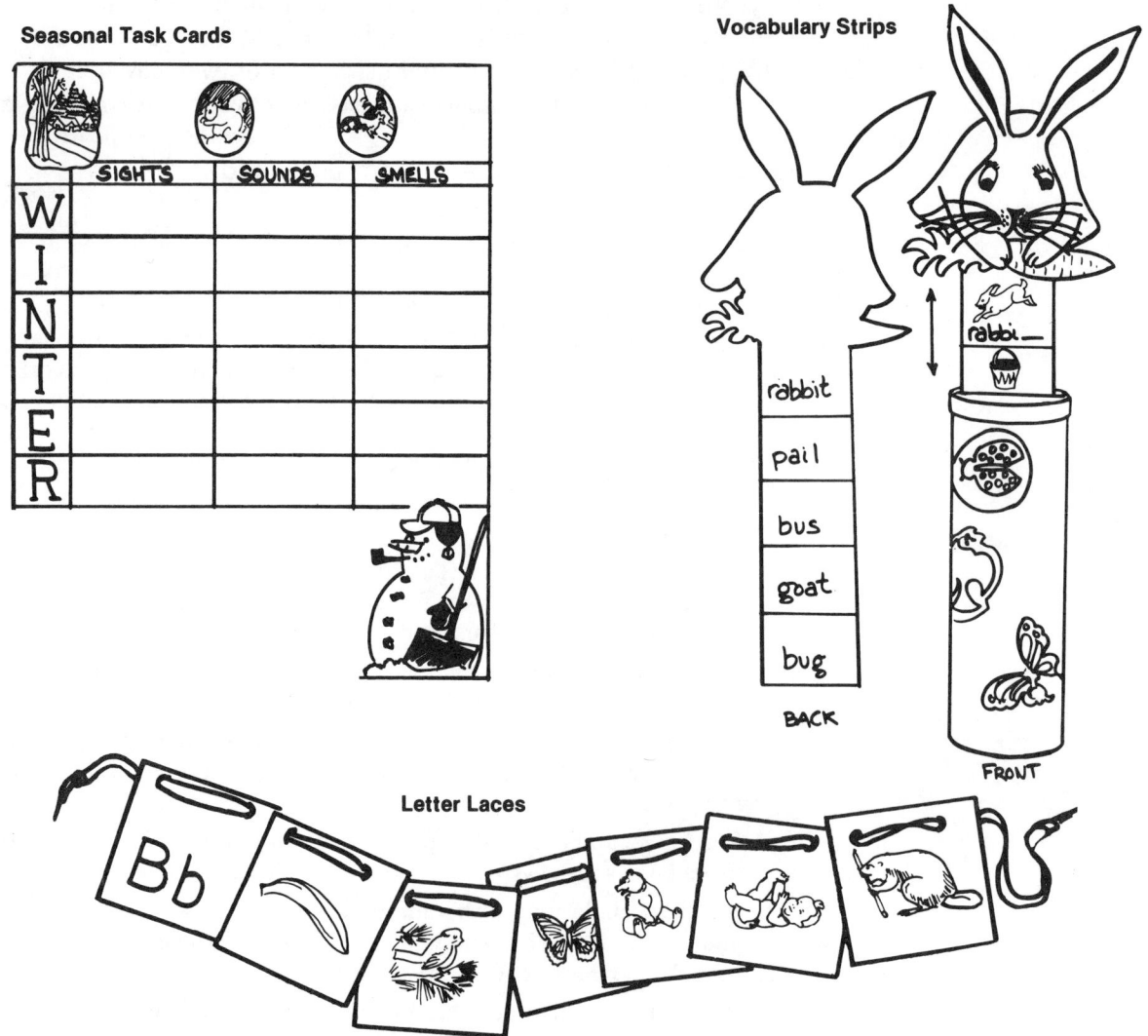

Children Who Speak with a Dialect or Who Use English as a Second Language (ESL)

When teaching word attack skills to children who speak with a dialect, or who speak English as a second language (ESL), additional problems may arise. These could be substantially reduced if some basic underlying differences between Standard English and the student's language were taken into consideration.

Reading scores for these students are usually lower than for speakers of Standard English, giving rise to the false assumption that the dialect (ESL) is the culprit in the reading problem. Research suggests, however, that it is not the dialect (ESL) but rather the cultural attitude toward it that may be at the root of the difficulty. The fact is that nonstandard dialects are neither deficient nor inadequate, but are controlled by rules in their particular linguistic context, just the same as with Standard English.

Each dialect of English is a complete and valid form of communication, differing in minor respects from the entirety of Standard English. The insistence on young children reading and pronouncing words exactly as they are spoken in Standard English may create reading problems where none should exist. It should also be remembered that minority children who speak with a dialect exhibit *some* of the characteristics of their dialect, but rarely exhibit all of them. Also, within dialects there is "regionality," so that within each region additional differences, and even degrees of differences, occur.

Some of the differences between these dialects and Standard English (SE) will be briefly discussed.

The Black Dialect[1]

Phonology

1. Short /ĕ/ and short /ĭ/ do not have the same degree of contrast as in Standard English.

   pin   pen
   tin   ten
   since   cents
   I have tin cints.

2. As a past tense marker, *ed* is often eliminated. (Black speakers, however, do have a past tense that becomes apparent when they use irregular verbs such as *told* and *kept*.)

3. There is a high degree of *r*-lessness and *l*-lessness. The following word groups frequently sound similar.

   toe   tore   toll
   too   tool
   foe   four

4. Final consonant clusters are frequently shortened, with the final consonant eliminated.

Cluster	st	ft	nt	nd	ld	zd	md
Standard	past	left	bent	bend	hold	raised	aimed
Dialect	pas	lef	ben	ben	hol	rais	aim

   The following three words would sound similar:
   men   meant   mend

5. Three letter consonant clusters such as *str* and *scr* are sometimes difficult to pronounce:

   stream   scream
   strap   scrap

6. Final *th* is often pronounced like an /f/, sometimes as /d/:

   Ruth   roof
   death   deaf
   with   wid

---

(1) Much of the material for this section is excerpted from Walt Wolfram and Ralph W. Fasold, *The Study of Social Dialects in American English* (Englewood Cliffs, N.J.: Prentice Hall, 1974). See also Wm. Labor, "Objectivity & Commitment in Linguistic Science. The case of the Black English Trial in Ann Arbor." *Language in Society* 11 (August 1982) pp. 165-201.

7. Diphthongs such as /oi/ and /ou/ are often shortened:
   boil might be pronounced as /ball/
   pour might be pronounced as /por/
8. Accent and Voice Pitch
   a. Particular words receive a different accent pattern.
      pó lice for policé
      Jú ly for Julý
   b. Wider pitch (at times a far higher pitch than normal) and a more rising level in the final speech contour.

Grammar

1. Third person singular (present tense) is eliminated.
   He see me.
2. Possessive is indicated by word placement, not the traditional /s/ sound.
   You book.   John cousin.
3. There is not always verb agreement.
   They was going.
4. The verb *be* is not always necessary and does not always convey the same meaning as in Standard English.
   I going.   He a bad boy.
   He be working means that the action is habitual. *He working* conveys that the person is working now.
5. Double negatives are common.
   I don't get none.
6. Constructions with *here are* and *it is* do not follow standard rules.
   The following type of sentence is typical.
   It is a whole lot of people.
7. Irregular verbs are often regularized.
   We throwed a party.
8. Past tense and past participle forms are often reversed.
   went for gone
   broke for broken
   seen for saw
   taken for took
9. Differing Sentence Syntax.
   The lady, she went home. (double subject)
   What you mean by that? (do eliminated)

Interestingly, many language forms that we insist on as Standard English are actually the result of historical incidence. For example, one of the reasons we do not use the double negative today (it was used extensively by English speakers in the past) is because 18th century mathematicians said that since two negatives make a positive in math, the same must hold true for language! (Double negatives are still common among dialect speakers today.)

Another interesting feature in Black dialect as outlined under "Grammar Differences" is the lack of final *s* with third person singular verbs. This is an irregular feature of Standard English. Example: I sing, you sing, he/she/it sing*s*, we sing, you sing (plural), they sing. The Black dialect simply regularizes this irregular feature of English. It might be well to comment at this time that attitudes toward pronunciation differences are not as negative as they are toward grammar differences.

A third factor to consider with dialect, vocabulary differences, are not included here due to space limitations.

Spanish-Speaking Children for Whom English Is a Second Language

In a study of Mexican-American childrens' reading preferences, Peterson (1982) concluded that their interests differed little from that of other American children. It is, however, the language interference and cultural differences that sometimes cause reading problems for Spanish-speaking children. Moreover, the tune or intonational pattern of Spanish is quite different. For example, directions in English by the teacher can often sound as a scolding to the Spanish-speaking child, probably because Spanish is a "soft" language compared to English. When Spanish is used, speakers generally stand much closer. Because of this, Spanish children are often puzzled when their English-speaking teachers back away from them.

The checklist[2] in Table 5.1 may be used by teachers of Spanish-speaking children to individually evaluate the student's oral language. It shows areas of difference with Standard English that may interfere with learning to read. Note again many similarities to the problems of other minority children.

Table 5.1

ORAL LANGUAGE RATING — SPANISH INTERFERENCE	5	4	3	2	1	0
School .... Date .... Name .... Grade ..... Teacher						
Pronunciation (Sounds): Distinguishes between vowel sounds such as *sheep-ship, cut-cat, cut-cot, pool-pull*, and between consonant sounds as *sink-zinc, vote-boat, sink-think, yellow-jello, cheap-jeep*.						
Pronunciation (Clusters): Pronounces initial consonant clusters as in *school, speak, study*, and final consonant cluster as in *land, fast, old, box, act, desk, pulled, touched*.						
Pronunciation (Suprasegmentals): Pronounces sentences with appropriate rhythm, stress, pause, and pitch.						
Pronouns: Uses appropriate pronoun forms in subject position (*I, he, she*, etc.) in object position (*me, him, her*, etc.) and possessives (*my, mine; her, hers;* etc.)						
Negatives: Uses *not* to express the negative after the forms of *be* (*Bill is not here.*) and between auxiliary and verb in other sequences (*Bill was not talking. Bill did not talk.*). Uses singular rather than double negative.						
Noun Modifier: Uses adjectives appropriately, as in *the big dog* as opposed to *the dog big* and *Is the dog big?* as opposed to *Is big the dog?*						
Comparison: Uses the correct form of comparison such as *bigger, biggest, more beautiful, most beautiful*, rather than *more bigger, beautifuller*.						
Present Tense: Uses the appropriate present forms of regular verbs, with subject-verb agreement when *he* or *she* is used as subject, as in *He walks*, rather than *He walk*.						
Plurals: Distinguishes between singular and plural in regular forms such as *dog-dogs, boot-boots, horse-horses*, and in irregular forms such as *foot-feet, knife-knives*.						
Past and Perfect Tenses: Uses the past forms of regular verbs as in *walk-walked, glue-glued, land-landed*, and of irregular verbs as in *go-went-gone, dig-dug, cut-cut*.						
Uses of Be: Uses appropriate forms of *be* as an auxiliary and as a verb.						
Uses of Do: Uses appropriate forms of *do* in questions, answers, and in negative statements.						
Future Tense: Uses the appropriate future forms of regular verbs as in *run-will run*. **Possessive:** Uses appropriate possessive forms as in *John's wagon*.						

SOURCE: *Michigan Oral Language Series* (New York: ACTFL, 1970).

(2) Available from the American Council on the Teaching of Foreign Languages (ACTFL), 62 5th Avenue, New York 10011.

In summarizing the language differences of the dialect/ESL student, Table 5.2 may serve as a guide for the teacher.

Table 5.2 Summary Chart of Major Areas of Differences Between Standard English and Dialect-Speaking/ESL Students

Phonology
1. Consonant clusters are sometimes modified or eliminated.
2. Third person singular and past tense forms are frequently eliminated.
3. /th/ often has the sound of /d/ or /f/.
4. /r/ modifies and changes the vowel; /r/ is often eliminated.
5. Vowel sounds are modified and sometimes do not show contrasts.
6. Diphthongs often eliminate the glide.

Grammar Differences
1. Verb and subject agreement are frequently lacking.
2. The verb *be* is used differently.
3. Irregular verb forms are frequently regularized.
4. Past tense and past participle forms are sometimes reversed.
5. *Do* and *don't* forms are inserted or used differently than in Standard English.
6. Multiple negation is common.
7. Possessives take different forms.
8. The expletives *there are/were* and *it is* are used differently.
9. Syntax is sometimes changed.

Teaching the Dialect Speaker

Past and present proposed teaching methods

Over the past decade many educators have presented their views on teaching reading to the dialect/ESL speaker. These include:

1. teaching Standard English first.
2. using dialect readers, and then gradually introducing Standard English.
3. neutralizing the dialect differences in early books so there is minimum interference between book language and students' dialect.
4. teaching reading to children totally in their dialect or native language.

While at present the issue is far from settled, few educators today would opt for any of the above methods. Instead, the present position is that standard materials may be used quite successfully, provided the teacher understands and appreciates dialect differences, and does not overcorrect when the dialect initially differs. This *does* not imply that teachers should not use, describe, and teach Standard English when such instruction would be most beneficial to the students.

Coping with a complex linguistic environment is a serious problem for the young dialect speaker who is beginning to learn to read. The situation can only be exacerbated by a teacher's unrealistic expectation of what is appropriate English. We will look at the actual transcripts of two students, one Black and the other Spanish, to draw some conclusions about teaching reading to the minority student.

Reading transcripts, their implication

The words in the boxes are actual reading errors while the words appearing above the text words are dialect renderings of the text (Masland, 1979).

John's Oral Reading

           go   sto   wiv
"I think he goes to the store with his

| friend | can he

mother. Ask her if he can stay home

| today | | he | con

this time. Then we can get the club-

    | starried | firs | maybe |

house started first thing Monday."

Transcript of reading by a third grader who speaks a Black dialect.

Carmen's Oral Reading

  theenk   go   duh   wid heez
"I think he goes to the store with his

| friend | eef

mother. Ask her if he can stay home

| today | | he | con ged duh

this time. Then we can get the club-

houz | stored | theeng | maybe |

house started first thing Monday."

Transcript of reading by a third grader who is bilingual.

The classroom teacher who is unaware of the influence of dialect in the reading process might conclude that all of these miscued words are errors, and do some unnecessary drilling on known words. When changes in the text are due to dialect, the teacher would do well not to demand Standard English pronunciation from the young reader, as there is little research evidence that comprehension is adversely affected by dialect (Goodman and Buck, 1973).

Constant overcorrection on the part of the teacher places the child in a quandary as s/he knows the word and reads the word, and yet is told that it is incorrect. For example, leaving off the *ed* of *jump* in the sentence, *He jump yesterday* is correct in the language of the dialect speaker, and perfectly understood; because in the sentence the word *yesterday* indicates past time. In their dialect/language, the *ed* inflectional ending is superfluous and unnecessary.

Moreover, when children's speech is constantly corrected, they usually refrain from active participation in oral and written activities of the reading program. Because it is here that their speech patterns receive the most criticism, they perceive reading as a hostile experience, turning away from the threat it represents.

In the reading situation, what should teachers do, when they understand the dialect system and appreciate the difficulties with which these young children must learn to cope as beginning readers?

1. During early reading activities the teacher accepts and values the oral and written language of children who are bilingual or speak with a dialect — s/he is selective in the nature of correcting errors.
2. Words or word parts to be learned are first presented orally and in meaningful context, related to actions and objects in real-life situations.
3. While the child reads orally, the teacher does not try to teach Standard English. The concern is whether or not the student comprehends the text!
4. The teacher refrains from insisting children read the standard form if such a feature is *lacking in the child's oral speech,* as this indicates s/he has not internalized this Standard English rule. It would be as if we who use Standard forms were ordered to read and translate them into nonstandard ones. (Try it, and you will see how difficult it would be.)
5. The teacher helps the class as a whole appreciate the wide variance in the way English is used, and that each form is a viable mode of communication.

Reading tests and the dialect/ESL speaker

Reading tests in word attack often penalize dialect/ESL speakers because their "sounding out" ability to discriminate between words such as *sole* and *sold*, and *walk* and *walked* are not the same as the SE speaker. When these words are in the context of a phrase or sentence, they do not cause the same difficulty; differentiation for dialect speakers is easier. When dialect-related items are removed from standardized tests, an entire grade difference in achievement is often noticed in the scores.

Learning standardized forms

Parents of most minority children want schools to teach their children Standard/ English, but there are several problems.

1. No one knows the most propitious time to engage in such teaching, nor how best to do it! Walter Loban, the noted linguist who has done many comprehensive studies on the language of minority children, concluded that prior to the age of eleven, it would be difficult for them to understand the importance of learning the standard form.
2. Studies by sociolinguists Wolfram and Fasold (1974) conclude that language or dialect learning is a unique kind of learning, depending heavily on the *psychological factor of group reference*. This means that the students must *want* to be part of the group using that language or dialect. While some nonstandard English speakers have such a positive attitude toward the Standard English-speaking community, others do not; and at present there does not seem to be any easy way for the classroom to provide that motivation.

Methods of teaching

When this group reference factor is present, the nonstandard speaker would probably learn Standard English, *provided there is interaction of language between him/her and standard speakers,* with or without formal teaching. In order, however, to accelerate the rate of learning, or motivate students to want to learn SE, some well-designed programs have been developed.

One of the best programs for learning SE by dialect speakers was developed by Irwin Feigenbaum (1970). His program uses quick drill techniques, with sentences of interest to the students. There is a sequential progression to the drills, each activity more difficult than the last, with final drills including the student's use of free expression, approaching conversational SE. The sequence includes: (1) presentation of the difference between the dialect and SE, (2) discrimination of the difference, (3) identification of the difference, (4) translation into SE or the dialect form, and (5) responses to the questions asked, in the same (SE or dialect) form as the questions.

For example, drills of the 4th sequential step would be as follows:

Teacher Stimulus	**Student Response**
He work hard.	He works hard.
He works hard.	He work hard.
Paula likes leather coats.	Paula like leather coats.
She prefer movies.	She prefers movies.

The Asian student

The large recent influx of Asian students, particularly the Vietnamese, also necessitates some consideration. In spite of an excellent attitude towards school, learning the English phoneme system can be quite difficult for the Vietnamese. Additionally, there are three dialects spoken in Vietnam: the Northern, Central, and Southern dialects. Fortunately, there is uniformity in the written language as the Vietnamese writing system derives from the Roman alphabet, adopted after World War I.

Based on the difference of the two sound systems, the following may be problems for native Vietnamese speakers:

1. These sounds, which exist in English but not Vietnamese, are difficult for any speakers of any dialect of Vietnamese.

    /ĭ/ as in s<u>i</u>t   /o͝o/ as in b<u>oo</u>k   /ă/ as in c<u>a</u>t   /t̶h̶/ as in <u>th</u>en

    /th/ as in <u>th</u>ank   /ch/ as in <u>ch</u>urch   /j/ as in bri<u>dge</u>   /r/ as in <u>r</u>ed

2. For speakers of certain dialects the following sounds are difficult because they do not occur in their dialects:

    /sh/ as in <u>sh</u>oes   /zh/ as in plea<u>s</u>ure   /l/ as in <u>l</u>ate

3. There is difficulty in hearing the contrast between sounds as /ē/ in s<u>ea</u>t and /ĭ/ in s<u>i</u>t; /o͞o/ in f<u>oo</u>l and /ŭ/ in f<u>u</u>ll; /ĕ/ in b<u>e</u>d and /ă/ in b<u>a</u>d; /sh/ in <u>sh</u>oes and /ch/ in <u>ch</u>oose. The Vietnamese hears these sounds as similar. On the production of these sounds, they cannot produce them accurately since there is only one sound for each pair in their language.

4. Sounds that occur in both English and Vietnamese but have different articulations also constitute problems. Usually the students will assume they have the same sounds in both languages when they do not. Examples are voiceless stops as p/t/k/.

5. Final position of nasals /m/n/ and also the /l/ sound are pronounced differently in Vietnamese. Also different are the voiced and voiceless consonants in Vietnamese. /k/ in dock or /g/ in dog are the same, Vietnamese pronouncing both of them as voiceless.

6. Clusters of consonants are particularly difficult, especially when they occur in the final position. When the final clusters contain voiced consonants, the difficulty becomes insurmountable. They drop the excess consonant, pronouncing only one sound. A word like *minds* will be pronounced as if it had one consonant, *min*.*

With all the complexities of dialect/ESL, it is impossible for a text of this nature to deal adequately with this problem. The author refers those who have special needs in this area to contact the Center for Applied Linguistics in Washington, D.C.

Summary

Parents are being asked to play a more active role in the school's reading program. Suggestions were given for some of the activities parents may employ with their children. For those children who speak with a dialect and children for whom English is a second language, there has consistently been difficulty in learning to read. Proposals in the past that would alter the reading texts for them have been discarded in favor of an approach that places standard materials in the hands of a knowledgeable teacher.

Differences between SE and the dialect/ESL students' English were contrasted. While these differences are small, considering the totality of the English lexicon (1,000,000 words), they can cause reading problems unless teachers differentiate between what is an error and what is dialect interference.

Reading tests in word attack skills penalize the dialect speaker unless words are spoken in context. This is important to remember in teaching — to place words pronounced similarly (as *toe*, *tore*, and *tool* in the Black Dialect) in a phrase or sentence.

No one knows at what age dialect/ESL speakers should be "taught" SE; and there is even some doubt as to whether it can be done, unless the minority student wants to be part of the group who uses SE, the present prestige dialect. Today there are a few programs that may be instituted to help accelerate the changeover to SE, but there remains some question of their efficacy.

The Asian student's needs must also be considered in teaching word attack skills. Differences between their phoneme system and English were described.

PART 5: FINAL REVIEW

1. Why is parental involvement important in the school reading program?
2. What major phonological and grammatical differences occur between dialect/ESL speakers and SE speakers?
3. What five principles must teachers be aware of when teaching the young dialect/ESL speaker?
4. When is the best time to try to teach SE to the dialect/ESL speaker?
5. Do the Vietnamese have the same writing system as English?

---

* For more detailed information see *Assessment of Vietnamese Speaking for Limited English Proficient Students with Special Needs,* To Thi Dien, Huynh Dinh Te and Thi Dang Wei. The CA State Dept. of Ed., Personnel Development Unit, May 1986.

PART
6
Appendixes

APPENDIX A Answers To Quick Self-Check

I. p. 7
1. a. *a, o, u*
    b. *e, i, y*
    c. The *c* generalization works most of the time; the *g* generalization works some of the time.
2. *S* can encode the sounds of /s/, /z/, and /sh/.

II. p. 9
1. a. *r, l, s,* and *tw*
    b. With *r* and *l* blends the *r* and *l* letter/sounds are second.
    c. With *s* the letter/sounds are first. Also the *s* blends may contain three letters.
2. a. *ld, nd, nt, nk,* and *lk*
    b. as phonograms.

III. p. 12
a. *ch* /ch/, /k/, /sh/
    gh, /g/, /f/, /-/
b. *th,* /t̶h̶/, /th/
    wh, /w or hw/, /h/
c. *ph,* /f/
    sh, /sh/

IV. p. 14
1. The first letter of each digraph is silent.
2. They encode one sound.
3. All follow a short vowel.

V. p. 18
1. a. *u,* /o͞o/
    b. *a, o, u.* They are sometimes taught as sight words.
    c. It is similar to the sound of /ŭ/, and is usually heard in unaccented syllables.

VI. p. 20
1. English words do not end in the letter *v* (prove).
2. A final vowel is needed to complete the final syllable; therefore the first vowel remains long (stable).
3. Final *e* gives *c* a soft sound (fence).
4. Final *e* indicates the preceding vowel has a long sound (stake).
5. Final *e* is an historical leftover (else).

VII. p. 21
1. English words do not end with *i. Ai* and *ay* encode a long /ā/ sound.
2. English words do not end with *u. Au* and *aw* encode the /ä/ sound.
3. The sounds encoded by these graphemes do not vary.

APPENDIX A ANSWERS TO QUICK SELF-CHECK **151**

VIII. **p. 24**
1. *ee*
2. *ei*
3. *ea*
4. *ey*
5. *ie*

IX. **p. 29**
1. *ou* /ow/ as in proud, /ŭ/ as in touch, /ō/ as in soul, /o͞o/ as in group
2. English words do not end with *i*.
3. *oa*, /ō/
4. /ow/ as in cow, /ō/ as in know
5. /o͞o/ as in moon, /o͝o/ as in book

X. **p. 30**
1. /o͞o/
2. t*o*, r*u*de, m*oo*n, gr*ou*p

XI. **p. 32**
1. At the beginning of words
2. yes — as a consonant
cry — as a vowel
play — as part of a digraph
royal — as part of a diphthong

XII. **p. 36**
1. All have the same sound
2. When the letter *w* precedes *or*, the *or* likewise encodes the /er/ sound.
3. It has a variety of sounds.
4. *Ai* and *ee*. /Âr/ as in pair and /ē-r/ as in peer

XIII. **p. 75**
1. did ✓   pepper
from ✓   for ✓
dragon   matching
about ✓   once ✓
2. Dolch
3. Each word is very carefully introduced followed by lots of review and practice.
4. Through wide and varied reading.
5. Drill with phrase cards, sentence cards, or matching exercises, pointing out pertinent details, creative graphics, configuration; comparing and contrasting words; games.

XIV. **p. 77**
1. Sometimes a compound word has the combined meaning of the two root words, but sometimes it does not.
2. Starwars, lunar module, cranapple
3. See pages 76–77.

XV. p. 94

1. Prefixes are usually found before a base word or root; suffixes are placed after. Prefixes usually change the word meaning but not the part of speech. Derivational suffixes may alter both.

2.
Absorbed	*Active*
recent	prepay
insist	uncertain
	dislike
	impersonal

3.
Inflectional	*Derivational*
singing	foolish
jumps	cleverness
called	safely

4. a. Drop final *e* when adding an ending that begins with a vowel.
   b. Double the final consonant when adding a suffix that begins with a vowel if the word
      1) ends in a single consonant.
      2) is preceded by a short vowel.
      3) is a one syllable word.
   c. Do not drop the letter *y* when adding *ing*.

5. Through wide and varied reading and through classroom discussions that clarify affixed words

6. No, it creates confusion as there is a lack of relationship.

7. See pages 89–92.

XVI. p. 98

1. An open syllable ends in a vowel, often long; a closed syllable ends in a consonant and the preceding vowel is often short.

2. Check to see if the word is compound, has affixes, double consonants, or two unlike consonants, or a final *le*. Do not divide blends or digraphs.

3. Syllables are clapped; words may be written in syllables, pronounced in syllables, and then blended together.

4. Some medial vowel sounds in words are no longer pronounced.

5. Our written language relates to a more 'formal' English code.

XVII. p. 104

1. Semantic and syntactic clues

2. Explanation, experience, series, restatement, contrast, inference

3. See pages 99–100.

4. Words are omitted (5th, 8th, 10th) that students supply. The group or class discussion focuses on the appropriateness of choices suggested. Sometimes clues are furnished to students.

XVIII. p. 109

1. Alphabetizing skills, understanding guide words, ability to use pronunciation key, understanding phonics respelling, and ability to select proper definition

2. Through use!

3. See pages 104–109.

Answers to Part 1, Section I: Review and Self-Check, p. 15

1. *c, g,* and *s; c, g;* and *a, o,* and *u* condition these letters to have the hard /k/ sound. *I* and *e* condition *c* and *g* to have the soft sound. Word examples are *cat, cot, cut* (hard *c*). *Cigar, cement, cycle* (soft *c*). *Game, gone gull* (hard *g*). *Germ, giant, gym* (soft *g*). The *c* generalization works most of the time. The *g* generalization works about 75 percent of the time.

2. gra*ph, ch*aise, *gh*astly, *th*ink, air*sh*ip, *wh*ile

ch	(3)	*ch*air, s*ch*eme, *ch*andelier
gh	(3)	*gh*ost, rou*gh*, throu*gh*
ph	(1)	*ph*one
sh	(1)	*sh*elf
th	(2)	*th*ick, *th*em
wh	(2)	*wh*at, *wh*o

3. | gn | /n/ | *gn*ome |
    |----|-----|------|
    | kn | /n/ | *kn*ow |
    | wr | /r/ | *wr*ist |
    | ck | /k/ | de*ck* |

4. | /k/ | de*ck* |
    |-----|------|
    | /j/ | bri*dge* |
    | /ch/ | sti*tch* |

    They all follow a short vowel.

Answers to Part 1, Section II: Review and Self-Check, p. 30

1. ă act
   ĕ elephant
   ĭ it
   ŏ olive
   ŭ upon

2. Similar to short *u* as in *u*p. Language is changing: *a*bout, tick*e*t, penc*i*l, sec*o*nd.

3. *a* encodes /ä/ as in father.
   o encodes /o͞o/ as in pr*o*ve.
   u encodes /o͝o/ as in p*u*sh.

4. *u*. Language change. /yū/ and /o͞o/.

/yū/	/o͞o/
c*u*be	d*u*ty
m*u*sic	l*u*te

5. *ai* and *ay*. English words do not end in *i*.

ai	**ay**
m*ai*d	tr*ay*
r*ai*l	spr*ay*

6. *au* and *aw*. English words do not end in *u*.

au	**aw**
v*au*lt	dr*aw*
*au*tumn	s*aw*

7. long /ē/.

    ee as in /ē/
    sl*ee*p
    j*ee*p

8. long /ē/, short /ĕ/, and long /ā/. Long /ē/ is most common.

ea as /ē/	ea as /ĕ/	ea as /ā/
br*ea*the	h*ea*d	br*ea*k
r*ea*p	spr*ea*d	st*ea*k

9. long /ē/ and long /ī/.

ie as /ē/	ie as /ī/
bel*ie*f	d*ie*
n*ie*ce	tr*ie*s

10. Decodes /ē/ after *c*. Sometimes as /ā/. Also as ĕ/ and /ĭ/.
11. as /ē/ and as /ā/

ey as /ē/	ey as /ā/
k*ey*	th*ey*
donk*ey*	pr*ey*

12. *igh*, s*igh*t, r*igh*t
13. Vowel digraphs have two letters with one sound. Vowel diphthongs have two vowel letters with a gliding sound between them.
    oa as /ō/, r*oa*d
    oo as /ōō/ and /ŏŏ/, m*oo*n and l*oo*k
    ou as /ow/, /ŭ/ /ō/ and /ōō/, ar*ou*nd, t*ou*ch, sh*ou*lder, gr*ou*p
    ow as /ow/ and /ō/, cr*ow*d and l*ow*
14. /ōō/, fr*u*it, bl*ue*, and st*ew*.
15. as in gr*ou*p, m*oo*n, pr*o*ve, r*u*de, t*o*, s*ui*t, fl*ew*, tr*ue*.

Answers to Part 1, Section III, IV, and V: Review and Self-Check, p. 38

1.
Consonant	Vowel	Digraph	Diphthong
yam	gym	play	employ
yellow	cycle	key	royal
	cry	they	

2. All encode the sound of /er/.
   When *w* precedes *or*, it also has the /er/ sound.
3. They are *ea, ai,* and *ee*. When *r* follows *ea*, the sound may be as in *ea*rth /er/; p*ea*r /âr/; or f*ea*r /ē-r/. When *r* follows *ai* the sound is as in the word *air*. When *r* follows *ee*, the sound is as in the word *peer*.
4. The sounds have changed but the spelling still reflects the sound formerly used: *ch* as in *ch*andelier and *sh* as in *sh*ine.

Answers to Part 1, Sections VI and VII: Review and Self-Check, p. 64

1. Discrimination abilities with letters and sound; maturity; social responsibility; family background; language proficiency; motivation to read.
2. To identify whether children understand the meaning of word, sentence, begins and ends with, letter, line, top and bottom.
3. a. Students identify the capitals and small letters that encode a particular sound.
   b. Students select words containing the specific sound from words containing related sounds and suggest words with the specific sound.

c. Students write the capital and lower case letters that represent the specific sound.
d. Students participate in purposeful activities applying the knowledge of the relationship between the letter and sound.

4. a. 4
   b. 1) No sounds are isolated.
      2) Individual phonemes are pronounced and then blended together.
      3) The vowel is pronounced first, followed by the first consonant sound, then the final sound.
      4) The ending phonogram is pronounced first, then the beginning consonant sound.
   c. The one that works best with particular students!

5. a. In general, with synthetic phonics, teachers tell the sound-symbol relationships and have students memorize certain rules. With analytic phonics, students conclude what the sound-symbol relationship is after studying certain known sight words. Linguistic phonics is simply a patterned approach.
   b. The terms have not been standardized, with people claiming synthetic phonics is code-emphasis and analytic phonics is meaning-emphasis. Both can be concerned with meaning, so some of the criticisms do not appear to be supported. "Linguistics" reading is thought of by some as being language experience.

6. See pages 53–60.

7. There are dittos, workbooks, software, and hardware, and even a computer. The problem is that teachers sometimes engage in these activities to the exclusion of real reading.

8. Students develop an extensive sight vocabulary so they can engage in fluent reading.

9. A generalization is a starting point. Emphasize that they must remain flexible when decoding, and look for additional clues.

10. Students are pretested on a series of skills, taught those in which they are deficient, and retested after each skill has been taught for a period of time, to see if the skill can be applied. There are several commercial programs on the market.

Answers to Part 1, Final Phonics Review

Words with Consonant Digraphs	Words with Blends	Words with Vowel Digraphs	Words with Vowel Diphthongs	Vowels With R-Conditioning
scheme	world	receive	destroy	world
coaching	bridge	treat	now	hair
back	treat	afraid	about	earn
breath	afraid	coaching	toil	fewer
*edge	destroy	flight	spoon	surprise
chaise	flight	breath	fewer	
athlete	surprise	coast		
*stitch	streamlined	chaise		
physics	breath	streamlined		
	stitch			
	spoon			

*Some would not call it a digraph, but a special consonant combination.

Answers to Part 2, Final Review

1. Sight words occur frequently with percentages cited that range from 50 to 60 percent of running words. Students must know these words at sight in order to read with any degree of proficiency.

2. The goal in reading is for students to eventually acquire a large enough storehouse of words so that most all the words s/he comes across are in his/her sight vocabulary.

3. See pages 66–70.

4. Sometimes but not always. Meanings of words originally 'coined' frequently change.

5. Active prefixes are in the initial position, joined to base words, and alter meaning. Absorbed prefixes are part of the word.

Active	*Absorbed*
unsure	contain
submarine	preclude
preview	exceed

6.
Inflectional	*Derivational*
jumping	courageous
smallest	attention
women's	merriment
draws	

    There are only a few inflectional suffixes, and they are taught in early reading. They do not usually change the part of speech. There are many, many derivational suffixes, and they often alter the part of speech, and sometimes even change the meaning.

    Inflectional affixes are much simpler to learn. Derivational affixes are more difficult, frequently changing the part of speech of the root word. Also, there are many more derivational affixes.

7. a. When adding a suffix that begins with a vowel, final *e* is usually dropped.
   b. When a word has one syllable, one short vowel, and one final consonant, double the final consonant before adding the syllable that begins with a vowel.
   c. When a consonant precedes *y*, change *y* to *i* and add the suffix.
   d. Final *y* is not dropped when adding *ing*.

8. Through wide and varied reading, and through classroom discussion.

9. Check to see if the word is (1) a compound word or has affixes, (2) has double consonant letters or two unlike consonants, (3) or a final *le*. (4) Do not divide blends or digraphs.

10. Car*a*mel, int*e*rest, mem*o*ry (see page 98 for other examples.)

11. Syntactic and semantic
    Through examining books to see how authors supply context clues
    Through specific exercises
    Through cloze technique

12. Alphabetizing skills
    Understanding guide words
    Ability to use the pronunciation key
    Understanding phonic/respelling
    Ability to select the proper definition
    These skills are best learned through use!

Answers to Part 3, Final Review

1. (a) Try the context first.
   (b) Look at the structure for compound words, roots and affixes.
   (c) Check for syllable clues.
   (d) Check for phonics clues.
   (e) Check dictionary.
2. Teacher shows student a word card and tells her/him the best way to decode it. She offers sentences with the word. So do the students. Students write and say the word and check it against the word card. Teacher shows second word card, one with the target word, the other with a word that differs in one or two letters. Student tells what is the same and what is different about the words. Daily timed practice is required.
3. (a) They need to read a little slower.
   (b) They only note the outer configuration of words.
   (c) They use whole word processing.
4. Use "smiling" faces. Use yes/no questions. Use a chart form.
5. (a) The Imitative Method (Student listens to a cassette tape of a story, following along in a book, until mastery is complete.)
   (b) Impress Method (Teacher and student read together, the teacher allowing the student to take the lead when comfortable.)
   (c) Repeated Readings (Student reads a selection of about 100 words several times, improving rate and giving the student the feeling of fluency for the first time.)
6. Students use their hands to form an "image" of the word.

Answers to Part 4, Final Review

1. (a) Immediate feedback.
   (b) Actively engaged.
   (c) Pleasurable.
2. (a) cost
   (b) teacher training
   (c) overemphasis on drill
3. For word attack skills.
4. (a) Does the program do something other less expensive programs cannot do?
   (b) Are program goals clear?
   (c) Do students need prior training?
   (d) Has the program been evaluated?
   (e) Are correct answers confirmed?
   (f) Is there a management system?

Answers to Part 5, Final Review

1. (a) Research shows parents can make a significant difference.
   (b) School budget cuts.
   (c) Importance of pre-school years.

2. (a) Consonant clusters are sometimes modified or eliminated.
    Third person singular and past tense forms are frequently eliminated.
    /th/ often has the sound of /f/ or /d/.
    /r/ is often eliminated or modified.
    Vowel sounds are modified and sometimes do not show contrasts.
    Diphthongs often eliminate the glide or modify it.
   (b) Verb and subject agreement are frequently lacking.
    The verb *be* is used differently.
    Irregular verb forms are frequently regularized.
    Past tense and past participial forms are sometimes reversed.
    Do and *don't* forms are inserted or used differently.
    Multiple negation is common.
    Possessives take different forms.
    The expletives *there are/were* and *it is* are used differently.
    Syntax is sometimes changed.
3. Value the oral and written language of the child.
   Present words/word parts orally in meaningful context, related to actions and objects in real-life situations.
   Concentrate on the child's comprehension of the text.
   Teach grammar patterns after the child has oral mastery of the pattern.
   Build an appreciation in the classroom for language variation.
4. The student wants to be part of the group that uses SE.
5. Yes.

APPENDIX B

Record Form for Informal Assessment of Code Consciousness

Name: _____ Assessment dates: #1 _____ #2 _____ #3 _____ #4 _____

                                                                                      Always   Usually   Seldom

1. Identifies boundaries of written words.
2. Matches words.
3. Matches sentences.
4. Builds a word from a model.
5. Supplies a spoken word which begins with the same phoneme as a given printed word.
6. Understands terms including:
   beginning
   end
   same
   different
   first
   last
   line
   top
   bottom
7. Can name letters (circle letters and enter date of observation)

____Aa____	____Gg____	____Ll____	____Qq____	____Vv____
____Bb____	____Hh____	____Mm____	____Rr____	____Ww____
____Cc____	____Ii____	____Nn____	____Ss____	____Xx____
____Dd____	____Jj____	____Oo____	____Tt____	____Yy____
____Ee____	____Kk____	____Pp____	____Uu____	____Zz____
____Ff____				

A List of Basic Sight Words for Older Readers

more	last	course
than	might	war
other	great	until
such	year	something
even	since	fact
most	against	though
also	himself	less
through	few	public
should	during	almost
each	without	enough
people	place	took
Mr.	American	get
state	however	government
world	Mrs.	system
still	thought	set
between	part	told
life	general	nothing
being	high	and
same	united	didn't
another	left	later
while	number	knew

From "A Supplement to the Dolch Word Lists," by Jerry L. Johns. *Reading* Improvement 7 (Winter 1971-1972): 91.

Phonogram List

ab	ead	ice	oar	ub
ack	eam	ick	oat	ug
ad	ean	id	on	ule
ag	eat	im	one	ull
ail	eal	in	ong	um
ain	eed	ind	ook	ump
ait	eel	ine	ool	un
ake	eep	ing	oom	ung
all	eet	ink	oon	unk
ame	eg	int	ore	unt
an	ell	ip	ort	up
and	en	iss	oss	uss
ang	end	it	ot	ut
ank	ent	ite	ote	ute
ap	et		ound	
at				
ate				

A Typical Scope and Sequence Chart from the Scott Foresman Reading Program K–8 (1987)

Key
- ◯ Exposure prior to major instruction
- ☐ Instruction
- ▽ Review, reinforcement, extension
- ◇ Maintenance

- [T] Tested in Quarter Test only
- T Tested in Quarter Test and End-of-Book Test

	K	R	PP	Pr	1	2/1	2/2	3/1	3/2	4	5	6	7	8
Word Study Skills														
Identifies Words (Decoding)														
Uses phonics														
Consonants														
Initial consonants														
Auditory discrimination	[T]	[T]	[T]	◇	◇	◇	◇	◇	◇	◇	◇	◇	◇	◇
Letter-sound relationships														
b/b/; g/g/; m/m/; s/s/; l/l/	[T]	[T]	[T]	▽	▽	▽	▽	▽	▽	◇	◇	◇	◇	◇
c, k/k/; r/r/; p/p/; d/d/; t/t/	[T]	[T]	[T]	▽	▽	▽	▽	▽	▽	◇	◇	◇	◇	◇
f/f/; h/h/; w/w/; n/n/	[T]	[T]	[T]	▽	▽	▽	▽	▽	▽	◇	◇	◇	◇	◇
j/j/; v/v/; y/y/; z/z/	[T]	[T]	▽	▽	▽	▽	▽	▽	▽	◇	◇	◇	◇	◇
c/s/; g/j/; qu/kw/					[T]	▽	▽	▽	▽	◇	◇	◇	◇	◇
kn/n/; wr/r/						[T]	▽	▽	▽	◇	◇	◇	◇	◇
Final consonants														
Auditory discrimination				[T]	▽	▽	◇	◇	◇	◇	◇	◇	◇	◇
Letter-sound relationships														
p/p/; d/d/; t/t/; r/r/				[T]	▽	▽	▽	◇	◇	◇	◇	◇	◇	◇
b/b/; m/m/; s/s/; g/g/; l/l/; n/n/				[T]	▽	▽	▽	◇	◇	◇	◇	◇	◇	◇
k, ck/k/				☐	▽	▽	▽	◇	◇	◇	◇	◇	◇	◇
x/ks/					[T]	◇	◇	◇	◇	◇	◇	◇	◇	◇
s/z/				[T]	▽	▽	◇	◇	◇	◇	◇	◇	◇	◇
gh/f/						☐	▽	▽	◇	◇	◇	◇	◇	◇
Double final consonants				[T]	▽	◇	◇	◇	◇	◇	◇	◇	◇	◇
Medial consonants					[T]	☐	▽	▽	◇	◇	◇	◇	◇	◇
Consonant blends														
Initial blends					[T]	▽	[T]	▽	▽	▽	◇	◇	◇	◇
Final blends						[T]	[T]	▽	▽	◇	◇	◇	◇	◇
Consonant digraphs														
Initial digraphs					[T]	☐	☐	[T]	▽	▽	◇	◇	◇	◇
Final digraphs					[T]	☐	☐	[T]	▽	▽	◇	◇	◇	◇
Consonant substitution				☐	☐	◇	◇	◇	◇	◇	◇	◇	◇	◇
Consonant variability principles														
A consonant sound is represented by different consonant letters.								[T]	▽	◇	◇	◇	◇	◇
A consonant letter represents different sounds.							☐	▽	▽	◇	◇	◇	◇	◇
Word families (*See* Vowels)														
Vowels														
Short vowels														

162 PART 6 APPENDIXES

	K	R	PP	Pr	1	2/1	2/2	3/1	3/2	4	5	6	7	8
a (can)														
Word families		○	□	▽	◇	◇	◇	◇	◇	◇	◇	◇	◇	◇
Letter-sound *a*/a/	○	○	T	▽	▽	□	▽	▽	▽	▽	▽	▽	▽	▽
i (pig)														
Word families		○	□	▽	◇	◇	◇	◇	◇	◇	◇	◇	◇	◇
Letter-sound *i*/i/	○	○	T	▽	▽	□	▽	▽	▽	▽	▽	▽	▽	▽
o (sock)														
Word families		○		□	◇	◇	◇	◇	◇	◇	◇	◇	◇	◇
Letter-sound *o*/o/	○	○	○	T	▽	□	▽	▽	▽	▽	▽	▽	▽	▽
e (bed)														
Word families		○		□	◇	◇	◇	◇	◇	◇	◇	◇	◇	◇
Letter-sound *e*/e/	○	○	○	T	▽	□	▽	▽	▽	▽	▽	▽	▽	▽
u (bus)														
Word families		○		□	◇	◇	◇	◇	◇	◇	◇	◇	◇	◇
Letter-sound *u*/u/	○	○	○	T	▽	□	▽	▽	▽	▽	▽	▽	▽	▽
Generalizations														
CVC, CVCC				□	□	□	▽	▽	▽	▽	▽	▽	▽	▽
Long vowels														
a-e (rake)														
Word families					□	◇	◇	◇	◇	◇	◇	◇	◇	◇
Letter-sound *a-e*/ā/	○	○		○	T	□	▽	▽	▽	▽	▽	▽	▽	▽
i-e (kite)														
Word families					□	◇	◇	◇	◇	◇	◇	◇	◇	◇
Letter-sound *i-e*/ī/	○	○		○	T	□	▽	▽	▽	▽	▽	▽	▽	▽
o-e (rope)														
Word family					□	◇	◇	◇	◇	◇	◇	◇	◇	◇
Letter-sound *o-e*/ō/	○	○		○	T	□	▽	▽	▽	▽	▽	▽	▽	▽
ee (bee); *ea* (heat)														
Word families					□	◇	◇	◇	◇	◇	◇	◇	◇	◇
Letter-sound *ee*/ē/; *ea*/ē/	○	○			T	□	▽	▽	▽	▽	▽	▽	▽	▽
u-e (mule)														
Word family					□	◇	◇	◇	◇	◇	◇	◇	◇	◇
Letter-sound *u-e*/ū/				○	T	□	▽	▽	▽	▽	▽	▽	▽	▽
Vowel digraphs														
ai (train); *ay* (day); *oa* (oat)						T	T	▽	▽	▽	▽	▽	▽	▽
e (we); *o* (go); *y* (by); *y* (baby)						□	□	◇	◇	◇	◇	◇	◇	◇
Generalizations														
CVCE						□	▽	▽	▽	▽	▽	▽	▽	▽
CVVC						□	▽	▽	▽	▽	▽	▽	▽	▽
CV						□	□	◇	◇	◇	◇	◇	◇	◇
Contrast (short and long vowels)						□	□	◇	◇	◇	◇	◇	◇	◇
R-controlled vowels														
ar (dark)							T	T	□	▽	▽	▽	▽	▽
er (her)							T	T	□	▽	▽	▽	▽	▽
ir (dirt)							T	T	□	▽	▽	▽	▽	▽

APPENDIX B A TYPICAL SCOPE AND SEQUENCE CHART

Key
- ○ Exposure prior to major instruction
- □ Instruction
- ▽ Review, reinforcement, extension
- ◇ Maintenance

- [T] Tested in Quarter Test only
- T Tested in Quarter Test and End-of-Book Test

	K	R	PP	Pr	1	2/1	2/2	3/1	3/2	4	5	6	7	8
or (for)						[T]	[T]	□	▽	▽	▽	▽	▽	▽
ur (turn)						[T]	[T]	□	▽	▽	▽	▽	▽	▽
Generalization VR							□	[T]	□	▽	▽	▽	▽	▽
Less common vowels														
ow (now, snow)						[T]	[T]	▽	▽	▽	▽	▽	▽	▽
oi (oil); *oy* (boy)						[T]	[T]	▽	▽	▽	▽	▽	▽	▽
oo (room, stood)								[T]	◇	▽	▽	▽	▽	▽
ea (thread, beat)								[T]	▽	▽	▽	▽	▽	▽
ou (sound, bought)						[T]	[T]	▽	▽	▽	▽	▽	▽	▽
au (taught); *aw* (lawn)						[T]	◇	▽	◇	▽	▽	▽	▽	▽
ie (chief)								□	▽	▽	▽	▽	▽	▽
eigh (weigh)								□	▽	▽	▽	▽	▽	▽
igh (mighty)								□	◇	◇	◇	◇	◇	◇
all (call)						[T]	◇	◇	◇	◇	◇	◇	◇	◇
Vowel variability principles														
A vowel sound is represented by different vowel letters.							□	[T]	▽	▽	▽	▽	▽	▽
A vowel letter represents different sounds.							□	□	▽	▽	▽	▽	▽	▽
Vowel generalizations														
Short vowel CVC, CVCC					□	□	▽	▽	▽	▽	▽	▽	▽	▽
Long vowel														
CVCE						□	▽	▽	▽	▽	▽	▽	▽	▽
CVVC							□	▽	▽	▽	▽	▽	▽	▽
CV							□	◇	◇	◇	◇	◇	◇	◇
R-controlled VR							□	[T]	□	▽	▽	▽	▽	▽
Uses structural analysis														
Root words without spelling changes before ending or suffix				[T]	▽	□	[T]	[T]	◇	◇	◇	◇	◇	◇
Root words with spelling changes before ending or suffix							□	□	▽	▽	▽	◇	◇	◇
Final consonant doubled						[T]	□	[T]	◇	▽	▽	▽	◇	◇
Final *e* dropped						[T]	□	[T]	▽	▽	▽	▽	◇	◇
Final *y* changed to *i*								[T]	◇	▽	▽	▽	◇	◇
Final *f* or *fe* changed to *v*								[T]	◇	▽	▽	◇	◇	◇
Endings				[T]	▽	[T]	[T]	[T]	▽	▽	▽	◇	◇	◇
Contractions					[T]	▽	▽	[T]	□	▽	[T]	[T]	◇	◇
Compounds						[T]	[T]	□	□	▽	[T]	[T]	◇	◇
Suffixes									[T]	[T]	[T]	[T]	[T]	[T]
Prefixes									[T]	[T]	[T]	[T]	[T]	[T]
Syllabication rules									[T]	[T]	[T]	[T]	[T]	[T]
Multisyllabic words														
2-syllable words with affixes										□	[T]	[T]	[T]	[T]
Multiple affixes										□	[T]	[T]	[T]	[T]
Common word parts												□	□	[T]	[T]

Reprinted with permission of Scott Foresman and Company from a Typical Scope and Sequence Chart, Scott Foresman Reading Program, K-8 (1987).

APPENDIX C

EXAMPLE WORD LISTS

Structural Elements Taught at Particular Levels

Initial consonants

b	c	d	f	g	h	j	k	l	m
baby	cab	dark	face	gag	hail	job	kangaroo	lace	mad
bag	cage	date	fact	gale	hall	jack	keep	lad	magic
ball	cake	day	fade	game	ham	jade	keg	ladder	magnet
band	call	den	fail	gang	hand	jam	kennel	lady	make
bang	can	dent	fan	garden	happy	jar	kettle	lake	man
bank	cane	desk	farm	gas	hat	jaw	key	lamb	map
bat	cap	dig	fat	gate	have	jeep	kick	lamp	mask
bed	car	dike	feed	gaze	hay	jello	kid	land	match
bee	cat	dill	feet	goat	head	jet	kill	lap	mice
belt	cave	dim	fig	gob	heat	jig	kind	last	milk
big	coat	dish	file	gold	help	job	king	lawn	mirror
bike	cob	doe	fin	golf	hen	joke	kiss	leaf	mitt
bill	coke	dog	find	gone	hike	jolly	kit	leg	mix
bird	cold	doll	fish	good	hill	joy	kitchen	lemon	money
box	cone	door	five	gorilla	hip	judge	kite	lend	mop
boy	cub	dot	fix	got	home	jug	kitty	letter	mother
bud	cube	down	fond	gull	honey	juice		like	mud
bug	cuff	duck	fox	gum	hop	jumbo		line	muff
bus	cup	dull	funny	gun	hot	jump		lion	mug
buzz	cut	dust	fuzz	gust	hug	jungle		listen	must

n	p	q	r	s	t	v	w	x	z
nag	page	quack	rabbit	sack	table	vacation	wade	Xmas	zeal
nail	pail	quail	radio	sad	tack	valentine	wag	X ray	zebra
name	pan	quake	rag	said	taffy	valley	walk		zero
nap	paper	quarrel	rain	sailboat	tail	van	wall	y	zest
near	paw	quart	rake	salt	tall	vane	war	yacht	zigzag
neck	peanut	quarter	rat	sat	teacher	vase	warm	yank	zinc
need	pear	queen	rattle	save	team	vast	was	yap	zing
needle	pen	queer	read	saw	teeth	veil	watch	yard	zinnia
net	penny	quick	red	seal	ten	vein	water	yarn	zip
never	pet	quiet	ride	see	tiger	velvet	web	yawn	zipper
nice	pickle	quirk	ring	sell	time	vent	wedding	year	zone
nickel	picture	quit	road	seven	tire	verb	well	yeast	zoo
night	pie	quite	roar	sew	today	verse	west	yell	
nine	pig	quiver	rob	sick	toe	vest	wet	yellow	
nod	pill	quiz	robin	sing	top	vet	wind	yelp	
nose	pizza		rock	sink	toy	vim	window	yes	
note	pop		rocket	sister	tug	vine	wing	yield	
now	puff		rope	six	tummy	violet	wink	yogurt	
number	puzzle		rose	sock	turkey	violin	wolf	yolk	
nurse			run	sun	turtle	visit	wood	you	
								young	
								yoyo	
								yule	

APPENDIX C   EXAMPLE WORD LISTS

Consonant blends

bl	cl	fl	gl	pl	br	cr
black	clam	flag	glacier	place	brace	crab
blade	clap	flake	glad	plan	braid	crack
blank	class	flap	glass	plant	brain	cradle
blast	claw	flash	gleam	planet	brash	cream
blaze	clay	flat	glee	plaster	brave	crayons
block	clean	float	glide	play	bread	crib
blond	clock	flock	glitter	please	break	crisp
blood	close	floor	glory	plenty	brick	cross
bloom	clothes	flower	glove	plot	bride	crow
blow	cloud	fluid	glow	plug	bring	crown
blouse	clover	flush	glue	plus	brittle	crust
blue	clown				brown	cry
bluff					bruise	

dr	fr	gr	pr	sc	sk	sl
dragon	fraction	grab	prance	scab	skate	slam
drain	frame	grand	pray	scale	skeleton	slap
drape	freckle	grape	press	scald	ski	sled
drawer	free	graph	pretzel	scalp	skillet	sleep
dream	freeze	grass	pride	scan	skin	sleeve
dress	fresh	gravy	prince	scar	skinny	slice
drink	friend	graze	princess	scare	skip	slime
drip	frizz	green	print	scarf	skirt	sling
drive	frog	grin	prize	scatter	skull	slip
drop	frost	grip	proud	scooter	sky	sliver
drown	frozen	grocery	prune	scout		slot
drum		grow				

sm	sn	sp	st	sw	tr	tw
smack	snail	space	stain	swam	tractor	tweed
small	snake	spat	stamp	swarm	trade	tweet
smart	snap	speak	stand	swat	traffic	tweezers
smash	snatch	spear	staple	sway	train	twelve
smear	sneak	speed	star	sweat	trap	twenty
smell	sneeze	spell	stay	sweep	treat	twice
smile	sniff	spend	stem	sweet	tree	twig
smirk	snitch	spider	step	swell	triangle	twilight
smock	snooze	spill	still	swerve	tribe	twin
smoke	snore	spin	sting	swift	trick	twirl
smoky	snow	spoon	stitch	swing	trip	twist
smooth	snug	spot	stop		trot	
smuggle	snuggle				truck	

Variant consonant sounds

c /k/	*c* /s/	*g* /g/	*g* /j/	*s* /s/	*s* /z/
cabin	cedar	galaxy	gelatin	sack	babies
cage	ceiling	gallant	gem	saddle	boys
cake	cell	gallon	general	safe	chairs
camel	cement	gallop	gentle	sail	cookies
camp	census	garage	geography	salt	enemies
card	center	garbage	geometry	sample	families
cat	century	goat	germ	sand	frogs
coconut	cider	golf	giant	satin	girls
coffee	cigar	goose	ginger	second	please
collar	cinnamon	gorilla	giraffe	seed	rose
collie	circus	gown	gym	send	sees
cube	city	guard	gyp	settle	shelves
cucumber	cycle	guess	gypsy	single	stories
cute	cyclone	guide	gyrate	soft	surprise
	cypress	guitar	gyro	some	wives
				soup	

Consonant digraphs

ch /ch/	*ch* /k/	*ch* /sh/	*gh* /g/	*ph* /f/	*sh* /sh/
chain	character	chalet	ghastly	phantasy	shade
chalk	chasm	champagne	ghetto	phantom	shake
champ	chemical	chandelier	ghost	phase	shame
change	choral	charade	ghoul	pharmacy	shape
chart	chorus	chef		pheasant	shark
chase	chlorine	chenille	*gh* /f/	phone	sharp
check	christen	chivalry	cough	phoneme	shave
cheese	chrome		enough	phonics	shawl
chest	chrysalis		laugh	phonograph	shed
chick	scheme		rough	phony	sheep
chief	school		tough	phosphate	shelf
child				photograph	shell
chill				phrase	shine
chin				physical	ship
choose					shirt
church					

th /th/ (voiced)	*th* /th/ (voiceless)	*thr* /thr/ (digraph-blend)	*wh* /wh/
than	thaw	thrash	whack
that	theater	thread	whale
the	theft	threat	wharf
their	theme	three	wheat
them	thick	thresh	wheel
themselves	thief	thrift	where
then	thimble	thrill	whiff
there	thin	throne	whimper
these	thing	through	whine
they	think	throw	whip
this	third	thrust	whirl
those	thirsty		whisk
though	thirty		whisper
	thorn		whiz
	thought		whopper
	thousand		
	thumb		
	thunder		
	Thursday		

Consonant digraph with first silent letters (Also *tch* and *dge* and *ng*)

gn /n/	*kn* /n/	*wr* /r/	*ck* /k/	*tch* /ch/	*dge* /j/	*ng* /ng/
align	knack	wrack	back	batch	badge	bang
campaign	knapsack	wrangler	brick	catch	bridge	flung
design	knead	wrap	crack	crutch	dodge	gang
foreign	knee	wrapper	chick	hitch	edge	gong
gnarl	kneel	wreath	clock	itch	fudge	hung
gnash	knelt	wreck	dock	latch	grudge	long
gnat	knew	wrestle	duck	match	ledge	lung
gnaw	knife	wring	flick	patch	ridge	prong
reign	knight	wrinkle	kick	pitch	sludge	song
resign	knit	wrist	lick	splotch		sing
sign	knob	write	lock	stretch		strung
	knock	wrong	look	stitch		thing
	knot	wrote	luck	watch		wing
	know	wrung	peck	witch		
	knuckle	wry	pick			
			quack			
			quick			
			shock			
			slick			
			stack			
			stick			
			tack			
			tick			
			thick			
			trick			
			track			
			truck			

Short vowels

ă	ĕ	ĭ	ŏ	ŭ
act	bed	bib	block	bud
add	best	big	box	bus
as	den	bit	clock	cub
ask	end	dig	cop	cup
ax	ever	fig	dot	fun
bad	hem	fish	fox	gum
bag	jet	hid	got	gun
cab	led	hit	hop	jug
cat	men	if	lot	jump
dad	nest	ill	mop	lunch
fast	net	in	odd	mud
gap	next	inch	ox	nut
hat	pep	its	pot	pup
map	pet	kick	rob	rug
nap	red	milk	rot	sun
pat	sent	nip	shock	truck
sand	ten	pin	sock	tug
sat	web	sit	spot	under
tan	wet	wig	stop	up
tap	yes		top	us

Long vowel and silent *e*

ā	ē	ī	ō	ū	u as o͞o
bake	extreme	bite	bone	abuse	brute
base	impede	dime	cone	cube	bugle
cave	obese	file	drove	cure	flute
date	scene	five	hole	cute	parachute
game	scheme	hide	home	fuel	prune
gate	serene	hike	hope	fuse	refuge
gave	stampede	life	joke	huge	rule
lake	supreme	like	poke	mule	salute
made		mile	nose	music	sue
race		pine	note	mute	tube
sale		pipe	robe	refuge	tune
take		ripe	rope	use	
tame		rise	smoke		
tape		time	tone		
wave					

y as a vowel

y /ī/	y /ē/*
by	busy
cry	dirty
dye	foggy
fly	foxy
fry	funny
my	heavy
myself	juicy
rye	penny
sly	pity
sty	plenty
style	pony
stylus	puppy
styrofoam	snowy
try	spotty
wry	

*in some dialects /ĭ/

Vowel digraphs

ai /ā/	ay /ā/	ea /ē/	ea /ĕ/	ee /ē/	ie /ē/
aim	away	beach	ahead	beef	achieve
bail	bay	bean	bread	bleed	believe
braid	clay	cheat	dead	creek	brief
claim	decay	clean	head	creep	chief
drain	gray	creak	read	deep	field
faint	may	cream	spread	flee	hygiene
grain	play	flea	thread	free	piece
hail	pray	heat	tread	geese	priest
mail	ray	peach		green	rabies
paid	relay	reach		jeep	relief
paint	slay	scream		peel	shield
rain	spray	seat		queen	shriek
sail	stay	steam		seed	thief
snail	stray	team		sleep	wield
train	tray	treat			
		wheat			

ie /ī/	ei /ē/	ei /ā/	ey /ē/	igh /ī/	oa /ō/
cried	ceiling	beige	barley	bright	boast
die	conceive	eight	donkey	fight	cloak
dried	deceive	freight	galley	flight	coal
fried	either	neighbor	hockey	fright	coast
lied	leisure	reign	honey	high	coat
pie	neither	rein	jockey	knight	float
pried	protein	skein	journey	might	foam
relied	receive	sleigh	kidney	night	goat
replied	seize	veil	medley	plight	load
spies		vein	money	sigh	
tie		weigh		sight	
tied				slight	
tried				right	
				tight	
				thigh	

Diphthongs

oi /oy/	*oy* /oy/	*au* /ä/	*aw* /ä/	*oo* /o͞o/	*oo* /o͝o/
appoint	ahoy	applause	awning	balloon	book
avoid	alloy	auto	brawl	bloom	hood
boil	boy	because	crawl	broom	hoof
choice	convoy	caught	dawn	cartoon	hook
coil	decoy	cause	draw	cool	look
coin	destroy	fault	fawn	drool	stood
foil	employ	haul	flaw	goose	took
join	joy	launch	hawk	moon	
moist	joyful	laundry	jaw	pool	
noise	loyal	naughty	law	school	
oil	oyster	sauce	lawn	scooter	
soil	royal	saucer	raw	smooth	
spoil	tomboy	taught	saw	spool	
voice	toy	vault	yawn	spoon	
				tooth	

ow /ō/*	*ow* /ow/	*ou* /ow/	*ew* /o͞o/	*ue, ew* /yū/
below	allow	blouse	blew	cue
blow	brow	bounce	brew	few
elbow	clown	cloud	chew	hue
flow	cow	found	crew	mew
follow	cowboy	ground	drew	view
glow	drown	house	jewel	
grow	flower	loud	new	
know	frown	mouse	newly	
pillow	gown	ouch	screw	
rainbow	plow	ounce	slew	
shadow	power	out	stew	
show	shower	pound	strewn	
snow	towel	round	threw	
sparrow	tower	shout		
throw	town	sound		

*Here, *ow* decodes as a long vowel sound.

R-controlled vowels

ar /ar/	*or* /or/	*er* /er/	*ir* /er/	*ur* /er/
alarm	born	clerk	birch	burn
arch	corn	fern	bird	burst
ark	ford	germ	birth	church
arm	horn	herd	chirp	curb
armor	morning	jerk	dirt	curve
artist	north	nerve	firm	hurl
barn	orange	perch	shirk	nurse
cart	order	perk	shirt	purse
chart	short	refer	skirt	surf
dart	sort	serve	squirm	surface
mark	sport	stern	squirt	turf
part	stork	term	stir	turkey
shark	torch	verse	twirl	turtle
	torn	worker	whirl	urge
	sworn	zipper		

The following lists of prefixes (active and absorbed), and suffixes, have a designated grade level following them. These levels are suggested by Edgar Dale and Joseph O'Rourke in *The Living Word Vocabulary*,[1] and are based on considerable research over the years. (Testing was not done at grades three, five, and seven.)

Teachers, however, should use their own discretion in determining whether students in their classroom would profit from learning to decode these words. Note how many words at the fourth, sixth, and eighth grade levels are derived by the use of the following prefixes: *dis, in, un;* and the suffixes *tion, less, ly, ment, ness,* and *ly.*

---

(1) From *The Living Word Vocabulary* by Edgar Dale and Joseph O'Rourke. © 1976 by Field Enterprises Educational Corporation.

Active prefixes

dis
discharge (6)
discolor (6)
discomfort (6)
disconnect (4)
discontent (6)
discontinue (6)
discourage (8)
discouragement (8)
discourtesy (6)
disentangle (8)
disfavor (6)
disharmony (8)
dishonor (6)
disinherit (6)
disinterest (6)
dislocate (6)
dislodge (8)
disloyal (4)
disloyalty (6)
dismount (4)
disobedience (6)
disobey (4)
disorder (4)
disorderly (8)
disorganize (6)
displace (8)
displeasure (6)
disqualify (4)
disregard (6)
disrespect (6)
disrespectful (6)
dissatisfaction (6)
dissatisfy (4)
dissimilar (6)
distrustful (6)

en
enclose (4)
encourage (4)
encouragement (4)
endanger (6)
endear (8)
enforce (6)
enjoy (4)
enjoyable (4)
enjoyment (4)
enlarge (4)
enlargement (4)
enlist (4)
enlistment (4)
enrage (6)
enrich (6)
enroll (6)
enrollment (6)
ensure (4)
entangle (6)
entrust (6)

for/fore
forearm (6)
forefathers (6)
foregone (6)
foreground (6)
foreknowledge (6)
foreleg (6)
foreman (4)
forenoon (4)
forepaw (4)
foresaw (6)
foresee (6)
foreseen (6)
foresight (6)
foretell (6)
forethought (6)
foretold (6)
forever (4)
forevermore (4)
foreward (8)
forewarn (6)
forgave (6)

im
(means not, also in)
immature (6)
immeasurable (6)
immigrant (6)
immigration (6)
immodest (8)
immortal (8)
immortality (8)
immovable (6)
immunize (8)
impassable (4)
impatience (6)
impatiently (6)
imperfect (6)
imperfection (6)
impersonal (8)
impolite (4)
import (6)
impossible (4)
impress (6)
impressive (6)
imprint (8)
imprison (4)
imprisonment (6)
improbable (8)
improper (6)
impure (6)
impurity (6)

in
(means not, also in)
inability (6)
inaccurate (6)
inactive (8)
inadequate (8)
inappropriate (8)
incapable (6)
inclose (4)
inclosure (6)
income (6)
incoming (8)
incomparable (6)
incompetent (8)
incomplete (4)
inconsiderate (6)
inconvenience (8)
incredible (6)
incurable (6)
indebted (6)
indebtedness (8)
indecent (6)
indecision (6)
indefinite (8)
independence (4)
independent (6)
indestructible (8)
indigestible (6)
indirect (8)
indirectly (8)
indisputable (8)
indistinct (8)
indoors (4)
inedible (8)
ineffective (6)
inefficient (8)
inestimable (8)
inevitable (8)
inexact (6)
inexpensive (6)
inexpressible (8)
infield (8)
inflammable (6)
inflammation (8)
ingratitude (8)
inhospitable (8)
inhuman (6)
inhumane (8)
inscribe (6)
inscription (8)
insecure (4)
insensitive (8)
inseparable (6)
insoluble (8)
insufficient (8)
intake (4)

inter
intermarriage (8)
intermediate (8)
intermixture (8)
international (8)
internationalize (6)
intersection (6)
interview (6)
interweave (8)

mis
misapply (8)
misbehave (4)
misbehavior (8)
misconduct (6)
miscount (4)
misdeal (4)
misfit (6)
misfortune (4)
misjudge (4)
mislay (4)
mislead (6)
misleading (6)
mismanage (6)
misplace (4)
misprint (4)
mispronounce (6)
misquote (8)
misread (4)
misrule (6)
misspell (4)
misspent (6)
mistrust (6)
misunderstand (4)
misuse (6)

non
noncombatant (8)
nonconductor (8)
nonprofit (8)
nonresident (4)
nonsense (4)
nonstop (4)

re (meaning again)
rebirth (6)
reborn (8)
rebound (6)
rebroadcast (4)
rebuilt (4)
recall (4)
recapture (6)
recombine (6)
recondition (8)
recycle (6)
rediscover (6)
refill (4)
reforest (6)
refresh (4)
regain (4)
removable (6)
rename (4)
renewal (8)
reopen (4)
reorganize (4)
repaid (4)
repayment (6)
replace (4)
reprint (4)
reproduce (8)
retake (4)

un
unable (6)
unacquainted (4)
unaffected (8)
unafraid (4)
unaided (6)
unarmed (4)
unattached (4)
unattainable (8)
unattended (8)
unattractive (6)
unavoidable (8)
unbalanced (4)
unbeaten (8)
unborn (4)
unbreakable (4)
unbroken (4)
unbuckle (4)
unbutton (4)
uncertain (4)
unchanged (4)
unchecked (6)
uncivilized (6)
unclasp (4)
unclothed (4)
uncomfortable (6)
unconcern (6)
uncontrollable (6)

undiscovered (6)
undisturbed (4)
unearth (8)
uneasily (6)
unemployed (6)
unequal (4)
uneven (4)
unexpectedly (6)
unfold (4)
unfortunate (6)
unfurl (8)
unguarded (8)
unhappily (6)
unkindness (4)
unlikely (4)
unlively (6)
unmerciful (8)
unnatural (4)
unoccupied (8)
unopened (4)
unorganized (6)
unpopular (4)
unreality (6)
unsaddle (4)
unscramble (6)
unscrew (6)
unselfish (4)

unsettled (6)
unskilled (4)
unsuccessful (6)
unsuitable (6)
untangle (6)
untiring (6)
untouchable (4)
untried (6)
untrue (4)
untwist (4)
unwashed (4)
unwelcome (4)
unwilling (4)
unwind (6)
unwisely (4)
unworthy (8)

Absorbed prefixes

con
conceal (6)
concern (6)
conclude (6)
condense (8)
conflict (8)
confuse (4)
connection (6)
consist (6)
construct (4)
contact (6)
contest (4)
contract (6)
contraption (8)
contrast (8)

com
combine (4)
comfort (4)
comment (6)
commit (8)
common (6)
compass (8)
compete (8)
compose (6)
composition (6)
compound (6)
compromise (8)

de
debate (6)
decay (4)
decent (8)
decide (4)
decision (4)
declare (6)
decline (8)
defeat (6)
define (6)
defrost (4)
delay (4)
deliver (4)
demand (6)
depend (4)
deposit (4)
detail (8)
detract (8)

ex
examine (4)
example (4)
excellent (4)
except (4)
excess (8)
excite (4)
exclaim (6)
exclude (8)
excuse (4)
execute (4)
exhaust (6)
exile (8)
exit (4)
explain (4)
explode (4)
expose (6)
express (6)
extend (8)

pre*
precipitation (6)
predict (6)
prefer (6)
premium (6)
preparation (4)
prepare (4)
present (4)
pretend (4)
prevent (4)
previous (6)

pro
procedure (8)
proceed (4)
process (6)
produce (6)
production (6)
program (4)
prolong (8)
promote (4)
propose (4)
protest (6)

*The prefix *pre* is also an active prefix in words as *predetermine, prejudge*, etc.

Derivational suffixes

able

acceptable (8)
accountable (6)
admirable (6)
allowable (4)
believable (4)
charitable (8)
comfortable (4)
dependable (4)
desirable (6)
fashionable (4)
favorable (8)
flammable (6)
honorable (6)
justifiable (6)
manageable (6)
movable (4)
navigable (8)
notable (8)
observable (6)
portable (4)
presentable (6)
punishable (6)
reasonable (6)
respectable (6)
sizable (8)
traceable (6)
treasonable (8)
usable (4)
valuable (4)
washable (4)

ance

acceptance (8)
acquaintance (8)
admittance (8)
allowance (6)
appearance (4)
appliance (4)
assistance (4)
ordinance (8)
performance (4)
remembrance (8)
repentance (8)
resistance (8)
tolerance (8)

ess

authoress (8)
duchess (8)
enchantress (8)
huntress (6)
lioness (6)
poetess (6)
princess (4)
stewardess (6)
tigress (6)

ful
beautiful (4)
blissful (8)
careful (4)
cheerful (4)
colorful (8)
cupful (4)
doubtful (6)
faithful (6)
forgetful (4)
graceful (6)
handful (4)
harmful (4)
joyful (4)
lawful (4)
masterful (6)
meaningful (6)
merciful (6)
mournful (6)
playful (4)
shameful (8)
sinful (6)
sorrowful (4)
spoonful (4)
thankful (6)
thoughtful (4)
trustful (4)
truthful (4)
wonderful (4)

ify
clarify (6)
classify (6)
crucify (6)
glorify (6)
horrify (6)
identify (6)
intensify (8)
justify (6)
magnify (6)
mystify (8)
notify (6)
pacify (8)
terrify (4)

ion
abbreviation (4)
accusation (8)
addition (4)
admiration (6)
admission (6)
adoption (4)
affection (6)
amputation (8)
application (8)
attention (6)
attraction (6)
construction (6)
division (4)
elevation (6)
expression (4)
formation (6)
introduction (4)
irritation (6)
navigation (8)
nomination (6)
persuasion (8)
presentation (8)
production (6)
protection (4)
radiation (4)
reflection (4)
sensation (6)
starvation (4)
supervision (4)
taxation (6)
temptation (6)
tension (6)
vaccination (6)
vegetation (8)
vibration (6)
violation (8)

ish
banish (8)
bookish (8)
boyish (4)
brownish (4)
childish (4)
devilish (6)
foolish (4)
girlish (4)
grayish (6)
reddish (8)

ism
alcoholism (4)
Americanism (4)
barbarism (8)
cannibalism (6)
Catholicism (6)
colonialism (6)
communism (6)
criticism (6)
idealism (8)
liberalism (8)
patriotism (6)
terrorism (8)
vandalism (6)

ist
abolitionist (8)
accompanist (6)
biologist (6)
botanist (8)
chemist (6)
columnist (6)
duelist (8)
finalist (8)
humorist (8)
opportunist (8)
organist (4)
panelist (8)
terrorist (6)
tourist (6)
violinist (4)
vocalist (6)
zoologist (8)

ity
ability (4)
activity (8)
actuality (8)
authority (6)
cavity (6)
community (6)
curiosity (8)
deformity (8)
elasticity (8)
humanity (8)
legality (8)
locality (6)
majority (6)
maturity (8)
minority (8)
nobility (8)
opportunity (6)
personality (4)
possibility (6)
prosperity (8)
rapidity (4)
regularity (6)
scarcity (6)
security (6)
sincerity (8)
stability (8)
stupidity (6)
utility (6)
vitality (8)

ive
attractive (4)
defensive (8)
locomotive (4)
possessive (6)
preventive (6)
productive (6)
sensitive (8)

ize
apologize (4)
legalize (6)
materialize (8)
modernize (4)
organize (6)
specialize (6)
sterilize (4)
terrorize (8)
vaporize (4)

less	**ly**	**ment**
aimless (6)	actually (6)	achievement (6)
bottomless (4)	awfully (4)	advertisement (4)
boundless (8)	carefully (4)	agreement (4)
brainless (4)	certainly (4)	ailment (4)
breathless (4)	cheaply (4)	amendment (6)
ceaseless (8)	correctly (4)	amusement (4)
cheerless (4)	currently (8)	announcement (4)
childless (4)	directly (8)	apartment (4)
defenseless (6)	doubly (6)	appointment (4)
doubtless (6)	earthly (6)	argument (6)
fatherless (4)	easily (4)	arrangement (4)
faultless (8)	especially (6)	assignment (4)
formless (4)	feelingly (6)	detachment (8)
friendless (4)	frequently (4)	development (6)
guiltless (6)	friendly (4)	employment (6)
helpless (4)	furiously (6)	enchantment (6)
hopeless (4)	hourly (6)	engagement (4)
landless (4)	knowingly (6)	environment (6)
largeness (4)	mannerly (4)	government (6)
listless (8)	mostly (4)	judgment (6)
matchless (8)	naturally (6)	pavement (4)
meaningless (6)	nearly (4)	payment (6)
merciless (6)	orderly (8)	punishment (4)
motionless (6)	ordinarily (6)	refreshment (4)
needless (8)	patiently (4)	replacement (4)
noiseless (4)	personally (4)	resentment (8)
painless (4)	positively (6)	retirement (4)
pointless (6)	probably (6)	sentiment (8)
regardless (6)	saintly (6)	settlement (4)
shameless (8)	scarcely (4)	shipment (4)
shapeless (4)	seemingly (8)	statement (4)
sleepless (4)	severely (6)	temperament (8)
spiritless (8)	shapely (4)	treatment (4)
spotless (6)	sincerely (6)	
stainless (6)	slightly (6)	
thoughtless (4)	sparingly (6)	
timeless (6)	stubbornly (6)	
treeless (4)	supposedly (8)	
valueless (6)	swiftly (4)	
voiceless (6)	variously (6)	
witless (6)	vertically (8)	
	vocally (6)	

ness

alertness (6)
attractiveness (4)
bashfulness (4)
bitterness (4)
blindness (4)
briskness (6)
closeness (6)
coarseness (6)
darkness (4)
dimness (4)
drowsiness (6)
drunkenness (4)
dullness (6)
duskiness (6)
emptiness (6)
exactness (6)
fatness (4)
feebleness (6)
filthiness (6)
fitness (8)
flabbiness (6)
foolishness (4)
freshness (4)
greatness (4)
greediness (6)
greenness (4)
keenness (6)
kindness (6)
lawlessness (6)
loneliness (4)
nearness (4)
nervousness (4)
nobleness (6)

pleasantness (6)
prettiness (4)
rashness (4)
readiness (4)
restlessness (6)
roominess (6)
rottenness (4)
seriousness (6)
shyness (4)
smoothness (6)
steadiness (8)
stiffness (4)
stillness (4)
strangeness (4)
suddenness (4)
sweetness (4)
swiftness (4)
tardiness (4)
tenderness (4)
thankfulness (4)
thickness (4)
thoughtfulness (4)
usefulness (4)
watchfulness (6)
weakness (4)
weariness (6)
whiteness (4)
willingness (6)

ogy

archaeology (8)
astrology (8)
biology (8)
criminology (8)
ecology (8)
geology (6)
mineralogy (6)

ous

courageous (4)
dangerous (4)
glorious (6)
humorous (4)
joyous (6)
luminous (8)
marvelous (4)
miraculous (6)
mountainous (6)
mysterious (6)
nervous (6)
numerous (6)
odorous (8)
poisonous (6)
prosperous (8)
studious (8)
treasonous (8)

Practice words for syllabication

2 syllables	3 syllables	4 syllables
captive	belittle	declaration
carbon	capital	deliberate
carefree	correctly	embarrassment
cortex	corridor	encouragement
extent	exposure	exceedingly
extreme	extension	impersonal
formal	external	introduction
fungus	fantastic	magnesium
furnace	foundation	majority
junction	important	mathematics
mailman	imposter	mechanical
picket	impression	necessary
picture	janitor	objectionable
proverb	magnetic	pacifier
provoke	mastermind	predetermined
return	matador	recognition
royal	mechanic	relationship
rubber	medicine	revolution
twilight	medium	sensational
upstream	opportune	spectacular
waistline	preamble	supervisor
waitress	prospector	totality
welfare	resident	unsuspected
	stimulus	violinist

APPENDIX D

TESTS

A Teacher's Test of Decoding Skills

Part I

1. Define a consonant digraph. (1) List and organize them into (a) digraphs with *h*, (b) digraphs with an initial silent letter, (c) '3' letter digraphs. (2) Indicate the sound/sounds each encodes. (3) Give a word/word example of each and underline the digraph in the word.

   Definition:

Digraphs	**Sound/Sounds**	**Word Example/Examples**
(a)		
(b)		
(c)		

2. Some single consonant letters in our alphabet encode more than one sound. What are these letters? What sounds do they encode? What vowels condition these sounds? Give word examples of each.

Letter	**Sound/Sounds**	**Vowels That Condition**	**Word Example/Examples**

3. The letter *y* functions as both a consonant and vowel. Explain and give word examples.

4. Define a consonant blend. Give two examples of each kind of blend, underlining the blend. What is/are the main difference/differences between them?

   Definition:

Blends	**Examples**

5. At the end of some words *ck* is used as the /k/ sound. At the end of other words *ke* is used as the /k/ sound. Explain.

6. Give word examples of the five short sounds of the vowels.

7. Some vowels encode a third sound in addition to the short and long sounds. What are these vowels? What sounds do they encode? Give word examples.

8. List four 'regular' vowel digraphs that follow the rule used by many primary teachers: "When two vowels go a-walking, etc." Give word examples.

   Vowel Digraph   **Word Example**

9. The /o͞o/ sound as in the word *spoon* can be encoded in many ways. List the six additional letter or letter combinations that encode this sound. Give word examples.

Sound	Letter Combinations	Word Examples
/o͞o/	oo	spoon

10. Give word examples to show the effect of a final *e* on words. You should have five different examples to indicate five reasons why final *e* appears.

11. Long *e* may be encoded many ways. List the letter or letters that combine to encode this sound. Give word examples.

    Sound   **Letter Combinations**   **Word Examples**

12. Define a diphthong. What sounds do these diphthongs encode? Give word examples.

    Definition:

    Diphthongs   **Sounds**   **Word Examples**
    oo
    ou
    ow
    oi
    oy

13. Long *i* may *usually* be encoded three ways in addition to the letter *i*. Give the letter combinations with word examples.

    /i/   **Letter Combinations**   **Word Examples**

14. What do *ir, er, ur,* and *wor* have in common?

15. What is the schwa sound? Where is it found? How is it written? Give example words.

16. What happens to words such as *jog* and *brim* when adding endings that begin with a vowel? Why is this?

17. Add the endings *ing* and *ed* to the nonsense words below.

   blath
   gute
   pem
   shane
   colnep
   theg
   cay

18. What suggestions would you make to students when they come to an unknown word?

Part II

1. Circle the vowel digraphs
2. Underline the blends
3. Place a square bracket around the consonant digraphs
4. Place a checkmark before a word with a diphthong

character	afraid	relative	coarse
shook	flight	back	chaise
receive	known	surprise	athlete
treasure	toil	illustration	whether

Part III

1. (a) Define the term sight words and give some examples.
   (b) What is the importance of these words?

2. What is the difference between an absorbed and regular prefix?

3. What is the difference between an inflectional and derivational suffix?

4. What is the difference between a semantic and syntactic context clue?

5. What syllabication principles would you suggest to students to incorporate when they meet an unfamiliar word?

Answers to a Teacher's Test of Decoding Skills

Part I

1. Definition: two consonant letters together encoding one sound
   - (a) ch   /ch/ /k/ /sh/   *ch*amp   *ch*aracter   *ch*ef
     - gh   /g/ /f/ /-/   *gh*ost   tou*gh*   bou*gh*
     - ph   /f/   *ph*armacy
     - sh   /sh/   *sh*ape
     - th   /th/ /th/   *th*icket   *th*em
     - wh   /w/ /h/   *wh*en   *wh*ole
   - (b) gn   /n/   *gn*ome
     - kn   /n/   *kn*ife
     - wr   /r/   *wr*inkle
     - ck   /k/   che*ck*
   - (c) dge /j/   bri*dge*
     - tch   /ch/   ca*tch*

2.
Letter	Sound/Sounds	Vowels That Condition	Word Example/Examples
c	/k/ /s/	When *a, o, u* follow *c*, *c* encodes /k/. When *i, e, y* follow *c*, *c* encodes /s/	camera, cycle

Letter	Sound/Sounds	Vowels That Condition	Word Example/Examples
g	/g/ /j/	When *a, o, u* follow *g*, *g* usually encodes /g/. When *i, e, y* follow *g*, *g* usually encodes /j/.	game, gem
s	/s/ /z/	none	same, rose, sugar

3. *y* may be a consonant at the beginning of a word — *yellow.*
   y may be a vowel in the middle of words — /i/ g*y*m, /ī/ c*y*cle.
   y may be a vowel at the end of words — /ē/ prett*y*, /ī/ appl*y*.
   y may be part of a vowel digraph as *ay* /ā/ st*ay*, and *ey* /ē/ mon*ey*.
   y may be part of the diphthong *oy* /oy/ t*oy*.

4. A consonant blend occurs when two or three adjacent letters encode consonant sounds that cluster together and are pronounced very rapidly.
   a. *r* *cr*eam, *pr*ize   b. *l* *bl*ame, *fl*ight   c. *s* *sn*ail, *str*eam   d. *tw* *tw*irl, *tw*ist

5. *ck* is used after a short vowel. *ke* is used after a long vowel

6. Answers will vary b*at*, b*et*, b*it*, b*op*, b*ut*

7. *ä* /ä/ father
   o /o͞o/ to
   i /u/ bush

8. *ai* maid   *ay* tray   *oa* oats   *ee* sleep

9. *ou* soup   *u* rude   *ui* fruit   *ew* few
   o prove   *ue* clue

10. *chance, change.* Final *e* indicates the preceding *c* and *g* have the respective sounds of /s/ and /j/.
    pipe. Final *e* indicates the preceding vowel is long. This differentiates pipe from pip.
    have. Final *e* is used after *v* because English words do not end in *v*.
    able. Final *e* completes a needed second syllable; otherwise the word would be unpronounceable as *abl*.
    awe. Historical reasons.

11. *ee* sheep   *ie* brief   *ey* monkey
    ea treat   *ei* conceive   *e*   candy

12. A diphthong is a gliding sound from one vowel to another.
    oo /o͞o/ /o͝o/   spool, shook
    ou /ow/ /ŭ/   crouch, touch
    ow /ow/ /ō/   crowd, snow
    oi /oy/   moist
    oy /oy/   employ

13. *y* cry   *ie* pie   *igh* right

14. They all encode /er/; *or* encodes /er/ when *w* precedes it.

15. The schwa is the vowel sound in unstressed syllables with a sound similar to short *u*.

16. The final consonant is doubled to show the preceding vowel is short. This differentiates between words as stripper and striper!

17. blath   blathing   blathed
    gute   guting   guted
    pem   pemming   pemmed
    shane   shaning   shaned
    colnep   colnepping   colnepped
    theg   thegging   thegged
    cay   caying   cayed

18. First see if the sentence context can help.
    Check for structural parts such as roots and affixes.
    Check for syllable and phonics clues.

Part II

[ch] aracter	af(r) (ai) d	relative	c (oa) rse
✓ [sh] ook	fl (igh) t	ba[ck]	ch (ai) se
rec (ei) ve	[kn] own	surp(r)ise	a [th] lete
t(r) (ea) sure	✓ toil	illus(t)ration	[wh] e [th] er

Part III

1. (a) They are "heavy duty" words such as *at, the, be, of* that appear frequently.
   (b) They must be recognized immediately as it is difficult to read any extended passage without meeting a large number of them.
2. A regular prefix changes the word's meaning as preview (to see before). In an absorbed prefix the pre or other like-seeming prefix is part of the word (presume).
3. Inflectional suffixes number only eight and are taught early in the reading program. They do not change the part of speech. Derivational suffixes are very numerous and are of four kinds: noun, verb, adjective, and adverb. These do change the part of speech, their main function.
4. A semantic clue is a meaning clue; a syntactic clue is a grammar clue.
5. See if a word is compound or has affixes.
   See if the word has double consonant letters or two unlike consonants.
   Do not divide blends or digraph.
   If the word ends in *le*, place the preceding consonant before it.
   Always check to see if the word makes sense!

An Example Test for the Diagnosis of Student Word Attack Skills (Teacher Form)

Useful for skill grouping and to check student progress.
For students who should have mastered most of the decoding skills.
Words are taken from Dolch's 1000 word list.

1. *Alphabet*
   The student recites and recognizes all the letters when out of order.
   B I C F P M K L T E D S A J H W Q V N O Y K X G U Z
   o l y v p i a z k t m n r u h c w f q e x d g b s j

2. *Consonant Sounds*
   The student says a word beginning with each letter sound. (Use flash cards with letters, holding one up at a time.)

1. m	4. f	7. s	10. l	13. z	16. k
2. b	5. w	8. v	11. j	14. n	17. y
3. p	6. t	9. d	12. r	15. h	18. g

   The student writes the first letter of each word after hearing each word.

1. *p*encil	7. *v*ery	13. *h*appy
2. *b*aby	8. *s*ing	14. *z*ipper
3. *m*oney	9. *d*ark	15. *n*ever
4. *w*agon	10. *r*ain	16. *y*ellow
5. *f*oot	11. *l*ady	17. *k*ing
6. *t*eeth	12. *j*ump	18. *g*ame

3. *Blending Consonants and Vowels*
   The student writes the first two letters of each word or nonsense word after hearing each word.
   Real Words
   1. penny
   2. dust
   3. find
   4. taste
   5. ram
   6. lot

   Nonsense Words
   7. rel
   8. wab
   9. sote
   10. kife
   11. wum
   12. bame

4. *Context Clues*
   The student uses context clues by supplying the missing words.

   Jane and Bill were playing in front of a house. A woman came up and asked, "Is your mother at _____?" "Yes," said Jane, _____ is at home." "Good," said the woman, "then I will ring the _____ ." So she _____ the bell, but no one came. She rang the _____ again, but still no _____ came.

   She rang again and again and _____ , but no one came. Then she said to Bill, "Didn't your sister tell me _____ was at _____?"

   "Oh, yes," _____ said, "She did."

   "Then why doesn't she answer the _____ when I ring?"

   "Because," said Bill, "Jan isn't my sister. Her mother *is* at home, but my mother is out shopping."

5. *Consonant Blends*
   The student writes the first two letters of each word or nonsense word after hearing each word.
   Real Words
   1. black
   2. scooter
   3. present
   4. smell
   5. grab
   6. snap
   7. slip
   8. spade
   9. fruit

   Nonsense Words
   10. bram
   11. clep
   12. flim
   13. swit
   14. crute
   15. plim
   16. trep
   17. glod
   18. stel

6. *Consonant Blends (Ending)*
   The student writes the last two letters of each word after hearing each word.
   1. bend
   2. lint
   3. talk
   4. almost
   5. held
   6. comb

7. *Consonant Digraphs*
   The student writes the first two letters of each word or nonsense word after hearing each word.
   Real Words
   1. shape
   2. chime
   3. thumb
   4. whistle
   5. photo
   6. those

   Nonsense Words
   7. thun
   8. leng
   9. chork
   10. tish
   11. phent
   12. whob

8. *Variants "c" and "g"*
   The student writes the first two letters of each word after hearing each word.
   1. city
   2. circus
   3. card
   4. colt
   5. cake
   6. cent
   7. game
   8. gym
   9. gum
   10. giant
   11. good
   12. gentle

9. *Long and Short Vowels*
   The student writes the vowel letter sound of each word after hearing each word.
   1. hit
   2. bat
   3. rice
   4. bite
   5. bet
   6. run
   7. go
   8. cot
   9. make
   10. sleep
   11. use
   12. home

10. *Vowel Diphthongs*
    The student reads the following words with vowel diphthongs.
    Real Words
    1. book
    2. coil
    3. moon
    4. toy
    5. mouse
    6. grow

    Nonsense Words
    7. moit
    8. faw
    9. taul
    10. voy
    11. doot
    12. haut

11. *"r" Controlled*
    The student reads the following real and nonsense words.
    Real Words
    1. tar
    2. over
    3. for
    4. fur
    5. stir
    6. word

    Nonsense Words
    7. mer
    8. tir
    9. worb
    10. murt
    11. gar
    12. torm

12. *Word Division*
    (a) The student reads the following words and records the number of syllables in each words.
    Real Words
    1. home
    2. captain
    3. elephant
    4. doctor
    5. accident
    6. strong

    Nonsense Words
    7. timb
    8. bisby
    9. tabman
    10. melgan
    11. stom
    12. aritent

    (b) *Word Division with Older Students*, Grades 5 and above

    The student reads the following nonsense words.
    (Prefixes)
    1. propan
    2. dispay
    3. reraw
    4. enread
    5. comjump
    6. conbent
    7. pregate
    8. instand
    9. uncry
    10. delike
    11. exwell
    12. perdent

    (Suffixes)
    1. sleepance
    2. skinive
    3. turnant
    4. leatness
    5. dorous
    6. cornable
    7. daytion
    8. waterful
    9. cupment
    10. dreamest
    11. plantly
    12. strivence

    (Prefixes and Suffixes)
    1. rebushful
    2. retrayment
    3. enlandance
    4. prowooding
    5. inrailest
    6. dispiller
    7. exmilkous
    8. unpostent
    9. prestandive
    10. conworktion
    11. comstipment
    12. disoutless

Resources for the Teacher

Books

Christensen, Ann and Green, Lee. *Trash to Treasures: An Idea Book for Classroom and Media Center Materials.* Libraries Unlimited, P.O. Box 263, Littleton, CO 80160-0263, 1982.

Tells where and how to locate free or inexpensive materials in your own community. Step-by-step instructions on how to turn seemingly useless items into a variety of classroom and media center games, kits, displays and presentation models. Included are ideas for construction, and storage.

Dettre, Judith. *1, 2, 3 Read!* Pitman Learning Inc., 6 Davis Drive, Belmont, CA 94002.

A four-senses approach to reading - recognizing sight words, listening to sounds, aural recall, and word card manipulation.

Educational Service, Inc., Stevensville, MI.

Publishes the time-honored classic, *Spice,* and a newer selection, *Rescue,* for many excellent teaching ideas in word attack skills. Correlated duplicating masters for both books are available.

Enrich Corporation. *Tagalong Teddie's First Stories.* San Jose, CA 95131, 1985.

Stories about a happy bear family. In addition to stories there are cutouts and stickers. Skill building activities presented through Mother Goose rhymes.

Forte, Imogene, MacKenzie, Joe, and Collier, Mary Jo. *Kids' Stuff.* Incentive Publishers, Nashville, TN, 1981.

Creative activities for kindergarten.

Hayes School Publishers. *Modern Mastery Drills in Reading.* Wilkensburg, PA, 1985.

Levels D-H or grades 4-8. Provides practice in both reading and writing skills. Includes stories and non-fiction selections.

Higley, J. *Activities Deskbook for Teaching Reading Skills.* Parker Publishing Co., NY, 1977.

This practical guide gives the elementary teacher a broad range of classroom tested ideas and activities for creating more effective reading lessons and improving pupil reading habits.

Instructo, Judy. *Plurals.* Minneapolis, MN 55406.

A matching working bulletin board set may be purchased. Other skills also have matching bulletin boards.

Joseph, Helen and Russ, Flora. *Apple for the Beginning Beginner.* Enrich-Ohaus, 2325 Paragon Dr., San Jose, CA 95131, 1983.

An easy and helpful intro to computers and programming.

Love, Marla. *Twenty Reading Games: Decoding;* and *Twenty Reading Games: Word Structure.* Pitman Learning Inc., 6 Davis Drive, Belmont, CA 94002.

These books provide game boards and fun sheets to help primary students learn about letter recognition, contractions, consonant blends, simple prefixes and suffixes.

Mallett, J. J. *Classroom Reading Games Activities Kit.* Center for Applied Research in Education, Inc., NY, 1975.

Contains over 100 complete, easy-to-make game activities for building specific individual reading skills in the elementary classroom.

Milliken Publications Inc. *Taking Off Series.* St. Louis, MO, 1985.

Preschoolers learn basic readiness skills such as the alphabet and beginning sounds.

Milliken Publications Inc. *Learning Series.* St. Louis, MO, 1985.

Includes several booklets on readiness skills at kindergarten and first grade levels.

1983 Classroom Computer News Directory of Educational Computing Resources. International Educations, Inc., 341 Mt. Auburn Street, Watertown, MA 02172, 1982.

Prepared by educators for educators and contains descriptions of periodicals, professional associations, ongoing projects, funding and many sources of ideas, information and materials on classroom computer use. Compilation of annotations and over 1000 listings arranged for quick and easy reference.

Sciara, Frank and Walter, Richard. *Reading Activities with the Tape Recorder.* Instructor Publications, Danville, NY 14437.

Teacher Created Materials. *Seasonal Bear Readiness Skills.* P.O. Box 301, Sunset Beach, CA 90742, 1985.

For each month different skills are stressed, such as shapes, classification, and sequencing.

Publishers

Barnell Loft, 958 Church St., Baldwin, NY 11510

A Word Recognition Program. A complete program: phonics, word elements using the context, structural analysis, and syllabication.

C. C. Publications Inc., P.O. Box 23699, Tigard, OR 97223

Word Endings. For students who can read simple material fairly well, but have trouble with word endings, omitting or confusing them.

Children's Press, 1224 W. Van Buren St., Chicago, IL 60607

Wise Owl's ABC Book. Wise Owl takes an alphabet walk and asks children to match alphabet letters with the first letter in an animal's name.

Communication Skill Builders, 3130 N. Dodge Blvd., P.O. Box 42050-F, Tucson, AZ 85733

What's the Word. Discusses characters, objects and events via posters relating the happenings to student experiences.

Curriculum Associates, 94 Bridge Street, Newton, MA 02158

Lively Letters: Physical Phonics (set and program). Multisensory involvement to help children remember the sound of letters.

Dexter & Westbrook, 958 Church St., Baldwin, NY 11510

Instructional Aid Kits, Decoding Skills. A decoding program for individuals or small groups. On one side of each card there is a basic letter cluster with a key word. On the reverse side, words with the same cluster are listed in order of ascending difficulty.

Educational Systems, 4401 W. 76th St., Minneapolis, MN 55435

Word Attack Worksheets. Colorful worksheets to teach each phonics skill.

Educational Teaching Aids, 159 W. Kenzie St., Chicago, IL 60610

Basic Vocal, Stages 1, 2, 3. Beginning vocabulary presented in small booklet format. Includes words, a sentence, writing, and testing. Particularly useful for children for whom English is a second language.

Educators Publishing Service Inc., 75 Moulton St., Dept. CPR, Cambridge, MA 02238

Worldly Wise Books. Students in grades 2-4 can learn to use words precisely in a variety of situations.

Ginn and Company, Lexington, MA 02173

The "Ginn Word Enrichment Program" provides a flexible, seven-level program of word attack skills through colorful workbooks that are adaptable to diagnostic teaching procedures.

Ideal School Supply Company, Oaklawn, IL

Charts with coordinated duplicating masters, along with games and puzzles, come together for a well-rounded word attack skills program. Also a sight word kit entitled "Fun With Sight Words." Includes sets of six booklets, ditto masters, and sight word sentence cards.

Kenworthy Educational Service, Inc., Buffalo, NY 14205

A variety of games and flip cards for zeroing in on students' needs in word attack skills instruction.

McGraw-Hill, Paoli, PA 19301 (Instructo)

Long and short vowels — Desk Tape. A personal reference guide to vowel sounds that may be taped to each student's desk.

Milliken Publishing Company, St. Louis, MO 63132

This company has a wide selection of excellent transparencies, duplicating masters, records, and task cards for teaching and reinforcing word attack skills.

Modern Curriculum Press, Cleveland, OH 44136

The "Phonics Workbook" and "Phonics Is Fun" series provide reinforcement in all word attack skills. Additional teaching aids are also available.

New Dimensions in Education, Inc., Plainview, NY 11803

A multisensory beginning Reading and Language Arts Program, emphasizing word mastery through phonics. Contains 'Letter People' as inflatable puppet such as Tall Teeth, masters, books, games, and guides for parental involvement.

Prentice-Hall, Englewood Cliffs, NJ 07632

Learning With Laughter. Multimedia phonics material that uses brightly colored filmstrips of amusing cartoon characters. Recordings use lively song and rhyme. Fifty-four interrelated kits that teach consonants, consonant blends, vowels, medial and final consonants, inflectional endings, and sight words.

Perfection Form Co., 1000 N. 2nd Ave., Logan, IA 51546

Vocabu-Lit Workbooks. Designed with a contextual approach to word study for the junior high student.

Rand McNally, Inc.

This company carries the famous Lyons and Carnahan "Phonics We Use" workbook series and the revised "Phonics We Use" learning games kit.

Random House

Mix or Match Storybook. Good for reading words in context. By flipping book sections, students create unusual stories with colorful cartoon animal characters.

Reading Joy, Inc., 2210 Wellington Court, Naperville, IL 60532

A remarkable set of how-to books containing ideas for reinforcement of many reading skills. Also includes word lists. Sets of ready-to-complete game materials are also available.

Frank Schaffer Publishers, Inc., Palos Verdes, CA 90274

Activity Book, Activity Cards, Game Boards, Duplicating masters covering all facets of word attack skills. Animated characters with very bright colors.

Trend Enterprises, New Brighton, St. Paul, MN 55112

This company has an outstanding selection of task cards, bulletin board posters, and puzzles for teaching word attack skills.

Troll Publishers, 320 Rt. 17, Mahwak, NJ

Two talking dictionaries sets that let kids see and hear what they're reading. Grades 1-4.

Jane Ward Co., Inc., 1642 S. Beech St., Lakewood, CO 80228

Flip Cards. For sound blending practice using nonsense words also T. Scopes. Strips with words (consonants, blends, digraphs, vowels) slide through scopes showing words in slot — with picture answer below.

Manufacturers and Distributors of Games — Some Names and Addresses

Milton Bradley
43 Cross Street
Springfield, MA 01101

Childcraft Education Corporation
52 Hook Road
Bayonne, NJ 07002

Creative Publications
3977 E. Bayshore Road
Palo Alto, CA 94303

Denoyer-Geppert
5235 Ravenswood Avenue
Chicago, IL 60640

Developmental Learning Materials
7440 Natchez Avenue
Niles, IL 60648

Educational Teaching Aids
159 West Kinzie Street
Chicago, IL 60610

Follett Educational Corporation
1010 W. Washington blvd.
Chicago, IL 60607

Garrard Publishers
1607 N. Market Street
Champaign, IL 61820

Good Apple
Box 299
Carthage, IL 62321

Houghton-Mifflin
110 Tremont Street
Boston, MA 02107

Ideal School Supply Company
11000 S. Lavergne Street
Oak Lawn, IL 60453

Instructo Corporation
180 Cedar Hollow Road
Paoli, PA 19301

Kenworthy Educational Service
P.O. Box 3031
Buffalo, NY 14205

McGraw Hill
Early Learning
Paoli, PA 19301

Media Materials, Inc.
2936 Remington Avenue
Baltimore, MD 21211

Montessori Educational Games
15 Central Drive
Farmingdale, NY 11735

Multi Media Education
747 Third Avenue
New York, NY 10017

NCS/Educational Systems
4401 West 76th Street
Minneapolis, MN 55435

New Dimensions in Education
160 DuPont Street
Plainview, NY 11803

New York Times Teaching Resources
100 Boylston Street
Boston, MA 02116

Playskool
3720 N. Kedzie Avenue
Chicago, IL 60618

Parker Brothers Games
P.O. Box 900
Salem, MA 01970

Phonovisual Products
12216 Parklawn Drive
Rockville, MD 20852

Remedial Education Press
Kingsbury Center
2138 Bancroft Place, N.W.
Washington, DC 20008

Scott, Foresman and Company
1900 E. Lake Avenue
Glenview, IL 60025

Frank Shaffer Publications
26616 Indian Peak Road
Palos Verde Peninsula, CA 90274

St. Regis Paper Company
Consumer Products Division
P.O. Box 6416
Birmingham, AL 35217

Trend Enterprises, Inc.
St. Paul, MN 55165

WFF 'N Proof
Learning Games Associates
1111 Maple Avenue
Turtle Creek, PA 15145

Manufacturers and Distributers of Reading Computer Software

Advanced Ideas
2920 San Pablo Ave.
Berkeley, CA 94702

American Educational Computer, Inc.
525 University Ave.
Palo Alto, CA 94301

American Guidance Services
Publisher's Building
Circle Pines, MN 55014

Avant-Garde
1907 Garden Ave.
Eugene, OR 97403

Bertamax Inc.
3647 Stone Way North
Seattle, WA 98103

CodeWriter Corp.
5605 West Howard
Nilas, IL 60648

COMPress
P.O. Box 102
Wentworth, NH 03282

Conduit
University of Iowa, Oakdale Campus
Iowa City, IA 52242

Cross Educational
P.O. Box 1536
Ruston, LA 71270

CUE Softswap
333 Main St.
Redwood City, CA 94063

D.C. Health
125 Spring St.
Lexington, MA 02173

Data Command
P.O. Box 548
Kankakee, IL 60901

Davidson & Associates
6069 Groveoak Place #12
Rancho Palos Verdes, CA 90274

DesignWare
185 Berry St., Bldg 3, Ste. 158
San Francisco, CA 94107

Developmental Learning Materials
One DLM Park
Allen, TX 75002

Didatech Software
549-810 W. Broadway
Vancouver, BC V524C9

Educational Activities
P.O. Box 392
Freeport, NY 11520

Educational Materials & Equip.
P.O. Box 17
Pelham, NY 10803

Educational Publishing Concepts
P.O. Box 715
St. Charles, IL 60174

ERIC Clearinghouse
030 Huntington Hall
School of Educ., Syracuse University
Syracuse, NY 13210

Gamco Industries
Box 1911
Big Spring, TX 79721

Hartley Courseware
P.O. Box 431
Simindale, MI 48821

Hi Tech of Santa Cruz
126 Lighthouse Ave
Santa Cruz, CA 95060

Holt, Rinehart, and Winston, Inc.
383 Madison Ave.
New York, NY 10017

Houghton Mifflin
One Beacon St.
Boston, MA 02107

HRM Software
175 Tompkins Avenue
Pleasantville, NY 10570

Imperial International
P.O. Box 548
Kankakee, IL 60901

InterLearn
P.O. Box 342
Cardiff By The Sea, CA 92007

Jostens Learning Systems, Inc.
600 West University Dr.
Arlington Heights, IL 60004

Kent Publishings
10 Davis Dr.
Belmont, CA 94002

Krell Software
320 Stony Brook Rd.
Stony Brook, NY 11790

Learning Company, The
545 Middlefield Rd., Suite 170
Menlo Park, CA 94025

Learning Technologies, Inc.
4255 LBJ Freeway, Suite 131
Dallas, TX 75244

Learning Well
200 South Service Rd.
Roslyn Heights, NY 11577

McGraw Hill
Princeton Rd.
Hightstown, NJ 08540

MicroPro International
99 Fourth St.
San Rafael, CA 94901

Microcomputer Workshops
225 Westchester Ave.
Port Chester, NY 10573

Midwest Software
Box 214
Farmington, MI 48024

Milliken
1100 Research Blvd.
St Louis, MO 63132

Paperback Software Internat.
2612 Eighth St.
Berkeley, CA 94710

EduWare
185 Berry St.
San Francisco, CA 94107

Random House
400 Hahn Rd.
Westminster, MD 21157

Research Design Assoc., Inc.
P.O. Box 848
Stony Brook, NY 11790

Scarborough Systems, Inc.
25 N. Broadway
Tarrytown, NY 10591

Scholastic
4466 Black Ave., Suite L
Pleasanton, CA 94566

Scott, Foresman and Company
630 Wendell Dr.
Sunnyvale, CA 94089

Simon & Schuster
1230 Ave. of the Americas
New York, NY 0020

Spinnaker Software
215 First St.
Cambridge, MA 02142

Springboard Software, Inc.
7807 Creekridge Cr.
Minneapolis, MN 55435

Sunburst
39 Washington Ave.
Pleasantville, NY 10570

Teacher Support
P.O. Box 7125
Gainesville, FL 32605

Weekly Reader
245 Longhill Road
Middletown, CT 06457

World Book-Childcraft Intl.
Merchandise Mart Plaza,
Chicago, IL 60654

Questions to Ask about Computer-Based Reading Programs

1. *Cost.* Is there:
   - program copy protection?
   - charge for back-up copies?
   - expense for supplemental or resource materials?
   - a single program disk or are multiple disks required?
   - provision for refunds or returns?
   - provision for program upgrading as new versions appear?

2. *Computer brands and special equipment.* Does the program need:
   - a color monitor?
   - two disk drives?
   - a student data disk?
   - a printer?
   - a speech synthesizer—which one?
   - anything else?

3. *Where might the program fit in my curriculum?*
   - What grade level?
   - What types of students?
   - What types of teaching styles?
   - What types of reading and language arts materials are compatible?
   - How long do the activities take?

4. *What is read on/off screen?* Do students:
   - read passages?
   - read sentences?
   - read individual words or phrases?
   - recognize letters?
   - read program or activity directions?
   - read or recognize anything else?

5. *Program content.* Do activities include these types:
   - instructional?
   - practice?
   - vocabulary?
   - comprehension?
   - study skills?
   - grammar?
   - syllable or alphabet?
   - game?
   - test?
   - other?
   - multiple activities on one disk?

6. *Video presentations.* Does the program:
   - present information with appropriate speed and legibility?
   - present print appropriately spaced and sized?
   - use graphics (with color) — what types, when, and why?
   - use animation — when and why?
   - have color that interferes with legibility of print?

7. *Audio (and speech) presentation.* Does the program:
   - use speech (synthesized space-age voice or digited human voice) — when and why?
   - use nonspeech sound — when and why?
   - allow us to control volume or eliminate the audio?

8. *Reading and language arts goals.* Does the program have stated objectives and goals:
   - for teachers (achievement, motivational, behavioral, management)?
   - for students?
   - for concerned others (parents, administrators, supervisors)?
   - that meet state, provincial, or local educational requirements?
   - that meet objectives and goals of tests I'm required to give?

9. *Prerequisite skills.* Of the following skills, what kinds are needed?
   - computer literacy?
   - keyboard?
   - spelling?
   - entry level reading?
   - background knowledge?
   - other?

10. *Reinforcement in the program.*
    - What behaviors are reinforced — why when, how?
    - What control do I have over the reinforcement?

11. *Program operation.*
    - Can the students use the program with little or no help from me?
    - Can I or the students:
      — change an activity's contents?

Reprinted with permission of the International Reading Association from Blanchard, Jay, "Questions to Ask about Computer-Based Reading Programs," THE READING TEACHER, November 1985, pp. 250-252.

- change activity formats?
- receive on-screen prompts or help?
- make mistakes or press keys accidentally without ruining the activity?
- correct our entries?
- work on unfinished sections of an activity without repeating completed sections?
- reread previous screens easily without restarting the activity?
- use the activities without changing to another program disk in the middle?
- use the activities if the program disk is removed from the disk drive?
• Can the program give pretests or posttests?
• Can the activity be used with either groups or individuals?

12. *Program reviews and field-testing.* What's available?
   • Critical reviews?
   • Descriptive reviews?
   • Reports of field-testing?

13. *Supplemental or resource material.* Are supplemental materials available for examining:
   • the contents of the activities before using them with the computer?
   • background information about the activity's content?
   • information about instructional strategies used?
   • other educational resources?

14. *Scoring and recordkeeping.* Does the program:
   • score and record student performance or other information — how?
   • permit students as well as teachers to see records?
   • allow the recall of information about students — what information, why?

Finally, ask the question, "What does this program offer my students that I cannot otherwise give them?"

A Model Sheet For Evaluating Reading Games

GAME TITLE:_____

PUBLISHER:_____

COST:_____

	Yes	So-So	No
1. Gives instructions for use that are clear and understandable.	_____	_____	_____
2. Is interesting and acceptable to students at designated age groups.	_____	_____	_____
3. Presents concepts or skills thoroughly and accurately.	_____	_____	_____
4. Uses language suitable for students who will be using the material.	_____	_____	_____
5. Provides for students to apply what they learned to other related areas.	_____	_____	_____
6. Presents follow-up activities for reinforcement.	_____	_____	_____
7. Provides for self-correction.	_____	_____	_____
8. Challenges students.	_____	_____	_____
9. Is easily presented to students.	_____	_____	_____
10. Provides the activity individually, or in a group.	_____	_____	_____

STRENGTHS: _____

_____

WEAKNESSES: _____

_____

Glossary

Affixes. Prefixes and suffixes.

Analogies. (plural) A correspondence between things otherwise dissimilar.

Analytic Phonics. A system of teaching sound/symbol relationships, whereby a student deduces the phonic principle involved.

Basic Sight Words. A list of high-frequency words as *the, up, about* that constitute between 50 and 66 percent of all running vocabulary.

Blend. Two or three consonant letters with their related sounds that cluster together and are pronounced very rapidly as *tr*ap and *str*eet.

Breve. A diacritical mark (˘) as in the word *mat* to indicate the short vowel.

CAI. Computer assisted instruction.

Cloze Technique. Students learn the importance of context through completing cloze exercises, or closing the sentence by supplying the necessary word in a blank. Cloze is also used for diagnostic purposes.

Consonant Digraph. Two consonant letters encoding a single sound/sounds as ch in *champ/school/chef*.

Context. The words, phrases, and sentences surrounding a word, giving clues to its meaning. (Context may be semantic or syntactic.)

Decode. Reading the word, phrase, or sentence.

Diphthong. Two vowels with a "gliding" sound as in the word *oil*.

Educanese. Newly coined terms from other disciplines applies to reading.

Encode. Writing the word, phrase, or sentence.

"Linguistic" Phonics. A patterned approach to teaching phonics that shows minimal differences between pairs of words.

Macron. A diacritical mark (-) as in the word *mate* to indicate the long vowel.

Microcomputer. A small computer.

Morpheme. (noun) Minimal letters or sounds that show meaning.

Morphemic. (adjective)

Orthography. A writing system.

Phoneme. One of the smallest units of speech that distinguishes one word from another.

Phonogram. A cluster of vowel and consonant blends as *ent* and *ild* to which beginning sounds are added, forming words as *sent* and *wild*.

Phonology. The science of speech sounds.

Prefix. A syllable before the root word that usually changes meaning as *prearrange*.

Printout. The end product of the computer.

R-Conditioned Vowels. The letter *r* following a vowel (in the same syllable) modifies the vowel sound as in *her* and *stare*.

Root. A base to which prefixes and suffixes may be added.

Schwa. A reduced vowel neither long nor short with the sound of short *u* as in apron. It is written with an upside down ə as in aprən.

Scope and Sequence Chart. A publisher's chart that shows at what grade level particular reading skills are taught.

Semantic. Relating to word meaning.

Software. Programs essential to the computer's operation.

Stem. A base word or word part to which affixes are added.

Structural Analysis. Understanding word parts as compound words, affixes, roots, and syllables.

Suffixes. *Derivational* —There are many of these suffixes such as *ment* and *ism*. They often change the part of speech of the root word and sometimes the word meaning.

Inflectional —There are only eight simple suffixes as *ing* and *en*. These do not change the part of speech. They are learned in the early stages of reading.

Syntactic. Relating to the grammar.

Synthetic Phonics. A system of direct teaching of sound/symbol relationships.

Vowel Digraphs. Two vowels together with one vowel sound as in *seat*.

References

Agnew, Ann T. "Using Children's Dictated Stories to Assess Code Consciousness." *The Reading Teacher* 35, no. 4 (January 1982): 450–53.

Ahmann, Linda. "Some Tips on Teaching Vowel-Sound Discrimination." *Academic Therapy* 17, no. 5 (May 1982): 570–71.

Alexander, Clara Franklin. "Black English Dialect and the Classroom Teacher." *The Reading Teacher* 33, no. 5 (February 1980): 571–76.

American Council on the Teaching of Foreign Languages. (ACTFL). 62 5th Avenue, New York 10011.

American Heritage Dictionary of the English Language, The, p. 444. New York: Dell Publishing Co., 1977.

Anderson, Richard C., Hiebert, Elfrieda H., Scott, Judith A., and Wilkinson, Ian A. G. *Becoming a Nation of Readers: The Report of the Commission on Reading*. Washington, D.C.: National Institute of Education, 1985.

Azar, Teri Oberstein. "Teaching the Short Vowel Sounds Using Visual Imagery." *The Reading Teacher* 38, no. 9 (May 1985): 926–928.

Balmuth, Miriam. *The Root of Phonics: A Historical Introduction*. New York: McGraw-Hill, 1982.

Baratz, Joan C. and Shuy, Roger. *Teaching Black Children to Read*. Arlington, VA: Center for Applied Linguistics, 1969.

Blanchard, Jay. "Questions to Ask About Computer-based Reading Programs." *The Reading Teacher* 39, no. 2 (Nov. 1985): 250–256.

Boraks, Nancy and Roseman, Amy and Allen. "A Program To Enhance Peer Tutoring." *The Reading Teacher* 30, no. 6 (February 1977): 479–84.

Burmeister, Lou E. "The Usefulness of Phonic Generalizations." *The Reading Teacher* 21, no. 4. (January 1968): 349–64.

Burmeister, Lou E. *Words — from Print to Meaning,* pp. 91-92. Reading, MA: Addison Wesley, 1975.

Carnine, Douglas, and Silbert, Jerry. *Direct Instruction in Reading*. Columbus, OH: Charles E. Merrill, 1979.

Carter, Thomas P. and Segura, Roberts D. *Mexican Americans in School: A Decade of Change*. College Entrance Examination Board, NY, 1979.

Casale, Ula Price. "Motor Imaging: A Reading-Vocabulary Strategy," *Journal of Reading* 28, no. 7 (April 1985): 619–621.

Chall, Jeanne. *Learning to Read: The Great Debate*. New York: McGraw-Hill, 1967.

Chall, Jeanne S. *Learning to Read: The Great Debate,* 2nd Ed. New York: McGraw-Hill, 1983.

Chomsky, Carol. "After Decoding: What?" *Language Arts* 53, no. 3 (March 1976): 288–96.

Coley, Joan D. "Self Evaluation Techniques for Young Children." *Reading World* 22, no. 3 (March 1983): 197–202.

Collins, Cathy. "Content Mastery Strategies Aid Classroom Discussion." *The Reading Teacher* 40, no. 8 (April 1987): 816–817.

Cook, Jimmie E. "Parents Who Take An 'Academic' Interest Get Real Results," *Early Years* (December 1982): pp. 18–21.

Cunningham, James W. "An Automatic Pilot for Decoding." *The Reading Teacher* 32, no. 4 (January 1979): 420–24.

Cunningham, Patricia M. "A Teacher's Guide to Material Shopping." *The Reading Teacher* 35, no. 2 (November 1981): 181–84.

Cunningham, Patricia M. "Teaching Vocabulary in the Content Areas." *NASSP Bulletin* 63, no. 424 (February 1979): 112–16.

Cunningham, Patricia M. "Teaching Were, With, What and Other 'Four-Letter' Words." *The Reading Teacher* 34, no. 3 (November 1980): 160–63.

Cunningham, Patricia M., Cunningham, James W. and Rystrom, Richard C. "A New Syllabication Strategy and Reading Achievement." *Reading World* 34, no. 3 (March 1981): 208–13.

Dahl, Patricia R. "An Experimental Program for Teaching High Speed Word Recognition and Comprehension Skills." University of Minnesota. Final Report. Project No. 3 — 1154, Washington, D.C.: United States Department of H.E.W., 1974.

Dale, Edgar and O'Rourke, Joseph. *Techniques of Teaching Vocabulary,* p. 183. Palo Alto, Calif.: Field Educational Publishers, Inc., 1971.

Dale, Edgar and O'Rourke, Joseph. *The Living Word Vocabulary.* Elgin, Illinois: Dome Press, Inc., 1979.

Devall, Yvonna. "Evaluating Microcomputer Software for Reading Instruction." *Journal of Reading* 26, no. 6 (March 1983): 553.

Dien, To Thi, Huynh Dinh Te, and Tam Thi Dang Wei. *Assessment of Vietnamese Speaking Limited English Proficient Students with Special Needs.* CA State Dept. of Education, Office of Special Education, Personnel Development Unit, May 1986.

Dreyer, Lois G., Futtersak, Karen R., and Boehm, Ann E. "Sight Words for the Computer Age: An Essential Word List." *The Reading Teacher* 38, no. 12 (October 1985): 12–15.

Durrell, Donald D. and Murphy, Helen A. "A Prereading Phonics Inventory." *The Reading Teacher* 31, no. 4 (January 1978): 385–89.

Editors, *Instructor.* "We Can Become a Nation of Readers," 95, no. 4 (November/December): 1985.

Editors, *Learning.* "What Teachers Had to Say About Using Computers in Today's Schools," 15, no. 3. (March 1986): 48–52.

Eeds-Kniep, Maryann. "The Frenetic Fanatic Phonic Backlash." *Language Arts* 56, no. 8 (November/December 1979): 909–17.

Eeds-Kniep, Maryann. "Phonics: Teach and Test." *Instructor and Teacher* 91 (October 1981): 136–38.

Ehri, Linnea C. "A Critique of Five Studies Related to Letter-Name Knowledge and Learning to Read." *Reading Research Revisited,* ed. by Lance M. Gentile, Michael L. Kamil, and Jay S. Blanchard. Columbus, OH: Charles E. Merrill, 1983.

Eldredge, Lloyd J. "Alternatives to Traditional Reading Instruction." *The Reading Teacher* 39, no. 9 (October 1986): 32–37.

Exemplary Center for Reading Instruction, 2888 Highland Drive, Salt Lake City, Utah, 84106.

Farr, Roger. *Reading Trends and Challenges.* West Haven, CT: National Education Assn., 1981.

Feigenbaum, Irwin. "Using Foreign Language Methodology to Teach Standard English: Evaluation and Adaptation." Linguistic-Cultural Differences and American Education, Special Anthology Issue of *The Florida FL Reporter.* Edited by Alfred A. Aarons, Barbara Y. Gordon, and William A. Steward, 1970.

Fox, Deborah. "The Debate Goes On: Systematic Phonics vs. Whole Language." *Journal of Reading* 29, no. 7 (April 1986): 678–680.

Fox, Paula. *The One-Eyed Cat,* New York: Broadway Press, 1984.

Frey, Sandra J. "The Long and Short of It." *The Reading Teacher* 35, no. 5 (August 1982): 54.

Fromkin, Victoria and Rodman, Robert. *An Introduction to Language,* p. 196. New York: Holt, Rinehart and Winston, Inc., 1974.

Frenzel, Norman J. "Children Need a Multi-pronged Attack in Word Recognition." *The Reading Teacher* 37, no. 6 (March 1978): 628–31.

Gates, Louis and Lowry Heath. "A Face Lift for the Silent e." *The Reading Teacher* 17, no. 1 (October 1983): 102–103.

Gillis, M. K. "Combining Phonics: Approaches for Problem Readers." *Academic Therapy* 17, no. 4 (March 1982): 389–94.

Goodman, Kenneth S. and Buck, Catherine. "Dialect Barriers to Reading Comprehension Revisited." *The Reading Teacher* 27, no. 1 (October 1973): 6–12.

Groff, Patrick. "Teaching Reading by Syllables." *The Reading Teacher* 34, no. 6 (March 1981): 686–91.

Groff, Patrick. "A Test of the Utility of Phonics Rules." *Reading Psychology* 4, (July-December 1983): 217–225.

Groff, Patrick. "The Maturing of Phonics Instruction." *Education Digest* 52 (January 1987): 40–41).

Groff, Patrick. "Resolving the Letter Name Controversy," *The Reading Teacher* 37, no. 4 (January 1984): 384–388.

Haddock, Maryann. "Teaching Blending in Beginning Reading Instruction Is Important." *The Reading Teacher* 31, no. 6 (March 1978): 654–58.

Hanna, Paul R.; Hodges, Richard E.; and Hanna, Jean S. *Spelling Structure and Strategies*, pp. 79–83. Boston, MA: Houghton-Mifflin, 1971.

Harris, Albert J. "What Is New in Remedial Reading." *The Reading Teacher* 34, no. 6 (January 1981): 405–10.

Heckelman, Robert G. "A Neurological Impress Method of Remedial Reading Instruction." *Academic Therapy* 5, no. 4 (1969): 277–82.

Hiebert, Elfrieda H. "A Comparison of Young Children's Self-Selected Reading Words and Basal Reading Words." *Reading Improvement* 20, no. 1 (Spring 1983): 41–45.

Janicke, Eugene M. "Massive Oral Decoding." *Academic Therapy* 17, no. 2 (November 1981): 157–60.

Johns, Jerry L. "A Supplement to the Dolch Word List." *Reading Improvement* 7 (Winter 1971–72): 91.

Johns, Jerry L. "The Revised Dolch List: Data and Rationale." *Reading World* 18, no. 1 (October 1978): 24–26.

Johnson, Dale D., and Baumann, James F. "Word Identification." In *Handbook of Reading Research*, ed. by P. David Pearson, New York: Longman, 1984.

Kraske, Robert. *The Story of the Dictionary*. New York: Harcourt, Brace, Jovanovich, 1975.

Krieger, Veronica K. "Differences in Poor Readers' Abilities to Identify High-Frequency Words in Isolation and Context." 20, no. 4 (May 1981): 263–69.

Labov, William. "Language Characteristics of Blacks," *Reading for the Disadvantaged: Problems of Linguistically Different Learners*. ed. by Thomas Horn. New York: Harcourt, Brace, Jovanovich, 1970.

Lauritzen, Carol. "A Modification of Repeated Readings for Group Instruction." *The Reading Teacher* 35, no. 4 (January 1982): 456–58.

Liebert, Burt. *Linguistics and the New English Teacher,* pp. 105-14. New York: Macmillan, 1971.

Liles, Bruce L. *Linguistics and the English Language,* p. 236. Pacific Palisades, CA: Goodyear Publishers, 1972.

Loban, Walter. *Language Development: K–12*. National Council of Teachers of English. Urbana, Illinois, 1976.

McCormick, Sandra and Collins, Betty M. *The Reading Teacher* 34, no. 6 (March 1981): 692–96.

Mason, Geo. E. "The Computer in the Reading Clinic." *The Reading Teacher* 36, no. 6 (February 1983): 504–507.

Mason, Geo. E. "Computerized Reading Instruction: A Review." *Educational Technology* 20, no. 9 (September 1980): 18–22.

Masland, Susan W. "The Reading Program and Its Potential Obstacles for Minority Children." *Elementary School Journal* 79, no. 4. (March 1979): 250–54.

Meagher, Judy. *Instructor* 95, no. 2 (1985): 148.

Moon, Louise and Scorpio, Carolyn M. "When Word Recognition Is OK — Almost!" *The Reading Teacher* 27, no. 9 (May 1984): 825–827.

Otto, Jean. "The New Debate in Reading." *The Reading Teacher* 36, no. 1 (October 1982): 14–18.

Palmer, Barbara. "Dolch List Still Useful." *The Reading Teacher* 38, no. 7 (March 1985): 708.

Peterson, Marilyn L. "Mexican-American Children: What Do They Prefer and Read?" *Reading World* 22, no. 2 (December 1982): 129–31.

Pikulski, John J. "Questions and Answers." *The Reading Teacher* 40, no. 8 (April 1987): 831–832.

Prescriptive Reading Inventory, The. McGraw-Hill Publishers, Del Monte Research Park, Monterey, CA 93940.

Read: An Individual Pupil Monitoring System. Boston, MA: Houghton Mifflin Publishers.

Rinsky, Lee Ann. "A, E, I, O, U and OO." *The Reading Teacher* 29, no. 2 (November 1975): 146–49.

Rosenshine, Barak and Stevens, Robert. "Classroom Instruction in Reading." In *Handbook of Reading Research,* ed. by P. David Pearson. New York: Longman, 1984.

Rosso, Barbara Rak and Emans, Robert. "Children's Use of Phonics Generalizations." *The Reading Teacher* 34, no. 6 (March 1981): 653–57.

Rupley, Wm. H. and Chevrette, Patricia. "Computer Assisted Reading Instructor: A Promising Tool for Enhancing Teacher Effectiveness." *Reading World* (March 1983): 236–40.

Shuck, Annette, Ush, Florence and Platt, John S. "Parents Encourage Pupils: An Intercity Parent Involvement Reading Project." *The Reading Teacher* 36, no. 6 (February 1983): 524–28.

Sippola, Arne E. "What to Teach for Reading Readiness — A Research Review and Materials Inventory." *The Reading Teacher* 39, no. 2 (November 1985): 162–163.

Sittig, Linda Harris. "Involving Parents and Children in Reading for Fun." *The Reading Teacher* 36, no. 2 (November 1982): 166–68.

Snyder, Geraldine V. "Learner's Verification of Reading Games." *The Reading Teacher* 34, no. 6 (March 1981): 686–91.

Spiegel, Dixie Lee. "Six Alternatives to the Directed Reading Activity. *The Reading Teacher* 34, no. 8 (May 1981): 916.

Stotsky, Sandra L. "Teaching Prefixes in the Elementary School." *The Elementary School Journal* 78, no. 4 (March 1978): 278–83.

Swaby, Barbara. "How Parents Can Foster Comprehension Growth in Children." *The Reading Teacher* 34, no. 2 (December 1980): 280–83.

Swaby, Barbara. "Using Repeated Readings to Develop Fluency and Accuracy." *The Reading Teacher* 36, no. 3 (December 1982): 317–18.

Venezky, Richard L. "Harmony and Cacophony from a Theory-Practice Relationship." *Theory and Practice of Early Reading*. Vol. 2, ed. by Lauren B. Resnick and Phyllis A. Weaver. Hillsdale, NJ: Laurence Eribaum, 1979.

Wardhaugh, Ronald. *Introduction to Linguistics,* pp. 198–99. New York: McGraw-Hill, 1972.

Wedman, Judy. "Reading Software: What's Out There." *Language Arts* 60, no. 4 (April 1983): 516–17.

Wedman, Judy. "Software: What's in It for Reading." *Journal of Reading* 26, no. 7 (April 1983): 642.

Williams, Joanna P. "The Case for Explicit Decoding Instruction." *Reading Education: Foundations for a Literate America*. ed. by Jean Osborn, Paul T. Wilson, and Richard C. Anderson. Lexington, MA: Lexington Books, 1985.

Wisconsin Design. The Educational Systems, 4401 W. 76th Street, Minneapolis, MN 55435.

Wolfrom, Walt and Fasold, Ralph. *The Study of Social Dialects in American English*. Englewood Cliffs, NJ: Prentice Hall, 1974.

Wood, Karen D. and Robinson, Nora. "Vocabulary, Language and Prediction: A Prereading Strategy. *The Reading Teacher* 36, no. 4 (January 1983): 392–95.

Zintz, Miles. *The Reading Process: The Teacher and the Learner,* p. 260. Dubuque, IA: William C. Brown Co., Publishers, 1975.